"Malcolm Jeeves brings to this highly readable book both a lifetime of eminent scientific research in neuroscience and psychology and all the wisdom of his accumulated theological reflections as a Christian. Anyone struggling to see how contemporary science, in all its complexity, can be consonant with committed theological belief should peruse this volume with care: it touches on all the major metaphysical and theological points of contention, and does so with clarity, insight, and compassion."

—SARAH COAKLEY
Editor of *Spiritual Healing: Science, Meaning, and Discernment*

"Drawing on a lifetime's experience in psychology and neuroscience, and with the perspective of his Christian faith, Prof. Malcolm Jeeves shows that many, perhaps most people today believe in shrunken gods that do not do justice to either the depth of scientific knowledge about the created world, or the biblical view of a sovereign creator God. In a magisterial overview of current understanding, he encourages us to expand our vision to embrace both the fruits of modern science and the insights of biblical scholarship to give a richer and fuller view of this amazing world in which we live, and of the place of humans within it."

—BOB WHITE
Emeritus Professor of Geophysics, Cambridge University,
and Emeritus Director, The Faraday Institute for Science and Religion

"Too often today we hear reductionist claims: *I have faith so don't need science!* or *I have science so don't need faith!* With an astonishing breadth of perspective, Malcolm Jeeves dispels both myths—and he does so with such easy-to-read and humble prose that we do well to stop and reflect on this book's practical wisdom. Here is an invitation to take up fresh, robust, and faithful ways of making sense of God's good creation."

—JOEL B. GREEN
Author of *Body, Soul, and Human Life: The Nature of Humanity in the Bible*

"How do you answer a cry for help from someone battling doubts about their Christian faith? Here is the lifetime experience of a distinguished professor of psychology and neuroscience faced with today's questions about origins, human nature, miracles, faith, and fakes. Malcolm Jeeves explores remarkable advances not only in the sciences but in biblical scholarship. Together, they help us to avoid the danger of shrinking our ideas about the living God."

—BRIAN HEAP
Past President of the European Academies Science Advisory Council

"Malcolm Jeeves, a pioneering cognitive neuroscientist and founder of one of the world's great psychology departments, is also one the world's wisest thinkers on matters of science and faith. After a lifetime's experience among great scientists and visionary people of faith, he invites us to sit beside him as he offers his final reflections. And how refreshing and inspiring it is—in an era when religion so often seems anti-science—to think with him as he unifies scientific and biblical wisdom about human origins and human nature, about miracles, and even about faith itself."

—DAVID MYERS
Professor of Psychology, Hope College

Why Science and Faith Belong Together

Why Science and Faith Belong Together

Stories of Mutual Enrichment

MALCOLM A. JEEVES

CASCADE *Books* • Eugene, Oregon

WHY SCIENCE AND FAITH BELONG TOGETHER
Stories of Mutual Enrichment

Copyright © 2021 Malcolm A. Jeeves. All rights reserved. Except for brief quotations in critical publications or reviews, no part of this book may be reproduced in any manner without prior written permission from the publisher. Write: Permissions, Wipf and Stock Publishers, 199 W. 8th Ave., Suite 3, Eugene, OR 97401.

Cascade Books
An Imprint of Wipf and Stock Publishers
199 W. 8th Ave., Suite 3
Eugene, OR 97401

www.wipfandstock.com

PAPERBACK ISBN: 978-1-7252-8619-1
HARDCOVER ISBN: 978-1-7252-8620-7
EBOOK ISBN: 978-1-7252-8621-4

Cataloguing-in-Publication data:

Names: Jeeves, Malcolm A., 1926–, author.

Title: Why science and faith belong together : stories of mutual enrichment / Malcolm A. Jeeves.

Description: Eugene, OR: Cascade Books, 2021 | Includes bibliographical references and index.

Identifiers: ISBN 978-1-7252-8619-1 (paperback) | ISBN 978-1-7252-8620-7 (hardcover) | ISBN 978-1-7252-8621-4 (ebook)

Subjects: LCSH: Religion and science | Bible and science | Theological anthropology—Christianity | Evolution (Biology)—Religious aspects—Christianity | Miracles

Classification: BL240.3 J44 2021 (paperback) | BL240.3 (ebook)

05/13/21

Scripture quotations marked as (KJV) are from the King James Version of the Bible. Scripture quotations marked as (NRSV) are from the New Revised Standard Version Bible, copyright © 1989 National Council of Churches of Christ in the United States of America. Used by permission. All rights reserved worldwide.

Scripture quotations marked as (NIV) are from the Holy Bible, NEW INTERNATIONAL VERSION, copyright © 1973, 1978, 1984, 2011 by Biblica, Inc. Used by permission. All rights reserved worldwide.

Scripture quotations marked as (ESV) are from the Holy Bible, English Standard Version, copyright © 2001 by Crossway Bibles, a publishing ministry of Good News Publishers. Used by permission. All rights reserved worldwide.

To Ruth, for her love and support through
more than six decades of my life.

Contents

Preface | ix
Acknowledgements | xvii

SECTION I: GAINING PERSPECTIVE
1 Is Your God Still Too Small? Echoes from the Past | 3
2 Anything New under the Sun? The Proliferation of Gods | 29
3 "Gods" on Offer: Sampling the Twenty-First-Century Marketplace | 42

SECTION II: STORIES OF MUTUAL ENRICHMENT
4 Human Origins: The Evidence from Science | 65
5 Human Origins: The Evidence from Scripture | 78
6 Human Nature: The Evidence from Science | 94
7 Human Nature: The Evidence from Scripture | 108
8 Miracles of Nature: Divine Upholder or Occasional Gap Filler? | 124
9 Miracles of Nature: Illustrative Examples | 142
10 Miracles of Health and Healing: Scriptural and Scientific Insights | 154
11 The Multifaceted Nature of Faith: The Evidence from Scripture | 176
12 The Multifaceted Nature of Faith: The Evidence from Science | 189

SECTION III: THEOLOGICAL REFLECTIONS
13 Divine Upholding and Divine Emptying: An Essential Balance | 209

Postscript | 227
Appendix: Going Deeper—Guidance for Study and Discussion | 229

Bibliography | 249
About the Author | 263
Name Index | 265
Subject Index | 271

Preface

NO ONE LIVING THROUGH the 2020 COVID-19 epidemic can have failed to notice the way in which world leaders, such the Prime Minister of the United Kingdom, make repeated references to the need to follow the best evidence from research in science and in medicine. Indeed, it would only be a slight exaggeration to say that the image presented is of science and medicine as our potential saviors in our current predicament. This constant reminder of the need to pay attention to advances in science and medicine further underlines the challenges to their Christian faith that college and university students face daily. These are graphically illustrated by the emails that I receive regularly from such students. For example, one student wrote to me recently:

> My name is [****] and I am currently a sophomore studying biology and minoring in health sciences so I can one day become a high school science teacher. . . . Though you do not know me and this may seem personal, since studying biology, as well as psychology for one of my education requirements, my faith has been put to a test and I have been battling doubts in my faith for six to seven months now. I understand this may be a shot in the dark, but I am really struggling trying to piece together my faith, which I have known for the nineteen years of my life, and the research I have been doing in my classes and in my free time. My faith seems to be getting shakier and shakier as time goes by, so . . . I have a handful of questions I would love to ask you if you would be willing to answer and help. *They range from biology, neurology, and the brain, and life sciences in general, but all have something to do with my faith.* If you would be willing to help me, I would be very, very appreciative (emphasis added).

Another student wrote:

> I am a Christian having trouble believing in a soul, afterlife, or higher power. A lot of people in your particular field are atheists. Does their atheism make you question your faith? Why or why not? Do you feel the mind is reducible to the brain? If consciousness was confined to the brain would that eliminate the idea of a soul/afterlife? Can you give me a few scientific/logical (preferably scientific) reasons to believe in an afterlife? If you respond to this I greatly appreciate it.

This student, in a later email, added:

> Also I hear that our morals can be completely attributed to scientific evolutionary processes. Do you think this is true? If it is, does that make them less valuable/precious?

These and similar emails from worried students reveal a tension between their Christian faith and their understanding of science. Some of the most frequently recurring questions concern human origins, human nature, miracles in nature, and miracles of healing—issues that are highlighted regularly by the BioLogos organization. In the USA, the results of national surveys by the Pew Research Center and the Barna Group make clear that these students are not alone in their concerns. For example, a 2015 Pew survey reported that 59 percent of Americans think that science and religion are in conflict.[1] The perception of conflict weighs heavily on young people, who are trying to make sense of the world and find their place in it, and many of them are turning away from the church. According to a 2018 Barna survey, those born between 1999 and 2015 have become a "post-Christian" generation—in which 49 percent of church-going teenagers agreed that "The church seems to reject much of what science tells us about the world."[2] Young people hear many voices—whether from school, church, or popular culture—saying that science and faith don't mix. When their questions go unanswered, they tend to accept the message that the church is "anti-science."[3]

All too often, as we try to understand ourselves and the world we live in, we look first to science—and only then, if gaps remain and puzzles continue, do we try to fill in these gaps with reference to God and our faith. Such a "god-of-the-gaps" approach has a long history and is sadly alive and well today. This book was written to provide an alternative approach, posing this basic question: *How can educated Christians maintain our intellectual*

---

1. Pew Research Center, "Religion and Science."
2. Barna Group, "Atheism Doubles."
3. Cootsona, "Apologetics."

honesty and, at the same time, be faithful both to Scripture and to science? In this book, I select examples of some of the liveliest "science vs. faith" issues today and suggest ways to think constructively about each of them. This perspective is reflected in the book's title, *Why Science and Faith Belong Together: Stories of Mutual Enrichment.*

THE CURRENT SCENE

Given the importance of science in our modern world, the concerns of the students quoted above prompted me to write this book. It is clear that there are many thoughtful young Christians who need help and guidance on these issues. How can college students maintain their commitment to truth when authoritative figures in local and national churches seem to be unaware of exciting developments in science that have theological implications at odds with what is preached from pulpits, or who deny the truth or relevance of such new knowledge? And it is not only the puzzled students who need help. Overworked pastors have very little time or opportunity to keep abreast of what is happening in the world of science. Pastors may be all too aware of the problems the bright young people in their congregations are struggling with, but still feel unable to help. With them very much in mind, I have tried to write in a manner that does not assume a university degree in science.

It is important to underline that it is not just in the USA that students have problems. The spring 2020 newsletter of Christians in Science in the UK has an interview with Gavin Merrifield, currently a committee member of Christians in Science. The first question he was asked was, "When did you become a Christian and did this change your view of science in relation to God?" He replied,

> I grew up in a Christian household where my father became a church minister by the time I was a teenager and I made a fairly early personal commitment to Christ. Similarly, I have always been fascinated by science. Understanding the world and universe around us as God's creation helped to nurture this interest as I grew up. *Unfortunately, when I was a teenager I fell for the particular vision of both science and theology presented by Young Earth Creationism (YEC). I think this was mainly because I was never presented with an alternative understanding of how science and the Bible can come together in the church circles I was involved in.* . . . This all changed at University, when I came across *Christians in Science* and the resources it provided for my

thinking. I was also challenged by the example of particular professors at my university who were passionate about their faith, but who had very different ideas on how science and faith come together to me.[4]

Later in the interview Merrifield was asked, "What challenges, if any, have you come across as a Christian and a scientist?" His reply: "The first challenge I encountered was that of creation and evolution, which I am happy to say I have resolved to my thinking. That's not to say evolution doesn't pose interesting questions for the Christian—it does! But these are questions now of consequence rather than conflict. *Conflict between the two is still a challenge for parts of the wider church and undermines attempts to produce a fruitful understanding of science in our churches.*"[5]

The popular idea of a conflict, a battle between science and Christianity, in which the latter is in a millennia-old retreat and losing ground to the former, is a modern tale. Those who propagate it often have a clear anti-Christian axe to grind. In fact, this so-called "conflict-retreat model" did not become popular until the final decades of the nineteenth century. R. L. Numbers traced its beginnings at least as far back as an 1845 article in a US newspaper,[6] which claimed that, "Every new conquest achieved by science, involved the loss of a domain to religion."[7] And the idea was arguably already implicit in the intellectual milieu of the Enlightenment. However, this conflict model is an oversimplification, since the history of relations between science and Christianity shows a richer and much more complex story. In later chapters I shall give a brief summary of a modern consensus concerning the relations of science and religion developed by dedicated scholars over the past half century.

A second reason for writing this book is to call attention to some fundamentals of the Christian faith that, in recent years, have tended to slip into the background of Christian thought. Christianity is about Jesus Christ. In Scripture Jesus Christ is described as "the Word." The opening lines in the Gospel of John declare, "The Word became flesh and dwelt among us . . . full of grace and *truth*" (John 1:14 ESV). In Mark's Gospel this same Jesus, who is full of truth, is also the one who exhorts his followers to "Love the Lord your God with all your heart and with all your soul and *with all your mind* and with all your strength" (Mark 12:30 ESV). Sadly, today the use of the mind has been greatly diminished, or even forgotten, in matters of

---

4. PréCiS, "Interview with Gavin Merrifield" (emphasis added).
5. PréCiS, "Interview with Gavin Merrifield" (emphasis added).
6. Boston Cultivator, "Science and Religion," 344.
7. Numbers, *Galileo Goes to Jail*, 4.

faith and life. Whenever the power of the mind is minimized or sidelined the risk increases of shrinking both our faith and our understanding of how great our God is. So concerned was Mark Noll, Professor of History at Notre Dame University, about the failure of some Christians to use the mind that he devoted a monograph to the topic of *Jesus Christ and the Life of the Mind*. This was a follow up to his earlier book *The Scandal of the Evangelical Mind*. Although, as we shall see, there has been some progress in remedying the situation so graphically exposed by both of Mark Noll's books, nevertheless, the drop off in numbers in church affiliation and attendance as young people move through their senior years at school and on to college continues.

A third reason for writing this book is to share with students—such as the ones quoted above—and with the wider community, some ways to think constructively about the most frequently raised issues at the interface of science and faith. In doing so, I am also keen to illustrate how knowledge from *both* developments in science *and* advances in biblical scholarship actually expands our understanding of the wonderful God in whom we believe.

My specialist training over half a century in psychology and neuroscience has equipped me to write about some of these issues from first-hand knowledge. Since becoming an emeritus professor, I have remained in close contact with my colleagues in the School of Psychology and Neuroscience at St. Andrews University. I have also kept in touch with theologians and biblical scholars in St. Mary's College, which shares a quadrangle with the psychologists and neuroscientists. Some of these sustained interactions have resulted in publications to which I contributed and which I edited. For example, *From Cells to Souls and Beyond, Rethinking Human Nature*, and *The Emergence of Personhood: A Quantum Leap?* It is natural therefore for me, when selecting illustrative examples of issues at the interface of science and faith—which produce many of the problems for thoughtful young students and which result in a variety of shrunken gods, which are in fact "no gods" (in the biblical sense of the word God)—to turn to issues where my day-to-day work in science enables me to write with first-hand knowledge. Two such issues are: first, the rapid advances in evolutionary psychology, in which St. Andrews scientists have played a leading role, and second, advances at the interfaces of psychology and neuroscience, in which I have myself been involved, serving for a period as the Editor-in-Chief of *Neuropsychologia*, one of the leading scientific journals in this field. Research in evolutionary psychology has contributed to fresh understandings of human origins, and research in neuropsychology has posed new questions and shed fresh light on our understanding of human nature. It is for this reason that four of the later chapters about contemporary illustrative issues are devoted to human origins and human nature. My aim has been to help the puzzled student to understand that, when scrutinized carefully, the up-to-date evidence from both science and biblical scholarship, taken together, produce an enriched understanding of the God in whom we believe. While highlighting the key recent scientific evidence, I have pointed the reader to much more detailed treatments of each topic than a small book such as this would allow.

Additional chapters are devoted to discussions of miracles, since this is a topic that is apt to generate more heat than light, especially when it concerns claims of contemporary healing miracles. It is also a topic that brings out into the open our assumptions about the relation of God to his creation, perhaps shrinking God from the "divine upholder" to an "occasional gap-filler."

Writing now in the midst of the COVID-19 pandemic, I noted above that we in Britain have daily been reassured by the government's Chief Medical Officer, Professor Chris Whitty, who has been described by BBC Health Editor Hugh Pym as "The man with our lives in his hands." We all know what Pym means. The phrase reminds us that throughout Scripture we are taught that our lives are in the hands of God our creator. For example, in his pain and anguish Job declared, "in his [God's] hand is the life of every creature" (Job 12:10 NIV). David, pursued by his cruel enemies who were threatening his life, put his trust in God, saying, "My times are in your hands" (Ps 31:15 NIV). Paul, speaking about God to the people of Athens—regarded at that time as the most civilized, philosophical, highly educated, artistic, intellectual population on the face of the globe—declared that God had made the world and everything in it, and that it is "in him we live and move and have our being" (Acts 17:24–28 NIV). Recently there was a salutary reminder from Paul Nurse, a former Nobel Laureate and currently Director of the Francis Crick Institute, that the excellent advice from scientists is not the last word. He said, "I know both Chris Whitty and Sir Patrick Vallance and I think they are excellent scientists. We should feel in safe hands, . . . but I think it's really important that scientists do not speak with the word of God."[8] The greatest scientists have always known their limitations, have recognized the changing face of science, and have been careful not to claim more than the current evidence warrants. Sadly, a similar humility has not always characterized the interpretation of Scripture by preachers and theologians. We cannot too often remind ourselves that:

> The way we come to conclusions about what the Bible teaches is an indispensable part of how we use the Bible. No one comes to the Bible with a blank slate. We come instead with a host of presuppositions and habits of mind, some conscious and deliberate,

---

8. Sylvester and Thomson, "Boris Knows."

others products of culture, family, denomination and our personal fallenness and finitude. The same was true of the classic commentators of the Christian past.[9]

A recurring problem remains that "Some Christians abhor such lack of resolution for the uncertainty it seems to impart to the Bible."[10] Such "felt uncertainty" is one of the reasons why we devote a chapter to examining the complex nature of faith in theory and in practice.

Finally, it must never be forgotten that the divine upholder is also the one who, in Christ, "emptied himself." Any balanced understanding of the relation of God to his creation must hold in delicate balance *both* divine upholding *and* divine emptying. Not an easy task. It must never be forgotten that the divine upholder is also the one who, in Christ, "emptied himself." We see these two aspects of the Godhead supremely embodied in Christ, the one in whom all things hold together and also the one who emptied himself in his self-giving in his incarnation and at Calvary.

---

9. Thompson, *Reading the Bible*, 183–84.
10. Thompson, *Reading the Bible*, 184.

Acknowledgements

ONLY WITH THE TIRELESS encouragement and support of Thomas Ludwig, who assisted with all aspects of the manuscript preparation, has this book reached publication. My colleagues at St. Andrews, Alan Torrance and Andrew Torrance, provided invaluable guidance on the questions for study and discussion.

SECTION I

Gaining Perspective

1

Is Your God Still Too Small?

Echoes from the Past

We can never have too big a conception of God, and the more scientific knowledge (in whatever field) advances, the greater becomes our idea of his vast and complicated wisdom.[1]

Will we let God be as he is, majestic and holy, vast and wondrous, or will we always be trying to whittle him down to the size of our small minds, insist on confining him within the boundaries we are comfortable with, refuse to think of him other than in images that are convenient to our lifestyle.[2]

It is comparatively easy to name yesterday's idolatrous systems. It is much harder to point to the equivalents in today's and tomorrow's world.[3]

THE CURRENT SCENE

WHY DO YOUNG PEOPLE who have grown up in church leave it in large numbers in their teens? Why have 50 percent of those who have grown up in the Southern Baptist Church of the USA left the church by the time they are

---

1. Phillips, *Your God Is Too Small*, 123.
2. Peterson, *Long Obedience*, 120.
3. Wright, *Day the Revolution Began*, 393.

thirty? According to numerous surveys, one of the reasons is that they are asked by their pastors to believe explanations about the world they live in that totally contradict and deny what God has enabled dedicated scientists to discover about the same world and about themselves. Commitment to truth through the diligent use of our minds is a Christian responsibility. It is also a pressing pastoral issue. In his book *Vanishing Grace*,[4] Philip Yancey underlines this by highlighting some of the challenging and disturbing results of recent Barna surveys focusing on the youth in the churches of the USA. He illustrates his concerns by giving the example of a blogger named Mark Yoder who wrote about "ten surprising reasons our kids leave church." It was based on interviews in Texas, a comparatively religious state. Typical of the questions raised by advances in science—which are the focus of differences between what the young people hear in Sunday from the pulpit and what they are learning in their schools and colleges—are: Where did human beings come from? Is there such a thing as a soul? What is the relation of my mind, my brain, and my soul (if I have one)? What am I to make of claims today of healing miracles in churches? Why pray? Is prayer for the sick effective? The cumulative effect of these pressing questions has been to alert young people to the fact that, sadly, at times they are being presented with extremely shrunken versions of the Christian God, who, according to Scripture, created all things—which are "very good"—and who "upholds them at all times by the word of his power" (Heb 1:3 KJV). He is not a God who pops back from time to time on Sundays or at evangelistic rallies to give a passing "emotional buzz" or do tricks of religious magic called miracles.

This is a theme taken up by James Bryan Smith when he writes,

> But for a variety of reasons the gospel message we often hear, the story often told, is shrunken and distorted. This is why we see so many frustrated, disappointed Christians. It is not that they are bad people, but they have never heard the magnificent story in its fullness.[5]

For very good reasons, when sharing the essence of the gospel, we focus on the wonders of God's grace. The centrality of grace in presenting the Christian gospel has been underlined and shared widely in books such as *What's So Amazing about Grace?* by Philip Yancey. Sadly, despite the earnestness and sincerity with which we continue to sing hymns such as "Amazing Grace," nevertheless, at times, as Yancey has documented, so degraded, distorted, and corrupted has become the common understanding

---

4. Yancey, *Vanishing Grace*.
5. Smith, *Magnificent Story*, 13.

of grace that he felt moved to write *Vanishing Grace?* as a follow up to his earlier book. But not only has the idea of grace become grossly distorted, sadly a similar fate has befallen our understanding of "truth." This book is in part a plea that we give as much weight to loving God with the mind and to the word "truth" in the description of Jesus Christ as "full of grace and *truth,*" as we do, quite rightly, to the word "grace." The notion that "the only Son was full of truth" seems, at times, to have been almost lost altogether. If, as Philip Yancey cogently argues, the biblical understanding of grace has been shrunk almost to vanishing point, the importance of truth is today being shrunk or ignored in a similar way. Fake news is everywhere.

In Britain exposure to televised presentations from mega-churches in the USA remains limited. It is however still sufficient to note how often a preacher will promise a more prosperous life or instant healing from sickness and disease, if those listening will pray a prayer under the preacher's guidance. Commenting on this tendency Philip Yancey, long-time observer and analyst of church life in the USA, has written, "I have visited churches where authority figures make sweeping promises about a higher plane of living, or about prosperity and good health, as if superior faith will elevate you into a privileged class. That message may get results for a while—until reality sets in."[6] In Britain we do however, from time to time, witness evangelistic crusades with a strong emphasis on miracles of healing. What are we to make of the claims, at times dramatic, made at such healing crusades? In seeking to answer that question we are fortunate that an experienced medical practitioner has undertaken a detailed study of healings claimed at one such crusade in Britain. Drawing upon his published findings a later chapter is devoted to a discussion of miracles and healing. A further chapter on miracles of nature draws on the well documented book by a distinguished Cambridge scientist on the miracles recorded in the book of Exodus. Taken together these two chapters afford an opportunity to reflect on how, all too often, the God of Scripture, "Who upholds all things by the word of his power" (Heb 1:3 KJV) is reduced to a "god-of-the-gaps" or a "divine magician." All such gods are in fact "shrunken gods."

LEARNING FROM THE PAST: A SMALL BOOK WITH A LARGE IMPACT

From time to time a small book makes a huge impact in Christian circles, for example, C. S. Lewis's *Mere Christianity*[7] was not only very widely read

---

6. Yancey, *Vanishing Grace,* 81.
7. Lewis, *Mere Christianity.*

but also highly influential in shaping the thinking of Christians for several decades. Around the same time, a very small book by J. B. Phillips, a friend of Lewis, had a similar effect. In 1952 he published *Your God Is Too Small*.[8] Phillips had already established his reputation as a scholarly and careful translator of the letters of St. Paul to the young churches into contemporary and accessible English. At last the ordinary reader, often mystified by the English of the Authorized Version, felt able to understand the impact of the message of Scripture. Phillips wrote of the problems confronting the honest seeker in Christian churches of all denominations in the mid-twentieth century, "It will always be by such an effort that he either worships or serves a God *who is really too small* to command his adult loyalty and cooperation."[9] Reflecting on the views of those outside the churches as they looked at the attitudes of Christian people, he wrote, "If they [Christians] are not strenuously defending an outgrown conception of God, then they are cherishing a hothouse God who could only exist between the pages of the Bible or inside the four walls of a church."[10]

The title for this book, *Why Science and Faith Belong Together: Stories of Mutual Enrichment*, is an invitation to the reader to sit beside me as I reflect on the current landscape of contemporary debates about how properly to relate faith with an informed scientific understanding of the world we live in, of which we are a product, and for which, according to Christian doctrine, we are to be responsible stewards. Since Phillips wrote his thought-provoking book, significant advances have occurred in many areas of science and of biblical scholarship. But we still produce "gods" that are too small, and we reduce the meaning of "faith" to various forms of "what is in it for me?" and a variety of short-cut "believeisms." In his penetrating and insightful analysis, J. B. Phillips spelled out the variety of "gods" on offer in the religious marketplace at that time—"gods" who, he believed, could best be described as the "Resident Policeman," the "Grand Old Man," the "Heavenly Bosom," the "Managing Director," and various others. Phillips's "Resident Policeman" highlighted the dangers of making "conscience into God." This, said Phillips, is a highly dangerous thing to do given all that we know about how conscience is formed and conditioned by social context and group pressures, often leading to false feelings of guilt.

While so much has changed in today's world when compared with Phillips's world of the mid-twentieth century, nevertheless some of the key themes of Phillips's book still resonate strongly with salient features of

---

8. Phillips, *Your God Is Too Small*.
9. Phillips, *Your God Is Too Small*, 7 (emphasis added).
10. Phillips, *Your God Is Too Small*, 7–8.

today's Christian landscape. In the 1950s, certainly in the United Kingdom, relatively few people owned a television. Computers were largely confined to scientific laboratories. Communication was primarily by letter or telephone. Instant access and instant communication were undreamt of. Today laptops, handheld computers, and smart phones boast computing power exceeding that of some of the biggest computers in science laboratories seventy years ago. Supermarkets were in their infancy. Convenience stores were unheard of. Today the world is overwhelmed with information overload through the development of multimedia. Within the USA, and to a lesser extent within Europe, these multimedia outlets are widely used by churches and Christian organizations. What we might call today's "religious supermarkets" have a high profile and are well-stocked with an almost bewildering range of "gods" on offer. In the "convenience sections" of the religious supermarkets you can immediately see what the current best-sellers are for ready access. The many "gods" on offer in Phillips' day have multiplied several times over and the claims and counter claims for particular gods are being sold with all the power of today's media. Well-developed marketing methods are extensively used. The net effect of all this is that there is on every side a bewildering array of "gods" on offer. And each of these "gods" makes claims and counter-claims. The question is: How do we evaluate these different "gods" and the claims linked to them? Is God there primarily to make us more prosperous, to make us happy, to provide a shortcut to health and healing? In a word, in many ways Phillips's diagnosis is as relevant today as it was in 1952. Writing of Christians at that time, he said,

> Many men and women today are living, often with inner dissatisfaction, without any faith in God at all. This is not because they are particularly wicked or selfish or, as the old-fashioned would say, "godless," but because they have not found with their adult minds a God big enough to "account for" life, big enough to "fit in with" the new scientific age, big enough to command their highest admiration and respect, and consequently their willing cooperation.[11]

In 1962, a decade after Phillips book appeared, a young pastor began preaching at Christ Our King Presbyterian Church in Hartford, Connecticut. He was to become one of the most widely read and highly respected authors of the late twentieth and early twenty-first centuries. In some ways, he continued Phillips's crusade to bring the message of the Christian gospel to the ordinary reader. In 1993 he published a personal paraphrase of the New Testament in a volume titled *The Message: The New Testament in*

11. Phillips, *Your God Is Too Small*, 8.

Contemporary Language,[12] adding the Old Testament in 2002.[13] In 2018, the publication of some of Peterson's collected sermons take up and extend Phillips's themes.[14] For example, Peterson wrote,

> There are some people who are always looking for a religion that makes no demands and offers only rewards, a religion that dazzles and entertains, a religion in which there is no waiting and no emptiness. And they can usually find someone like Aaron who will help them make it up, some sort of golden calf religion. . . . And then in a moment of boredom, some of us turn our backs on all this and say to someone or other, "Make us gods, entertain us, pamper us, amuse us, give us some supernatural gewgaw that we can play with." . . . We abandon the awesome silence of worship and fill the air with third-rate jingles. We get tired of participating in the strenuous but invigorating life of freedom and faith.[15]

Today Phillips's "Grand Old Man" has, given our knowledge of the age of the universe, become very much older even than he was when Phillips wrote. Of the "Managing Director" concept of God, Phillips noted that, at first sight, it appears to be really lofty and splendid. Nevertheless, a close examination shows it to be yet another shrunken idea. Phillips wrote, "It is to think that the God who is responsible for the terrifying vastnesses of the universe cannot possibly be interested in the lives of the minute specks of consciousness which exist on this insignificant planet."[16] Once again, he refers to science when he says, "To have even the beginnings of an appreciation of the greatness of the power controlling the incredible system that science is beginning to reveal to us is a staggering but salutary experience."[17] One consequence of this view of the unimaginable size of God, wrote Phillips, is that "I cannot imagine such a tremendous God being interested in me."[18] Phillips concluded that "To hold a conception of God as a mere magnified human being is to run the risk of thinking of him as simply the Commander-in-Chief who cannot possibly spare the time to attend to the details of his subordinates' lives."[19] But, he continued, "We need a God with

---

12. Peterson, *Message: New Testament*.
13. Peterson, *Message: The Bible*.
14. Peterson, *As Kingfishers Catch Fire*.
15. Peterson, *As Kingfishers Catch Fire*, 32.
16. Phillips, *Your God Is Too Small*, 41.
17. Phillips, *Your God Is Too Small*, 41.
18. Phillips, *Your God Is Too Small*, 41.
19. Phillips, *Your God Is Too Small*, 43.

the capacity to hold, so to speak, both Big and Small in his mind at the same time. This, the Christian religion holds, is the true and satisfying concept of God revealed by Jesus Christ."[20]

The final unreal God identified by Phillips was the "Pale Galilean." Phillips wrote of how unhappy worshippers are "bound to their negative God by upbringing, by the traditions of a church or party, by the manipulation of isolated texts of Scripture, or by a morbid conscience."[21] Phillips felt that this negativity and manipulation was not faithful to the New Testament, which he described as "a book full of freedom and joy, courage and vitality."[22] He later comments,

> This pathetic idea of being "something special" is clung to with desperation, so that we find worshippers of the negative God who knowing in their secret hearts that their lives cannot really exhibit any superior qualities to those of their "worldly" or "worldly Christian" friends. Clinging tightly to their rules of "separateness" they feel that they are marked out as the special favorites of their God![23]

He adds "All this is very unattractive and unpleasant, but it is quite common among religious people."[24] Any honest assessment of the present scene would have to agree that things have not changed as much as one would wish.

Mindful of the rapid progress made by social psychologists studying group dynamics and cognitive psychologists studying the nature of belief systems, today we can better appreciate the force of the picture painted by Phillips. For example, around the time that Phillips was writing, groundbreaking books by psychologists were appearing that shed new light on how personality factors shaped individual's belief systems. Some were flexible, some highly inflexible. Such books included *The Authoritarian Personality*[25] and *The Open and Closed Mind*.[26] The research has moved on, and with hindsight we can better appreciate the force of the picture painted by Phillips. Today, we are certainly much more aware of the multiplicity of factors at work in shaping our beliefs. For example, in his recent revision of his textbook *Social Psychology*, David Myers wrote,

20. Phillips, *Your God Is Too Small*, 43.
21. Phillips, *Your God Is Too Small*, 51.
22. Phillips, *Your God Is Too Small*, 52.
23. Phillips, *Your God Is Too Small*, 52.
24. Phillips, *Your God Is Too Small*, 53.
25. Adorno et al., *Authoritarian Personality*.
26. Rokeach, *Open and Closed Mind*.

> In the political realm, even correct information may fail to discount implanted misinformation. . . . When, during the 2016 Presidential campaign, Donald Trump repeatedly claimed violent crime was increasing, media stories consistently rebutted his statements with FBI statistics showing crime had actually declined markedly since 2008. Nevertheless, 78 percent of Trump supporters continue to believe crime was increasing. . . . Such politically biased information processing is bipartisan, report Peter Ditto and his colleagues (2018). They found "clear evidence of partisan bias in both liberals and conservatives, and at virtually identical levels." When evidence supports our views, we find it cogent; when the same evidence contradicts our views, we fault it.[27]

What happens in forming beliefs in the political realm also applies in the realm of the formation and operation of religious belief systems. Most recently a paper in the prestigious *Journal of Experimental Psychology: General* was entitled "The Partisan Mind: Is Extreme Political Partisanship Related to Cognitive Inflexibility?" The article begins by referring to the two books named above by Theodor Adorno and colleagues and by Milton Rokeach. While the focus of the research in this paper is on political partisanship and thus on political beliefs, its findings regarding mental rigidity and cognitive flexibility would seem to be very relevant to religious partisanship. They write, "The results of this study, together with those across studies, suggest that the cognitively inflexible mind may be especially susceptible to the clarity, certainty, and safety frequently offered by strong loyalty to collective ideologies and doctrines, regardless of their subject matter and motivation. . . . This is in line with Rokeach's (1954) argument that adherents of both extreme left-wing and right-wing ideologies would exhibit tendencies toward rigidity."[28] Today it is not difficult to think of extreme religious ideologies displaying something of the same rigidity when asked to consider fresh interpretations of over-familiar passages of Scripture.

Eugene Peterson echoed some of Phillips's major themes. Writing of "small gods" designed to serve our purposes, Peterson argued, "His [Abraham's] relation to God was not mercantile, not utilitarian. He wasn't taking pains to stay on good terms with God so he might get a good inheritance. His altar-building doesn't seem to have been an insurance policy against disaster. His altars were spontaneous acts of friendship and gratitude, expressions of respect."[29] He continued, "You can buy a religion of promises and

27. Myers and Twenge, *Social Psychology*.
28. Zmigrod et al., "Partisan Mind," 416.
29. Peterson, *As Kingfishers Catch Fire*, 20.

wise sayings and interesting answers to big questions for fifteen or twenty dollars. The world is full of such stuff. But what most of us want to know is does it happen? Can it happen here? And is it living? We must ask the stubbornly practical questions when we come to God and to church. I have no patience with a truth that cannot be lived, and I don't want you to have any patience with it either."[30]

N. T. Wright has underlined Phillips's main theme as a contemporary issue in his book *The Challenge of Jesus*. Wright listed what he calls "Gods of our own making." He wrote, "There has been a resurgence of interest, in our post-secular world, in all kinds of vaguely religious or spiritual matters. . . . *There are, then, plenty of gods currently on offer.* . . . But, do any of them have anything to do with Jesus? . . . It is vital that in our generation we enquire once more: to what, or rather whom, does the word God truly refer?"[31] Later Wright wrote, "You can push God, or the gods, upstairs out of sight, like an elderly embarrassing relative. But history shows again and again that other gods quietly sneak in to take their place."[32] Wright continued,

> These other gods are not strangers. The ancient world knew them well. Just to name the three most obvious: there are Mars, the god of war, Mammon, the God of money, and Aphrodite the goddess of erotic love. One of the fascinating things about modern Western ideas has been the work of the "masters of suspicion" Nietzsche, Marx, and Freud, claiming to reveal the motives that lie hidden beneath the outwardly smooth and comprehensive surface of the modern world. It is all about power, declared Nietzsche. Everything comes down to money, said Marx. It's all about sex, said Freud. In each case these were seen as forces or drives that were there whether we like it or not; we might imagine we are free to choose, but in fact we are the blind servants of these impulses.[33]

Scientists also have taken up this theme. Twenty-one years ago—in the book *How Large Is God?*—there were pleas from leading scientists not to diminish the God we worship. Physics professor Howard Van Till wrote, "I invite my fellow theists, particularly those who continue to hold the special creationist picture of God's creative activity, *to enlarge their portrait of the Creator.* Allow that portrait to be large enough to include the expectation that the universe to which this Creator has given being has been generously

---

30. Peterson, *As Kingfishers Catch Fire*, 24.
31. Wright, *Challenge of Jesus*, 71 (emphasis added).
32. Wright, *Surprised by Scripture*, 152.
33. Wright, *Surprised by Scripture*, 152.

gifted from the outset with a formational economy sufficiently robust to make possible its self-organization into the full array of physical structures and biotic forms that have ever been actualized."[34] This point was eloquently made by Peterson when he was preaching about miracles. He said, "*Naming an event a miracle doesn't mean we can't understand it.* It means we can't anticipate it. It means we can't produce it. We cannot control it. There's more going on than we can comprehend. There's more to life than we can account for. Miracle is a word Christians used to name events, at least some of them, that God brings about."[35] Given the enduring relevance of these views of miracles and given the fact that, on close scrutiny, there remains today a seemingly almost unstoppable tendency to interpret miracles, ancient and modern, *as occasional interventions from an otherwise preoccupied God returning to fill an explanatory gap* in our understanding of the world we live in, we shall devote later chapters to detailed consideration of miracles ancient and modern.

SHRINKING GODS: THEOLOGICAL ALARM BELLS

High-profile theologians on both sides of the Atlantic continue to highlight the ever-present danger of shrinking our ideas of God. In the USA, Eugene Peterson wrote about "Trying to whittle him [God] down to the size of our small minds."[36] Peterson asks, "Will we let God be as he is, majestic and holy, vast and wondrous, or will we always be trying to whittle him down to the size of our small minds, insist on confining him within the boundaries we are comfortable with, refuse to think of him other than in images that are convenient to our lifestyle? But then we are not dealing with the God of creation and the Christ of the cross, but with a dime-store production of something made in our image, usually for commercial reasons."[37] In the UK, N. T. Wright, one of the best known and highly respected theologians and biblical scholars of the twenty-first century, echoes this theme when he writes that we are surrounded with "gods of our own making." His frequent references to the proliferation of "gods" underlines the spectacle of "shrinking gods" as a contemporary issue.

In April 2018, a report by the Pew Research Center in the USA revealed the ambiguity evident in the diversity of "gods" in whom Americans say they believe. The report tells us, "Nine-in-ten Americans believe in a

---

34. Van Till, "No Place for a Small God," 113 (emphasis added).
35. Peterson, *As Kingfishers Catch Fire*, 22 (emphasis added).
36. Peterson, *Long Obedience*, 114.
37. Peterson, *Long Obedience*, 120.

higher power, but only a slim majority believe in God as described in the Bible."[38] This same report underlined an age trend: "Compared with older adults, those under age 50 generally view God as less powerful and less involved in earthly affairs than do older Americans. At the same time, however, young adults are somewhat *more* likely than their elders to say they believe that they personally have been punished by God or a higher power in the universe."[39]

Another repeated trend in recent Pew surveys is that highly educated Americans are less likely to believe in the God of the Bible. "Among US adults with a high school education or less, fully two thirds say they believe in God as described in the Bible. Far fewer adults who have obtained some college education say they believe in God as described in the Bible (53 percent). And among college graduates, fewer than half (45 percent) say they believe in the God of the Bible."[40] The take-home message: Many of the "gods" in the marketplace today *are either rejected outright or not taken seriously by educated young people because they feel they are asked to commit intellectual suicide.* They are asked to do this by denying most of what they have learned, for example, in their science courses. They are asked to believe in diminished "gap-filling gods." All of which takes us back to J. B. Phillips's argument that we construct undersized gods. We explain the shrinking gaps in our knowledge by referring to a "celestial Santa Claus" that justifies our tribal purposes.

RESHAPED GODS: TECHNOLOGICAL ALARM BELLS

One feature of today's world is strikingly different from J. B. Phillips's mid-twentieth-century world. It is a change that impacts the whole population. I refer to the almost unbelievable diversity and speed of ways of communication between individuals and groups developed in the intervening years. A visitor from space visiting the small university city where I live would be fascinated by the number of students walking along, either with one hand held to their ear, or with wires dangling from both ears while they apparently speak animatedly to themselves. If this same space visitor were to look at the January 12, 2019 issue of the international journal *The Economist,* she would find a clue to understanding this strange behavior. In an article headed "Bad news for Apple. Good news for Humanity," we read that "smart phone sales have peaked and seem to be levelling off at around 1.4 billion

---

38. Pew Research Center, "Americans Say They Believe."
39. Pew Research Center, "Americans Say They Believe."
40. Pew Research Center, "Americans Say They Believe."

units a year."[41] The piece continues, "People have voted with their wallets to make the smart phone the most successful consumer product in history: nearly 4 billion of the 5.5 billion adults on the planet now have one. And no wonder. They connect billions of people to the internets of information and services."[42] This is just one example of the almost unbelievable changes in the diversity and speed of ways of communicating between individuals and groups. *Such almost universal and instant communication in today's world, including knowledge of God and religion, has implications for the spread of knowledge that we are only just beginning to understand.* It means that in what I have referred to as the religious marketplace we may expect great competition both in the marketing and in the selling of the "gods on offer," including the "gods that are no gods," what I have called "shrunken gods."

How may we take advantage of the vast range of new technologies developed since Phillips wrote his book in 1952 without distorting the Christian message? Using developing technologies to share the gospel is not new. What is new are the many different ways of summarizing, presenting, and commenting on information, along with the exponential growth of communication technology. *These are not simply "neutral" technologies, they have the capacity to actually affect the messages being communicated in subtle, and not such subtle ways.* They can *change the message.* If we forget this, we make the mistake of forgetting these effects despite the impact of Marshall McLuhan's 1964 book, reminding us that "the medium is the message"[43]

When capitalizing on and adopting the benefits of these modern technologies for sharing the gospel, we need always to be alert to the ever-present dangers of, in the process, unthinkingly "shrinking the God" of the Christian gospel we are so keen to share. At times, for example, we shrink God to a "tick-box God." At times, we shrink God to "another way of satisfying our consumer instincts." Some words of Campbell and Garner may help to safeguard against the ever-present dangers of *shrinking both faith and God.*

> Walking humbly with God is a lifelong journey, and many of the spiritual exercises, disciplines, and realities of the Christian life *do not deliver everything instantly with little or no effort.* One strand of use of media and technology in our worship and church communities is to recognize people's short-term expectations and *chronos*-centered lives—to use Kevin Miller's terminology—and then assist and encourage them to deepen

---

41. Economist, "Maturing Smartphone Industry."
42. Economist, "Maturing Smartphone Industry."
43. McLuhan, *Understanding Media.*

their walks with God by helping them to develop a longer view of time.[44]

The Printing Press Changed Everything: Now Multimedia Is Changing Everything Again

In his book *The Hidden Power of Electronic Culture: How Media Shapes Faith, The Gospel, and the Church,* Shane Hipps notes that,

> In the fifteenth century, Johannes Gutenberg found an innovative use for a wine press, and the modern age of the printing press was born. With this simple invention, Gutenberg unknowingly set off an explosion of such overwhelming power that we continue to feel its reverberations today. Printing made the alphabet perfectly uniform and infinitely repeatable. This mass production placed literacy into the hands of everyone, subsequently launching the Protestant Reformation.[45]

In a word, the development of printing was extremely instrumental in facilitating the wide effects of the Protestant Reformation. This means that the new technology not only affected the communication of the Christian message but also affected the *content* of the Christian message for thousands and its wider dissemination witnessed by the fruits of the Reformation. The print not only had beneficial effects and affected our theology it also had other effects, which had both benefits and downsides. Hipps notes some of these.

First, he believes that print made us more individualistic and this means that "The modern age conceived of a gospel that *matters primarily for the individual*. The gospel was reduced to *forgiveness as a transaction*, a concern for personal morality, and intellectual pursuit of doctrinal precision. In this view the Bible became little more than an individual's handbook for moral living and right thinking. As a result, printing had a *tendency to erode the communal nature of faith*."[46] Note the "shrunken gods" implied by a gospel that matters primarily for the individual and how "the Bible became little more than an individual's handbook for moral living and right thinking," The effect was a "shrinking faith" that eroded the communal nature of faith—what in a later chapter I refer to as "faith in action." A theme taken up

---

44. Campbell and Garner, *Networked Theology,* 175 (emphasis added).
45. Hipps, *Hidden Power of Electronic Culture,* 51.
46. Hipps, *Hidden Power of Electronic Culture,* 54 (emphasis added).

by Dietrich Bonhoeffer in the mid-twentieth century with his emphasis on discipleship and community.

Secondly, says Hipps, print introduced the notion of objectivity. This has benefits, but also possible drawbacks. Hipps writes, "However, if objectivity is taken to its extreme, it leads to the belief that we can read and discover biblical truth with an unbiased clarity of vision. We presume the Bible presents an objective set of propositions that everyone will discover if they just read it properly. This inflated sense of objectivity, fueled by printing, breeds an unfortunate and arrogant illusion of omniscience. It leaves little room for subjective experience in the work of the Holy Spirit."[47]

Third, print makes us think more abstractly. Hipps argues that, "Another effect of this emphasis on abstraction was that Protestants became preoccupied with getting the doctrine straight. *Anyone who didn't hold a particular set of abstract propositions* in their head was deemed a heretic. As the modern age of print continued, Christians began scanning the Bible to extract propositional truth from disparate places and contexts in order to organize their theology into abstract categories."[48]

Finally, argued Hipps, print intensifies linear, rational thinking. Hipps writes, "Printing amplified and greatly extended this symbol system, leading to modernity's age of reason, in which linear, rational thought came to be the sole means of discovering truth. In the life of faith, the reasoning skills fostered by print extend our capacity for discernment."[49] He notes, "Paul was a highly literate person, and his letters reflect the kind of abstract if/then reasoning characteristic of a literal mind. This sits in contrast to the Gospels, which are *characterized by concrete storytelling rooted in the old tradition.* . . . This is one reason why Martin Luther's rediscovery of Romans resonated with post-Reformation culture in a way it couldn't have before that point."[50]

Hipps provides a recent example of the application of this emphasis on rational thinking. He writes,

> The modern preference for linear reasoning and suspicion of feelings is also well illustrated by "the four spiritual laws," an evangelistic tract by the late Bill Bright. In this pamphlet, Bright laid out *the syllogism of four abstract propositions one must believe in order to be saved.* Once the doctrines have been believed through reason and Christ is accepted through cognitive assent,

---

47. Hipps, *Hidden Power of Electronic Culture*, 55.
48. Hipps, *Hidden Power of Electronic Culture*, 57–58 (emphasis added).
49. Hipps, *Hidden Power of Electronic Culture*, 58.
50. Hipps, *Hidden Power of Electronic Culture*, 58 (emphasis added).

Bright issues a stark warning under the heading "Do Not Depend on Feelings." . . . The relegation of emotion to the caboose is unfortunate, for it reduces our view of people to little more than cognitive rational beings.[51]

The effect is still apparent today in some forms of what, in our discussions of the "religious superstore," we describe as "tick-box Christianity." Again, this brings to mind my reminder that faith involves cognition, conation, and emotion. This approach also fails to recognize the diverse roots of real faith in real lives, which is shaped by biological influences, psychological influences, and sociocultural influences, as is illustrated with examples in later chapters.

Potentials and Pitfalls of Technology

Some Christians, aware of the potential impact of expanding technologies on both the way the Christian gospel is portrayed in modern media and the methods being used to share the gospel, have alerted us to the need for analysis and action. One such early attempt was Shane Hipps's book mentioned above. Another, a decade later, was the book by Heidi Campbell and Stephen Garner titled *Networked Theology: Negotiating Faith in Digital Culture.*[52]

Hipps, drawing attention to an idea found in McLuhan's book, wrote, "We shape our tools, and afterward our tools shape us."[53] Hipps explored the wider effects on the Christian church of some of the rapid advances in communication technologies. A central theme of Hipps's book was not simply about how the technological advances have affected the range of media available today and about how they are used but, as he writes, "Rather, it seeks to provide the tools to help us interpret our electronic culture and understand the implications for our faith and our corporate life together. Behind everything that follows is a conviction that within the forms of media and technology, regardless of their content, *are extremely powerful forces that cause changes in our faith, theology, culture, and ultimately the church.*"[54]

---

51. Hipps, *Hidden Power of Electronic Culture*, 59–60 (emphasis added).
52. Campbell and Garner, *Networked Theology.*
53. The quote was actually written by Father John Culkin, SJ, a professor of communication at Fordham University in New York and friend of McLuhan. But though the quote is Culkin's, it is usually argued that the idea is McLuhan's, as it comes up in an article by Culkin about McLuhan. Culkin, *Schoolman's Guide to McLuhan.*
54. Hipps, *Hidden Power of Electronic Culture*, 17 (emphasis added).

The relevance of the issues discussed by Hipps is illustrated by a further quote. Commenting on the impact of Marshall McLuhan, a devout Catholic, through his 1967 book *The Medium Is the Massage*, Hipps writes, "McLuhan had much to say about the church, but his insights on the subject were largely ignored and rarely heeded. For example, just as the mega-church movement was gaining momentum in the early 1970s, he said, 'Christianity—in a centralized, administrative, bureaucratic form—is certainly irrelevant.'"[55] Most people didn't believe him then, but his prediction is increasingly coming true. While certain corners of the church (i.e., Pentecostals and Anabaptists) always practiced decentralized leadership, it is now becoming the model in many mainstream evangelical churches.

It is extremely important to realize that the possible effects of new technologies, not only upon the *communication* of the Christian faith, but also about the *content* of the Christian faith, has been amply demonstrated in the history of the Christian church. As Hipps notes by way of illustration, "The formation of the phonetic alphabet was an important element in shaping Western thought, but *its true impact became apparent only after it was channeled through the medium of print.* Printing amplified the effects of the alphabet with exponential force and completely restructured the culture—and therefore the church—in the process."[56]

MAKING GODS IN OUR OWN IMAGE: INSIGHTS FROM SOCIAL SCIENTISTS

David Myers, author of the bestselling college textbook in psychology for the last forty years, noted that for religious believers there is an enduring temptation to idolatry—that is, fashioning a God in their own image and worshipping this false god. Myers pointed out that three recent social science investigations have demonstrated the lure of this temptation and its relevance to today's culture and politics.[57] Myers asked the question, does God care about politicians' personal morality? He noted that in 2011, the Public Religion Research Institute (PPRI) asked voters "If an elected official who commits an immoral act in their personal life can still have can still behave ethically and fulfil their duties and their public and professional life." Only three in ten White evangelical Protestants concurred that politician's personal lives have no bearing on their public roles. But by July 2017, seven in ten White evangelicals were willing to separate the public and personal.

55. Hipps, *Hidden Power of Electronic Culture*, 32.
56. Hipps, *Hidden Power of Electronic Culture*, 50 (emphasis added).
57. Myers, "For Irreligious Evangelicals."

It was a head-spinning reversal, said the PRRI CEO—a shift explained by political researcher Michele Margolis finding that "It's not just that our religious beliefs affect our politics—it's that our politics affect our religious choices."[58] As William James wrote a century ago, sometimes "Piety is the mask" that covers and justifies our passions and politics: "At most we may blame piety for not availing to check our natural passions, and sometimes for supplying them with hypocritical pretexts."[59]

Myers went on to note that social psychologist Nicholas Epley and his colleagues explored *the human tendency to make God in our own image*. Most people, they found, believe that God agrees with whatever they believe. No surprise there. Perhaps folks are just letting their religious understanding guide their attitudes. But consider that when the researchers persuaded people to change their minds about affirmative action or the death penalty, they then assume that God believed the new view. As I am today, so is God. Myers also noted that people likewise project their social beliefs into their religious texts. As he has noted elsewhere, this phenomenon enables partisans on culture-war issues, such as immigration or sexual orientation or gender equality, *to read their Scriptures as supporting whatever beliefs they bring to them*. As my colleagues and I wrote in a recent publication, it is all too easy for those of us who are people of faith to be "not really listening to the Bible, but simply hearing our own voices echoing off the pages."[60] The final study noted by Myers seeks to answer the question, what does God look like? He says that a new study by a University of North Carolina research team led by Joshua Jackson exposed 511 American Christians to sets of faces overlaid with visual noise (making them appear fuzzy). When asked which best fit their image of God, most folks imagine God in ways similar to themselves in seeming age, attractiveness, and to a lesser extent, race. But liberals saw God as relatively more feminine and African American. Conservatives envisaged an older God. Perhaps, the researchers concluded on a note of hope, teaching people how their perceptions of God vary "may help increase religious tolerance."[61]

But is there a remedy for such idolatry? Part of the answer is a new humility. Believing that humans are imperfect creatures, not little gods, is a basis for humility. Theists may take a leap of faith, believing that sometimes (as when marrying or voting) life bids them to commit themselves to something about which they are 51 percent sure. Even so, they may also

---

58. Margolis, "When Politicians Determine Religious Beliefs."
59. James, *Varieties of Religious Experience*, 331.
60. Lucas et al., "Bible, Science, and Human Origins," 99.
61. Jackson, "Faces of God."

acknowledge that some of their beliefs surely err. When tempted to view themselves as did Shakespeare's Hamlet, "in apprehension how like a god," they should remember: if an infinite creative being exists, their comparatively meager minds are closer to what T. S. Eliot understood as a "headpiece filled with straw."[62] They can, therefore, push themselves to take God's perspective rather than their own.

Humility has, in the past, been a hallmark of leading scientists. But it is not always so. Scientists also have a personal agenda. At times they energetically make overblown claims. For example, on the day in April 1953 when James Watson and Francis Crick announced their model of the structure of DNA in Cambridge, they are recorded as describing it down at the local pub as having solved "the secret of life." They would have done well on their way to the pub, as they hastened through the portals of the Old Cavendish Laboratory, opened in 1874, to have noted the Latin inscription over the archway from the book of Psalms: "The works of the Lord are great, sought out of all them that have pleasure therein" (Ps 111:2 KJV). This is a timely reminder that equally great scientists before and after Watson and Crick have been humble and committed Christians.

SHRUNKEN FAITH AND SHRUNKEN GODS

As we identify exemplars of "shrunken gods," we need to pause and ask a related question, *is our God too small, not only because our idea of God has shrunk, but also because our understanding of the nature of faith has shrunk as well?* Given that question, I devote two chapters putting faith—as it is talked about, understood, and practiced today—under the microscope. Could it be that our seemingly over-readiness to worship shrunken gods is because we have accepted shrunken and unbiblical ideas of what is meant by faith and belief? As I will describe later, there is much to be learned from the lives of great people of faith of past generations. Since faith involves cognition, affect, and conation, and since all of these aspects of our mental lives can go wrong, I will illustrate from the lives of people such Martin Luther, John Bunyan, John Wesley, William Cowper, and J. B. Phillips how they, at times, struggled to cope with challenges to their faith. Hopefully we may learn from their lives and their struggles as we seek, in our day, to live the life of faith in all its fullness.

---

62. Eliot, "Hollow Men," 79.

Gods-of-the-Gaps and Shrunken Gods

As one considers Phillip's "unreal gods," many of them could be characterized as temporary "stop-gap" gods with a strictly limited scope and shelf life. His frequent reference to developments in science makes ready links with widespread contemporary discussions in the literature relating Christian faith to the scientific enterprise where the ever-present temptation to produce a variety of "gods-of-the-gaps" is never far away. "Stop-gap gods" are not new. Witness the widespread prevalence today, frequently associated with attempts to relate what we know of God from Scripture with what we infer about God from advances in philosophy and science, of a fallback position that in the past so often became "explain as much as you can without reference to God and if there remains a gap in your knowledge bring in God to fill the gap." The exposure and critique of the so-called "god-of-the-gaps" approach will always be associated with the Oxford mathematician Charles Coulson.[63] Coulson was critiquing a view that can be illustrated with a quotation from theologian W. A. Whitehouse, who wrote,

> I am myself inclined to think that the mystery of God's providence lies deeper than the eruption into nature of such interferences (he is thinking of the possible control of matter by mind) and I am attracted by the fact that the scientific explanations and predictions rest now on "the law of great numbers"; that fundamental physical laws are statistical, not exact in the popular sense. Why this should be so is an interesting metaphysical speculation. It may provide a sufficient room for manoeuvre beneath the observable, regular processes, for the personal care of God to be actively exercised.[64]

The key phrase is "room for manoeuvre," which implies that nature has things more or less tied up, but there may be a few gaps in which God can still have his own way. It is not only theologians who at times have written in this way; so also have some distinguished scientists, such as a leading astrophysicist who wrote approvingly of "the notion of God continually intervening, with deft touches now here, now there, to direct the material particles in the universe so as to conform to rationally deduced laws."[65] This interventionist "god-of-the-gaps" way of thinking was criticized by philosopher/theologian Austin Farrer,[66] who suggested that God's action in the

---

63. Coulson, *Science and Christian Belief*.
64. Whitehouse, *Christian Faith*, 121.
65. Milne, *Modern Cosmology*, 156.
66. Farrer, *Faith and Speculation*.

universe should be described in terms of "double agency." He argued that it is impossible to conceive of God's ways of acting in terms of our own, and therefore the causal joint between God's action and ours will always be hidden. Consequently, each event in the universe must have a double description and can therefore be spoken of in terms of the providential action of God while at the same time having a full natural explanation. Later we shall offer several illustrative examples of this important principle. Today, varieties of "god-of-the-gaps" are not only alive and flourishing but are spreading their influence.

In contrast to the historic emphasis in Christian theology on understanding God as the Creator and Sustainer of all things, there is today an almost bewildering diversity of smaller and limited "gap-filling gods" on offer in the religious marketplace. This observation resonates with the writings of leading contemporary high-profile figures in both theology and science who have documented the proliferation of "gods" in the religious marketplace. As we shall document later, some of these scholars have written about how the traditional Christian understanding of God has continued to be distorted and diminished. Because the "gods-of-the-gaps" are still alive and well, we shall spend time later examining them more closely. To be aware of them may help to see them for what they are, using God as a "stop gap" when our other efforts at understanding ourselves, our mysterious human nature and the world we live in through the scientific enterprise are, at the moment, incomplete. The clue is the phrase *"at the moment, incomplete"* because such is the nature of the scientific endeavor that given time and more research these current gaps will be filled in and thus the "gods" filling them will shrink and eventually become redundant. We shall give examples of how this has already happened, not only as the result of advances in science but also of advances in biblical scholarship which have helped us to see how, at times, in the past, we have misunderstood Scripture.

Referring to Phillips's book and reflecting on the question "How large is God?" the Lutheran church historian Martin Marty wrote,

> From time to time, a religious thinker will write, as J. B. Phillips did some years ago, a book with a teasing title such as *Your God is Too Small*. Such works usually have to do with the limits some prayerful folk put on the power of a personal God, so that this God cannot be of much help to them, whether as judge or savior or comforter. While they may not use the precise formulaic version "How Large is God," believers do ask something like this of others when some of them come to grief. Is the thou to whom you pray and whose comfort you seek great enough to hear and to provide support? How large is God? one may also ask in times

of doubt or despair, when this thou seems remote or eclipsed, silent or dead. Is your God so small that you feel abandoned? Is your God so reduced that you can get no affirmations to counter your doubts or despair?[67]

In developing his theme Marty raised the question "Why do you ask how large is God?" He believes the question is to be answered by a threefold response:

> Because if you are to deal with the concept of God at all, then if God, your God, the God in your world of conception and ideas and practice, is small, you will, first, do justice to reality—and all responsible people should seek to be true, to speak the truth as well as they can. Second, you will simply be left behind in the intellectual marketplace by those who ask non-God or anti-God questions. Or, third, you will constrict the imagination and obstruct the will, at a time when *our cultures need vast imaginations to deal with vast problems. They also need liberated wills, so that people in these cultures can make proper moral address to the issues of the day.*[68]

In response to these profound questions raised by Martin Marty, we shall, throughout this book, seek to do justice *both* to all that we are learning about ourselves and the creation of which we are a part through our scientific endeavors *and* at the same time seek to do full justice to those things that are revealed to us in Scripture and that, thanks to the continuing efforts of dedicated biblical scholars, continue to give us new insights into the greatness of our God. The details of advances in science are presented in each chapter as we discuss human origins, human nature, miracles, healing, and so on. What is not so widely recognized, and needs to be, is that just as there is progress in science there is also progress in New Testament and in Old Testament studies.

When Steve Walton gave his inaugural lecture as Professor of New Testament at the London School of Theology in 2012, he chose to title it, "What Is Progress in New Testament Studies?" He began by describing how an eminent scientist had posed to him the question "So, I know what is progress in my discipline. What's progress in your discipline, in New Testament studies?"[69] Walton goes on to point out that his answers to this question have implications both in the academy and in the wider church. And, as we've already seen, some of the members of the wider church are thoughtful

---

67. Marty, "Voices of Theologians and Humanists," 170.
68. Marty, "Voices of Theologians and Humanists," 171–72 (emphasis added).
69. Walton, "What Is Progress."

students at universities and colleges and they need to be aware that there are advances not only in science but also in biblical studies. If they knew this, they would be better able to think through some of the so-called conflicts we have listed already and will discuss in detail in later chapters. Walton's detailed response helps those of us who are mere scientists and lay people first of all to remain aware that in New Testament studies, research advances and views change, and also to avoid the temptation to put too much faith in a particular interpretation of particular texts at a particular time in history by a particular group of theologians, rather than putting their faith in the central figure in all of those researches. Our faith as Christians is not in a particular interpretation of a particular proof text in the early twenty-first century, our faith is in the living God revealed to us supremely in his only Son Jesus Christ.

That advances are occurring and that there is progress in New Testament studies is exemplified in Walton's lecture. He gives examples of how interpretations at any time are culturally embedded. He cites the example of how, for a time, German New Testament scholarship in some quarters was able to close its eyes to the Holocaust and to the tragic consequences of one way of interpreting the New Testament. Similarly, the South African government's policy of apartheid, the separate development of different ethnic groups, was justified by ways of reading the New Testament (and of the Old) which underlie the differences among ethnic groups rather than recognizing their common humanity. He notes that Richard Burridge has shown how the Dutch Reformed Church defended apartheid as in harmony with Scripture. Walton also points out that scholarship also has its academic fashions, which come and go. He notes that questions are asked and sometimes castles are built in the air on the slenderest of foundations. To illustrate his point, he refers to Richard Bauckham's plenary paper at a 1995 British New Testament meeting addressing the question, "For whom were the Gospels written?"[70] Bauckham cogently attacked the foundations of redaction critical study of the Gospels by arguing that the Gospels were written for a broad Mediterranean audience rather than particular individual local Christian communities. Walton says that Bauckham persuasively argued that New Testament scholarship had been down a blind alley for fifty years in reconstructions of "the Lukan community" and the like, and thus change—development of redaction criticism's reconstructions of communities—was not progress. In concluding this section of his lecture, Walton argues, "but the point remains: the method, developing hypotheses and then testing them against the data, is common to scientific enquiry and

---

70. Bauckham, "For Whom Were the Gospels."

New Testament studies. This implies that in both science and New Testament studies our knowledge is provisional: it is unwise to claim certainty for in both areas we deal in degrees of probability, highly probable to highly improbable. Intellectual honesty (and, a Christian would add, intellectual humility) requires that we recognize this and do not claim too much."[71]

Walton points out that archaeologists are constantly making fresh discoveries that are relevant for New Testament scholarship. Walton notes, for example, that "the most significant find of the twentieth century for New Testament scholarship must be the discovery the Dead Sea Scrolls in 1947."[72] Walton also underlines the need to read the New Testament against its sociocultural context. Of this, he writes, "Peter Oakes has considerably illuminated both Philippians and Romans by his fine work on the physical and social contexts of Philippi and Pompei. In both studies, Oakes uses knowledge gleaned from archaeological, epigraphical and literary sources to reconstruct the kind of community found in the cities and then seeks to 'hear' Paul's writing through the ears of the kind of people who most likely received the letters."[73]

Towards the end of his lecture, Walton makes a comment that relates closely to a point underlined repeatedly in a later chapter of this book— namely the need to be fully aware of the kind of reader that the New Testament authors presuppose. Their target audience are disciples. The target audience are not dilettantes, they are not a group of people searching for shortcuts to an easy life, rather, as Walton puts it, these texts are addressed "to a person who is committed to worshipping Jesus as Lord and living in tune with that commitment"[74]

More than a decade before Walton gave his inaugural lecture, another distinguished New Testament scholar, Martin Hengel of Tübingen University, had published a paper with the title "Tasks of New Testament Scholarship." The summary at the head of his paper set out his agenda clearly. It read as follows,

> New Testament scholarship must move beyond its current preoccupation with faddish methods (as evidenced by several variations of the so-called new literary criticism) and return to a solid grounding in history, primary source materials, archaeology, and competence in the pertinent languages. This also entails

71. Walton, "What Is Progress."
72. Walton, "What Is Progress."
73. Walton, "What Is Progress."
74. Walton, "What Is Progress."

familiarity with early Judaism, the Greek and Roman world, and early patristics.[75]

The theme of Martin Hengel's paper is a message that needs repeating today when there seems to be preoccupation with "certainty" in every realm of the religious life. He wrote,

> New Testament scholarship has always been in good part *a science of conjecture* and has become even more so. This fact should make us more modest. It is frequently a matter only of weighing probabilities, plausibilities, or even mere possibilities, and too often there exists the danger of confusing what is precisely possible with what in fact is really probable. An equation with several unknowns cannot be solved! . . . We must learn to recognise our limits at the point at which we can no longer establish probability but can only guess. We should not therefore be ashamed to speak candidly of our great uncertainty.[76]

Reading the Bible in Its Historical and Literary Contexts

Every advance in technology results in ever more rapid communication between different nations throughout the world. One side-effect of this increasing intercommunication between nations and peoples has been a fresh realization that every group and every nation has its own habitual ways of thinking, its own presuppositions about the world in which we live. This applies also to the presuppositions all of us carry, frequently unconsciously and of which we are unaware, that influence how we interpret events and people we meet and the literature that we read. The reading of the Bible is not exempt from the powerful effects of these unconscious and unspoken presuppositions. As a result, there have been an increasing number of books by Christians highlighting our past and present failure in the West to understand and take note of the presuppositions that those without our "Western set of eyes and presuppositions" bring to the reading of Scripture. Professional Old and New Testament biblical scholars have, of course, known the effects of these presuppositions for centuries, but the results of their scholarly endeavors frequently take a very long time to permeate through to the consciousness of the average pew dweller, that is if they ever do.

One result of our failure to be aware of the advances in biblical scholarship is that our interpretations of the Bible are anchored in the past and

---

75. Hengel, "New Testament Scholarship," 67.
76. Hengel, "New Testament Scholarship," 75–76 (emphasis added).

our thinking is impoverished by our failure to be enriched by the fruits of more recent scholarly labors. Recently there have been several books aimed at helping us be aware of the cultural embeddedness of Scripture. Typical of these is the book by E. Randolph Richards and Brendan J. O'Brien titled *Misreading Scripture with Western Eyes: Removing Cultural Blinders to Better Understanding the Bible*. Richards and O'Brien remind us that, "In whatever place and whatever age people read the Bible, we instinctively draw from our own cultural context to make sense of what we are reading.... We can easily forget that Scripture is a foreign land and that reading the Bible is a cross-cultural experience. To open the Word of God is to step into a strange world where things are very unlike our own. Most of us don't speak the languages. We don't know the geography or the customs or what behaviors are considered rude or polite. And yet we hardly notice."[77] It was these considerations that prompted Richards and O'Brien to write their book. They wrote, "The core conviction that drives this book is that some of the habits that we readers from the West (United States, Canada, and Western Europe) bring to the Bible can blind us to interpretations that the original audience and readers in other cultures see quite naturally."[78] Richards and O'Brien are fully aware that, "Making generalized statements about *Eastern* and *Western* cultures is ill-advised." But, as they say, we have to start somewhere. As we do so it is good to remember the advice of Richards and O'Brien that, "The best way to become sensitive to our own presuppositions about cultural mores—what goes without being said for us—is to read the writing of Christians from different cultures and ages. Being confronted with what others take for granted helps us identify what we take for granted."[79] They quote C. S. Lewis in his introduction to Athanasius's *On the Incarnation*, where he writes, "Every age has its own outlook. It is especially good at seeing certain truths and especially liable to make certain mistakes. We all, therefore, need the books that will correct the characteristic mistakes of our own period. And that means that the old books.... Not, of course, that there is any magic in the past. People were no cleverer then than they are now; they made as many mistakes as we. But not the same mistakes."[80] It is also important to remember, as Richards and O'Brien note, that, "Like the world we inhabit today, the worlds of both the Old and New Testaments were ethnically diverse and richly textured by an assortment of cultures, languages, and customs. And also like today, ancient peoples had a number of ways of

---

77. Richards and O'Brien, *Misreading Scripture*, 11.
78. Richards and O'Brien, *Misreading Scripture*, 15.
79. Richards and O'Brien, *Misreading Scripture*, 49.
80. Lewis, "Introduction," 7.

distinguishing between locals and out-of-towners, friends and enemies, the elite and the marginalized. Prejudice comes in all varieties, yesterday, today, and tomorrow. Time immemorial, humans have held prejudices against others based on their ethnicity, the color of their skin or factors such as where they come from and how they speak."[81]

One of the recurring themes in later chapters of this book will be the ways in which Christian faith may be enriched and our understanding of the God we worship may be enlarged by paying attention not only to what we read in the Bible but also to what we continue to learn about ourselves and the creation from the dedicated researches of scientists. This applies to this present chapter, where it is relevant to remember that psychological researches have underlined with an abundance of evidence what thoughtful people have long believed, namely, that our expectations, beliefs, and prejudices influence how we see the world, including other people, and how we interpret what we read. Psychologists have accumulated an abundance of evidence that gives us insights into how some of these mechanisms work at the basic level of visual perception, at the level of cognition (the effects of our beliefs and presuppositions), and at the level of the influence of social factors.

---

81. Richards and O'Brien, *Misreading Scripture*, 57.

2

Anything New under the Sun?
The Proliferation of Gods

THE STORY IS TOLD of how the film director Cecil B. DeMille was asked why he did not reproduce his famous silent film "The King of Kings," seen by an estimated 800 million people, with sound and color. He replied, "I will never be able to do it, because if I gave Jesus a southern accent, the northerners would not think of him as their Christ. If I gave him a foreign accent, the Americans and British would not think of him as their Christ. As it is, people of all nations, from every race, creed, clan, can accept him as their Christ."[1] This underlines the seemingly almost universal human urge to create "gods" of one sort or another, and all too often to re-make God in their own image. It is a further example of the results of the surveys mentioned in the previous chapter showing how we all too easily make our "gods" to match our own self-image.

Anthropologists have documented the urge for people of all times and places to create gods they can worship. Although the functions of "gods" varies widely across time and in different cultures, nevertheless there are common themes—such as the desire to have a god who will fulfil felt human needs and who will protect their worshippers. But what do we mean by a "god"? A little under a century ago, Cyril Valentine wrote a book titled *What Do We Mean by God?* In it, he referred to the writings of Xenophanes

---

1. Graham, *Wisdom for Each Day*, 358. Today we are even more highly sensitized to matters of color and race. With the benefit of hindsight, we can see that even Cecil B. DeMille was reflecting the blindness of his own time by presenting an obviously Anglo-Saxon Jesus.

of Colophon, who lived more than five hundred years before Christ and was already skeptical about the truth of some of the popular ideas of gods. Valentine says that, "In his quaint verse he makes a ruthless attack upon anthropomorphism."[2] What Xenophanes said so long ago is worth remembering today:

> Men imagine that the gods are born as they are, and have perception as they have, and also voice and form. . . . Yes, but if oxen or horses had hands and could paint to produce works of art as men do, horses would paint the god like horses and oxen like oxen. Ethiopians make their gods black and snub-nosed, and the Thracians give theirs red hair and blue eyes.[3]

The temptation to thinkingly or unthinkingly mold our idea of God to fit our presuppositions and momentary felt needs is very much in evidence today. It is underlined by the results of numerous surveys in the USA studying the beliefs of contemporary American Christians. For example, social psychologist Nicholas Epley and his colleagues have studied this human tendency to make God in our own image. Most people, they reported, believe that God agrees with whatever they believe. When the researchers persuaded people to change their minds about affirmative action or the death penalty, those people then assumed that God believed their new view.[4] *As I am*, the thinking goes, *so is God*.

The full impact of the repeated messages from numerous surveys in the USA in the past two decades monitoring the nature and the occurrence of changing religious beliefs can all too easily get lost amongst the maze of statistics. At times, to bring home the full impact of what some of the statistics really mean, and what lies behind them, we need to listen to first-person accounts of the journey to faith. One such is the letter from the young US student referred to above. Another is the 2017 book *The Magnificent Story* by the high-profile author James Bryan Smith. In it he gives an honest, at times heartrending, account of how he came to a living faith in Christ. I believe his story is typical of all too many thoughtful young Christians today. Chapter 2 of his book is called "Falling for Shrunken Stories," a title that echoes one of the major themes of this present book.[5] Smith tells us of how he grew up as what he calls "a Christmas and Easter Methodist." He goes on to tell how he and a close friend decided "to connect with God, but we did not know how." So together they set out seeking to learn about God. Their

---

2. Valentine, *What Do We Mean*, 11.
3. Clement, "Stromata," 5:14 and 7:4 (Fragments 14 and 15 from Xenophanes).
4. Epley et al., "Believers' Estimates."
5. Smith, *Magnificent Story*.

first attempt was by attending a meeting that in their church bulletin was called "a seekers meeting." But they say that they were sadly disappointed. When they asked, "What is the point of Christianity?" the reply they were given was "It is trying to be a good person and to do good things. Trying to live an ethical life, to right society's wrongs, and to engage in social justice causes." They were left with the feeling, as they say, that "God is distant and uninvolved." They write, "This shrunken story has had its day, particularly in the twentieth century. Two world wars and countless other wars, terrorism, and school shootings indicate that we have not progressed as much as we thought. This story is too small. It is centered on humans, who are puny. It had its chance and is found wanting."[6]

The next gospel they were confronted with in their search is what they call "the shaming and scary gospel." Having come to rudimentary faith in Christ, Smith went off to college where he was confronted by the leader of a parachurch ministry for college students who told him that he was not a real Christian because he had not prayed "the sinner's prayer." For a while, he writes, this scary and shaming gospel sounded convincing, but eventually Smith decided that "it was neither good, beautiful, nor true." As Smith wrote, "The gospel of Fred (the leader of the parachurch ministry) can be summed up like this: you are bad, God is mad, but Jesus took your beating. So try harder and you might make it to heaven." Smith goes on to say, "Each of the shrunken stories contains a measure of truth. We *are* sinners. Jesus *did* die for us. Scientific progress *has* been a great blessing to humans. We *should* make the world better. They are convincing because they contain a measure of truth."[7] Of these and the various other stories that James Bryan Smith confronted he asked the question, "what is at stake in getting it wrong?" He continues, "*The stories are too small because they start with us.* The social gospel puts humans at the center of the universe. Humankind as a generator of science, progress, and justice. The shaming gospel also starts with us, 'you are a sinner, salvation is about getting us into heaven . . . .'"[8] This tendency to allow prevailing and constantly changing public opinions to influence our professed religious beliefs depends in part on how involved and active our religious life is at any particular time. As social psychologist David Myers has recently noted, "It's no secret that many self-described 'evangelicals' are actually not religiously engaged. During the Republican primaries, Donald Trump's base was substantially non-churchgoing 'evangelicals.'"[9] In a 2016

---

6. Smith, *Magnificent Story*, 21.
7. Smith, *Magnificent Story*, 27.
8. Smith, *Magnificent Story*, 32 (emphasis added).
9. Myers, "Frontiers in Psychological Science."

survey by American National Election Studies, barely more than one-third of evangelicals who attended church weekly supported Trump, as did more than half of "evangelicals" who rarely attended. These non-attenders were also "more likely to agree with racist and anti-Muslim views."[10]

IDOLATRY AND CREATING OUR OWN GODS

Valentine noted that,

> Xenophanes refused the name of God to the religious beliefs of his time, but did not deny the reality of God. . . . If we may trust Aristotle at this point, Xenophanes considered that the name God was rightly used when it was made to designate the principle of unity and wholeness which for him was ultimate reality. The statement of Aristotle may be translated thus, . . . "Fixing his attention upon the universe as a whole, he said that in its unity it was God." In this way Xenophanes places God upon the objective side together with the universe and thus releases the idea from the subjective side where stand the mythologies. The pictures of God may hang upon the insubstantial walls of the mind's self-taught habitation, but the fact of God is embedded in the wide reality beneath and beyond. . . . God is not just another name for the universe; neither is he just a fantasy to satisfy human needs. Conceived as merely the universe, he cannot satisfy human needs; but neither can he satisfy human needs when he lacks the reality which the universe possesses. The problem is to understand how God can be as real and objective as the universe, and yet at the same time be what the universe is not. For God, to be God, must enter into the human heart and accomplish there such moral and spiritual changes as the universe is bankrupt to achieve.[11]

Within the Hebrew-Christian tradition, this pervasive need for, and record of, the creation of gods is well documented. Indeed, one way of telling the story of Old Testament religion would be in terms of a persistent tension between the spiritual conception of God and of worship, the hallmark of the genuine faith of Israel, and the continual pressures evident in the temptations to idolatry which debased and materialized the national religious consciousness and practice. In the Old Testament there is no simple upward development from idolatry to the pure worship of God. Instead we

---

10. American National Election Studies, "2016 Time Series Study."
11. Valentine, *What Do We Mean*, 11–12.

find the people of God possessing a pure worship and spiritual theology but nevertheless fighting, with the help of their spiritual leaders, continual religious seductions to devalue and debase pure religion. For example, Eugene Peterson, writing about the prophet Isaiah, reminded us that, "Everyone more or less believes in God or gods. But most of us do our best to keep God on the margins of our lives, or, failing that, we refashion God to suit our convenience. Prophets insist that God is the sovereign center, not off in the wings awaiting our beck and call. And prophets insist that we deal with God as God reveals himself, not as we imagine him to be."[12] Peterson continues, "the God of whom the prophets speak is far too large to fit into our lives. If we want anything to do with God, we have to fit into God."[13] Eugene Peterson has reminded us that Egypt, the country in which the people of Israel were enslaved, was itself deeply religious. He writes,

> Egypt was religious through and through, one of the most religious cultures in the history of the world. All the art and architecture was religious, either as a temple or a tomb that ensured a continuing afterlife.... Archaeologists and tourists alike continue to be dazzled by them. And the religion? Impressive, to say the least. It was a religion designed to keep order and control, to make things happen. It guaranteed a happy immortality, controlled the rising and falling of the Nile so the land would be fertile, controlled the people's every move so there would be law and order. The Egyptians talked endlessly about gods, addressed prayers to gods, built temples for gods. But the religion in Egypt was always what they were doing or had done.... Egypt was a thoroughly religious society.... If you want to control the personal family or society, there's no better way than through religion. That is just as true today as it was in ancient Egypt.[14]

We may ask, as we move from the ancient pervasive presence of idolatry via the apostle Paul to today's religious supermarkets, has anything changed? The need to be alert to the ever-present temptations to devalue or debase religion is underlined today when one salient feature of the contemporary religious scene is the bewildering range of offers in the "religious supermarket." It is well stocked with tempting special offers that promise a "god who will do something for you," such as offering an easy path to prosperity or to instant healing.[15]

---

12. Peterson, *As Kingfishers Catch Fire*, 115.
13. Peterson, *As Kingfishers Catch Fire*, 116.
14. Peterson, *As Kingfishers Catch Fire*, 29.
15. Peterson, *Long Obedience*, 16.

The pervasive polemic against idolatry found throughout the Old Testament, carried on mainly by the prophets and the psalmists, recognizes the same truth that the apostle Paul was later to affirm: that idols are nothing, nevertheless there was a demonic spiritual force to be reckoned with. Idols therefore constituted a positive spiritual menace. In Isaiah 44:6–21 we find a long section warning of the ever-present temptation to create idols. For example, we read (Isa 44:9 NIV), "All who make idols are nothing, and the things they treasure are worthless." Continuing later (Isa 44:10), "Who shapes a god and casts an idol, which can profit nothing? People who do that will be put to shame; such craftsmen are only human beings." The idol is nothing; a man has made it all (Isa 2:8). Its very construction and composition declare its futility (Isa 40:18–20; 41:6–7). This is a theme taken up by the apostle Paul when writing to the Corinthian Christians. He writes, "We know that an idol is nothing at all in the world and that there is no god but one. For even if there are so-called gods, whether in heaven or on earth (as indeed there are many 'gods' and many 'lords'), yet for us there is but one God, the Father from whom all things came and for whom we live; and there is but one Lord, Jesus Christ, through whom all things came and through whom we live" (1 Cor 8:4–6 NIV). In the New Testament we find a reinforcement and amplification of Old Testament teaching. There is, in the New Testament, a recognition that idols, while they are nonentities, nevertheless are dangerous spiritual forces. In chapter 1 of his letter to the Christians at Rome, Paul expresses the Old Testament view that idolatry is a decline from true spirituality and not a stage on the way to a pure knowledge of God. However, the new theme found in the New Testament underlines the fact that the perils of idolatry exist even where material idols are not being worshipped. For example, the association of idolatry with sexual sins (Gal 5:19–20) or the equating of covetousness with idolatry (1 Cor 5:11; Eph 5:5; Col 3:5), including sexual covetousness (Eph 4:19 and 5:3; 1 Thess 4:6; 1 Cor 10:7, 14). In similar terms, the apostle John, having underlined the finality and fullness of the revelation in Christ, warned that any deviation from this is idolatry (1 John 5:19–21). In short, the idol is whatever claims the loyalty that belongs to God alone (Isa 42:8). As we shall see later, some of today's false gods, today's "other gods," are distortions of Christian gods, which continue to have a powerful attraction, seemingly, for so many people.

MAKING GOD IN OUR OWN IMAGE

We all have needs. They seem more urgent at some times than at others. Some we want fulfilled at once. For some we can wait a little longer—as long as it is not too long! There is clear evidence historically and today of how all too easily our "needs" shape the "god" we believe in. The Bible has many things to say about human nature and human motivation. Psalm 8, for example, reminds us of the theocentric context of scriptural statements, in that they deal primarily with humans in relation to God as Creator, Sustainer, and Redeemer. This is a timely reminder that many of the questions posed by twenty-first-century writers, especially scientists, were not even considered by the biblical authors, let alone answered by them. The ever-present temptation, motivated by our felt needs, to read our personal views into Scripture was underlined by John Stott in his commentary on Paul's letter to the Romans. Commenting on the seventh chapter of Romans, Stott wrote, "*It is never wise to bring to a passage of Scripture our own ready-made agenda,* insisting that it answers *our* questions and addresses *our* concerns. For that is to dictate to Scripture instead of listening to it. We must lay aside our presuppositions, so that we can consciously think ourselves back into the historical and cultural settings of the text. Then we shall be in a better position to let the author say what he does say and not force him to say what we want him to say."[16] This was a view echoed recently by a group of UK scientists and biblical scholars writing following a detailed study of the early chapters of Genesis. They noted how people of faith often "are not really listening to the Bible, but simply hearing [their] own voices echoing off the pages."[17] N. T. Wright echoes this thought and poses the question, "By what right do we take Scripture and find ways to make it talk about things that we want it to talk about?"[18]

HOW HUMAN NEEDS AND MOTIVES SHAPE OUR GODS: PSYCHOLOGICAL CASE STUDIES

Why do people do the things that they do? What drives them to commit acts of hatred and violence, or acts of compassion and love? What needs are they seeking to meet? Theologians and philosophers have pondered these questions for centuries, and for the past century psychologists have joined in the discussion. Theories of personality contain basic assumptions and claims

---

16. Stott, *Message of Romans*, 189 (emphasis added).
17. Lucas et al., "Bible, Science and Human Origins."
18. Wright, "Reading Paul," 70.

about human nature. Each theory presents a model composed of various hypothetical constructs or entities that are said to interact in specified ways, both within the individual and with the environment. The outcome of such interactions guides our thoughts, feelings, and behavior. All such models aim at increasing our understanding of optimal, as well as dysfunctional, behavior and mental processes. Not surprisingly, since all these models attempt to explain the same events, they do possess certain common features and share certain pervasive themes. One such theme involves identifying common human needs, locating their roots, and investigating what goes wrong when such needs are unfulfilled. The ever-present desire to fulfil both immediate and long-term needs has been noted by some of the leading personality theorists of the twentieth century. In turn we can see how at times fulfilling these needs has shaped our views of the God in whom we claim to believe.

For example, Sigmund Freud's psychoanalytic theory proposed that the personality consists of three components—id, ego, and superego—along with a small number of basic psychic processes whose mutual interactions shaped the personality and mental health of an individual. Freud wrote, "The forces which we assumed to exist behind the tensions caused by the needs of the id are called instincts."[19] He saw the strident demands of the id as arising from innate drives for survival and reproduction. These sexual and aggressive drives are opposed by the superego's moral standards, derived from expectations of parents and society. The ego, as the executive part of the personality, must somehow reconcile those opposing forces—satisfying the id's drives without offending the superego—in order to accomplish the tasks of daily life in the real world. Freud claimed that the way those internal, unconscious conflicts were handled would determine the mental life and interpersonal relationships of that individual.

Several decades later, Freud's model was extended by one of his disciples, Erik Erikson, a very influential figure in the history of psychoanalysis, as Freud's theory came to be called. Erikson originally worked within the standard Freudian framework, which emphasized the unconscious conflicts within an individual's personality, often entangled in the childhood relationship with the parents. However, Erikson gradually moved toward a "life cycle" view of personality as developing across eight chronological periods in a person's life.[20] Within each period, Erikson identified a specific need or challenge that must be mastered at each stage. The first four stages cover infancy and childhood, as the infant first forms a special bond with

---

19. Freud, *Outline of Psycho-Analysis*, 5.
20. Erikson, *Childhood and Society*.

the parents (developing trust), then spends the childhood years gradually disengaging from the parents (developing *autonomy* and *initiative*), then building a sense of individual *competence*, to prepare for an independent life in adulthood.

Two other well-known twentieth-century personality theorists were Abraham Maslow and Carl Rogers. Both in their different ways emphasized the role of satisfying needs as central to personality development. They've often been described as the architects of the "humanistic movement" in modern psychology. Unlike Freud, who emphasized the antisocial "evil" aspects of human motivation, Maslow believed that human nature is essentially good. Left to themselves, individuals will naturally move in the direction of reaching their full potential—which Maslow called self-actualization.[21] He proposed that humanity shares certain basic motives that can be arranged into a "hierarchy of needs." The needs at lower levels (physiological needs and safety needs) must be addressed and satisfied before those at higher levels (affiliation needs and achievement needs) begin to dominate a person's motivation. Maslow explicitly considered the relationship between religion and his theory (as part of the broader humanistic psychology movement that he founded). He proposed that humanistic psychology could serve as a secular surrogate for religion. He wrote,

> The human being needs a framework of values, a philosophy of life, religion or a religion-surrogate to live by and understand by, in about the same sense that he needs sunlight, calcium or love. Without the transcendent and the transpersonal, we get sick, violent, and nihilistic, or else hopeless and apathetic. We need something "bigger than we are" to be awed by and to commit ourselves to in the new, naturalistic, empirical, non-churchly sense.[22]

Carl Rogers incorporated Maslow's ideas—about the positive potential of humans and the movement toward self-actualization—as the basis for his new method of psychotherapy, which he called "client-centered therapy" to distinguish it from other therapeutic approaches.[23]

A final example of the emphasis on the role of human needs in personality formation and functioning is in the work of Erich Fromm. He was strongly influenced by Sigmund Freud and Karl Marx, as well as by ideas from the Orthodox Judaism of his childhood. He took Freud's intrapersonal dynamics and sought to apply them to a deeper psychological understanding

---

21. Maslow, *Psychology of Being*.
22. Maslow, *Psychology of Being*, iv.
23. Rogers, *Client-Centered Therapy*.

of groups and societies. He believed that human personality can be understood as the coexistence of animal qualities and human characteristics. While the animal aspect of human nature produced physiological drives such as hunger, thirst, and sex, other uniquely human needs also must be satisfied to achieve true happiness. These needs, Fromm believed, included caring relationships; a sense of identity, freedom, and independence; and actively striving for and accomplishing worthwhile goals.[24] In the modern world, human nature is being shaped by the economic and social structures in which people live, but is still constrained by these basic psychological needs. The important point here is that Fromm made the presence and the fulfillment of human needs a crucial part of his psychological theory.

This very brief illustrative overview is given to make it obvious that the list of *psychological needs* suggested by these different personality theorists contain common themes, such as the idea that human motivation goes well beyond the drives based on individual survival, that a sense of identity is important, and that optimal functioning requires both a sense of social connection and the freedom to make independent choices. But these theories contain remarkably divergent perspectives on issues such as whether people are basically good or evil, whether human motivation is primarily conscious or unconscious, and whether tension within the personality helps or hinders personal growth. How are we to decide which, if any, of these lists of needs to accept? The difficulty in deciding among them should certainly trouble anyone claiming a scientific basis for these theories. If personality psychologists want to attach the label "scientific" to their models, they would need to provide evidence showing how well the models fit the established research findings about typical patterns of adaptive and dysfunctional behavior. As yet none of the models in the marketplace has succeeded in gaining widespread acceptance amongst psychologists. Much work remains to be done.

HOW HUMAN NEEDS AND MOTIVES SHAPE OUR GODS: THEOLOGICAL CASE STUDIES

While in the past century it has been the psychologists who have studied and written about human needs, it was not always so. Long before psychologists appeared it was the theologians who wrote with great insight about human needs. A brief consideration of some of the leading theologians of past centuries and of *their views on human needs* well illustrates how their views of what they believed were dominant human needs influenced their theology.

24. Fromm, *Heart of Man*.

St. Augustine (354–430), widely regarded as the greatest of the Latin church fathers, believed that every human being's predicament before a holy God *resulted in universal basic needs* that only God could satisfy. Augustine contrasted the depths to which humanity has fallen through sin with the heights to which it can be raised by the redemptive grace of God. This theme permeated much of Augustine's writings and has been described as "the cornerstone of Augustinian anthropology."[25] For example, in his *Confessions* we read about his own struggles that still resonate with life in the twenty-first century. Augustine had no doubt that without the direct intervention of God's grace, humans had no hope of redemption. Obviously, Augustine's perspective was very different from that of the "self-actualization" or "self-fulfillment" humanistic psychologists mentioned above. This is underlined when one reads of Augustine's profound analysis of the impossibility of any human being ever attaining happiness apart from God. He wrote,

> The simple truth is that the bond of a common nature makes all human beings one. Nevertheless, each individual in this community is driven by his passions to pursue his private purposes. Unfortunately, the objects of these purposes are such that no one person (let alone the world community) can ever be wholly satisfied. The reason for this is that nothing but Absolute Being can satisfy human nature.[26]

Thomas Aquinas (circa 1225–74) is our second example. He is another major figure who exerted an enduring influence on Western Christendom. He sought to systematize aspects of Aristotelian philosophy with Christian theology. Aquinas frequently *referred to the notion of human needs* giving rise to motivation for actions, with an overarching goal of *achieving* "happiness" (in the form of fulfillment or well-being). Following Augustine, Aquinas believed that humans were not capable of achieving complete happiness without the presence of God in their life. According to Thomas, because we all have an inherited tendency to sin, humans are basically evil, in the sense that we are constantly in opposition to God's will. Thus, as Étienne Gilson has observed, "At the basis of Aquinas's philosophy, as at the basis of all Christian philosophy, there is a deep awareness of wretchedness and need for a comforter who can only be God."[27] *We need God's* comfort to relieve our fears and anxieties, and we need God's grace to restore the good within us so that we can live according to God's will.

---

25. Sullivan, *Image of God*.
26. Augustine, *City of God*, 18.2.
27. Gilson, *Philosophy of Aquinas*, 375.

Jonathan Edwards (1703–58) is our third example. He is from a very different era, a different tradition, and held a very different theological position. The writings of Jonathan Edwards were largely shaped by his religious experiences. In his view, the themes of God's sovereignty, holiness, and grace stand alongside those of human sinfulness and the need for redemption. Steeped in the older Puritan authors, his views illustrate key features of the Reformed (Calvinist) tradition with regard to human needs. He certainly recognized and taught the need for a basic change in the condition of the human heart by the power of the Spirit of God. Indeed, the transformation that he saw as necessary was as radical as that which takes place in going from death to life. He wrote,

> Affections that are truly spiritual and gracious, do arise from those influences and operations on the heart, which are spiritual, supernatural, and divine. . . . And the influences of the Spirit of God in this . . . [to] communicate himself, and make the creature partaker of the divine nature, this is what I mean when I say that "truly gracious affections do arise from those influences that are spiritual and divine." . . . And natural men are represented in the sacred writings as having no spiritual life, no spiritual being; and therefore conversion is often compared to opening of the eyes of the blind, raising the dead, and a work of creation. . . . It is grace that is the seed of glory and dawning of glory in the heart, and therefore it is grace that is the earnest of the future inheritance.[28]

Thus, *the human needs of which Edwards wrote* were *the fundamental need* for the restoration of the broken *relationship* with God and the need to place all one's affections and hopes in God's promises of a future inheritance in Christ.

Karl Rahner (1904–84) is a final example. He has been called "the father of the Catholic Church in the twentieth century." Rahner set forth an approach that has been described as transcendental-existential. He saw the basic freedom of a person as the ability to move toward the love of God or away from it. Humans do have biological needs, but because humans are more than biological, they have needs that transcend the physical—needs that human effort cannot satisfy. Rahner stressed that the approach to God must be for God's own sake; God cannot be shaped to fit our needs.[29] As British theologian John Stott wrote, "We cheapen the gospel if we represent

---

28. Edwards, *Concerning Religions Affections*, 128, 135–36, 175.
29. Rahner, *Faith in a Wintry Season*, 2.

it as a deliverance only from unhappiness, fear, guilt and other felt needs."[30] According to Rahner, the attempt to reduce God to a mere fulfillment of human needs is "the unique heresy of our time."[31]

Here then we return to a major theme of this present chapter, the ever-present temptation to make our Gods to fulfil our present felt needs. This theme occurs frequently in the preaching of Eugene Peterson. For example, in one of his sermons Peterson imagines the apostle John preaching to his first-century local congregation and trying to encourage them in the face of adversity. Peterson comments "But for all their Jesus knowledge and Jesus enthusiasm in the mountains, none of it seems to make much difference in the valley."[32] Peterson further imagines one of his twentieth-century congregation saying to him, "You know, sometimes I just can't wait for Sunday so I can get up in the mountains for a little peace and quiet, climbing those Jesus Peaks and having a quiet time alongside Hallelujah Creek. By the way, Pastor, someone told me the other day of a prayer I could pray that is guaranteed to boost my salary and prevent cancer. Cancer runs in my family, and I've been a little worried lately. Would you teach me that prayer?"[33] It is not easy to know when our "wants" slip too easily and unthinkingly into becoming what we feel are our legitimate "needs." We must always ask the question, are our felt needs "kingdom needs" or "temporary self-satisfying needs"?

---

30. Stott, *Message of Romans*, 88.
31. Rahner, *Faith in a Wintry Season*, 27.
32. Peterson, *As Kingfishers Catch Fire*, 361.
33. Peterson, *As Kingfishers Catch Fire*, 362.

3

"Gods" on Offer

Sampling the Twenty-first-Century Marketplace

Say a little prayer for me: Alexa app helps users to connect with God.... The idea is to give information to newcomers to Christianity and spiritual succour for believers. In other words, users might ask Alexa to give them a prayer or a quick theology lesson.[1]

Our father, who art in cyberspace: Churches turn to the internet to reach their flocks.[2]

FOLLOWING RAPID DEVELOPMENTS SINCE 1970, advertisers have capitalized on the overwhelming power of images, not only to display their products, but *also to manufacture needs and desires in people that don't naturally exist.* This has resulted in a culture that penetrates almost every aspect of our lives today. One side-effect of this has been that some within the church, anxious to capitalize on these new developments saw these new advertising methods as ways of promoting their particular lifestyle choices and of making them available to the "religious consumers." Cashing in on the success of the techniques and structures already developed by large corporations, churches began to use sophisticated strategies to target their "consumers."

---

1. Bridge, "Say a Little Prayer."
2. Economist, "Our Father in Cyberspace," 51.

For example, one outcome was the development of extravagant weekend services designed primarily to attract the attention of as many people as possible and at the same time maximizing the worthy purpose of encouraging individual transformations and deepening personal relationships with Christ. Sadly, one manifestation of this has been the tendency all too often to create gods to fulfil our needs, a tendency evident in the past, reappearing in the twenty-first century.

The omnipresent social media have the potential and power for enormous benefits. The lead article in the 2019 Christmas issue of the international journal *The Economist* was titled "Pessimism versus Progress," with the subtitle "Contemporary Worries about the Impact of Technology Are Part of a Historical Pattern." The authors comment that,

> Today's gloomy mood is centred on smart phones and social media, which took off a decade ago. . . . For any given technology its drawbacks sometimes seem to outweigh its benefits. When this happens with several technologies at once, as today, the result is a wider sense of techno-pessimism. . . . That points to another lesson, which is that the remedy to technology-related problems very often involves more technology. . . . The most important lesson is about technology itself. A powerful technology can be used for good or ill. . . . Technology itself has no agency: it is the choices people make that shape the world.[3]

Earlier in 2019, the Archbishop of Canterbury wrote in *The Times*, "Social media have transformed the way we live our lives. . . . Each time we interact online we have the opportunity either to add to current cynicism and abuse or to choose instead to share light and grace."[4] As the church falls increasingly under the sway of today's consumer culture and social media it needs to be alert to the reciprocal effects of the medium on the message and vice versa, a theme developed by Heidi Campbell and Stephen Garner in 2016 in their book *Networked Theology*. However, before exploring these challenges in detail, it is important to remember that "Technology itself has no agency: it is the choices *people* make that shape the world."[5] We need to accept that it is a false distinction to draw a line too clearly between the medium and the message. The medium is not simply a conduit but may, in the process of being a medium, subtly change the content of the message.

Commenting on these recent developments, Shane Hipps wrote, "The medium of these churches is primarily a worship service designed to attract

---

3. Economist, "Pessimism v Progress," 13.
4. Burgess, "Thou Shalt Not Tweet" (emphasis added).
5. Economist, "Pessimism v Progress," 13 (emphasis added).

a crowd, respond to the overwhelming demands of a consumer society, and facilitate personal transformation. *This way of doing church amplifies and reinforces the modern gospel that affirms individualism and the privatization of faith.* . . . As a result, those who attend the services gain a personal relationship with Jesus, *but are left with an impoverished theology of both community and the church.*"[6] They have impoverished their theology and reduced their God. Hipps notes, "This is in stark contrast to the biblical vision of the church in which individuals exist for the sake of the community and the community exists for God's mission in the world."[7]

Networked Theology: Enrichment or Impoverishment?

Networked theology has the capacity either to enrich the Christian life or to impoverish it, to shrink our idea of God and of the Christian life or expand them. The data speak for themselves. "The Barna Research Group reported significant increases in church leaders' use of the internet (from 78 percent in 2000 to 97 percent in 2014)."[8] They noted an increase in pastors' perception of the internet as useful for facilitating spiritual religious experiences (15 percent to 39 percent). According to a 2014 report, nine out of ten pastors believed that it is "theologically acceptable for a church to provide faith assistance or religious experiences to people through the Internet." Campbell and Garner wrote, "Overall, many churches in America view the internet as having moved from being a luxury to being an essential tool for ministry. . . . As the Internet increasingly becomes a place where people meet and live a large portion of their social lives, the call has been sounded ever louder to meet them there with the gospel of Christ."[9] For example,

> In 2014 the Billy Graham Evangelistic Association recorded over 6 million online conversions connected to their websites and resources, in contrast to only fifteen thousand converts made through face-to-face outreach. Similarly, Global Media Outreach—a ministry that leverages the Internet, mobile devices, and social media—claimed that more than thirty-four million people made decisions to follow Christ through its digital evangelization work.[10]

---

6. Hipps, *Hidden Power of Electronic Culture*, 99–100 (emphasis added).
7. Hipps, *Hidden Power of Electronic Culture*, 100.
8. Campbell and Garner, *Networked Theology*, 1.
9. Campbell and Garner, *Networked Theology*, 1.
10. Campbell and Garner, *Networked Theology*, 1.

What we do *not* know is how many of the six million online conversions reported by the Billy Graham Evangelistic Association or the thirty-four million making decisions through Global Media Outreach were linked up to a local, worshipping, witnessing, serving, church community and were becoming Christian disciples in the steps of first-century Christians and the twentieth-century Christian Dietrich Bonhoeffer, for whom discipleship meant martyrdom.

Taking an extremely well-informed and hard-headed approach to their understanding of what they call the possibility of "networked theology," Campbell and Garner wrote, "The network is embedded with both positive and negative narratives, offering us hope for a better future through technology, along with the seeds of fear that our technologies will seduce or enslave us."[11] In the context of this present book, it is clear that technology may play a role in "shrinking our faith" and/or "shrinking the God" in whom we believe.

Campbell and Garner suggested that understanding "networked religion" has direct implications for Christianity and Christian communities:

> We argue that careful attention to how religion is seen online can teach us about how people's faith is manifested and informed by the structures and culture of networked society in general. *It also reveals the specific ways new media technologies may shape the practices of people of faith and reflect changing assumptions about the nature of their spiritual lives.*[12]

They further identify what they believe are "core issues or questions a Christian theology of the network might need to address in light of how new media technologies and spaces potentially shape the Christian life." They ask the question, "Who [is] our neighbor in a digitally networked world? We have friends on social media, email and phone contacts, links to other individuals' digital profiles through our online networks, and a wide range of other current digital connections. *Are any of these our neighbors in the theological sense?*"[13] For these authors, the key to a proper Christian understanding of the issues *focuses on the nature of humanity itself* and their argument is that *at core humans are relational beings*. They see this as part of networked theology. They write "Networked theology is inherently relational, with the network motif expressly describing various relationships within the network." Referring to the writings of Irenaeus, Augustine, Karl Barth, Emil Brunner, Gerhard von Rad, and others, they argue that "Christianity

11. Campbell and Garner, *Networked Theology*, 62.
12. Campbell and Garner, *Networked Theology*, 61–62 (emphasis added).
13. Campbell and Garner, *Networked Theology*, 82 (emphasis added).

is seen as an inherently relational faith in that it is based on the belief in the Trinity, that God is both three and one."[14] This key aspect of our nature and of what it means to be made in the image of God will be taken up in detail later. In spelling out the importance of this focus on relationality, Campbell and Garner draw attention to one possible aspect of the effects of the new technology on the nature of religious faith. They write, "Philip Meadows argues that Christians are called to be concerned with the transformation of this world and that a perception that an online life is more engaging or preferable to one in the physical world *could generate an escapist mentality where the physical world is ignored, and that transformative mission is lost.*"[15] This provides yet another hint of the dangers of how "shrinking faith" becomes mere self-serving escapism.

Technology's Impact on Spirituality and Faith

Any effect of modern media and technology *that diminishes our faith or diminishes the God in whom we believe* is to be challenged for what it is. Campbell and Garner continue,

> For all who follow Christ and the call to reflect him in the everyday world, the passage raises the question of what this should look like in the world of networked media and technology environments. In particular, it raises key questions about who the "poor" are in an information society, how they might be suffering and depressed technologically and what our response in Christ is to address that. We move beyond trite questions like "Would Jesus use social media?" to a more profound reflection on how to mirror the character of Christ in how we live with and talk about technology and media.[16]

As Campbell and Garner remind us, "a biblical starting point highlights particular aspects of what loving God, loving neighbor, and recognizing the humanity of others looks like."[17] These authors remind us that, at the start of Jesus's ministry as recorded in the Gospel of Luke, Jesus describes the good news he has come to proclaim. Jesus takes the scroll of the prophet Isaiah and reads aloud:

---

14. Campbell and Garner, *Networked Theology*, 82.
15. Campbell and Garner, *Networked Theology*, 87 (emphasis added).
16. Campbell and Garner, *Networked Theology*, 121.
17. Campbell and Garner, *Networked Theology*, 122.

> The spirit of the Lord is upon me,
> because he has anointed me
> to bring good news to the poor.
> He has sent me to proclaim release to the captives
> and recovery of sight to the blind,
> to let the oppressed go free,
> to proclaim the year of the Lord's favor. (Luke 4:18–19 NRSV)

How can we consistently meet this challenge and not shrink our conception of God? Campbell and Garner most helpfully see a clue to the answer in the words of the prophet Micah, where we read what we might call an appropriate Christ-informed response to technology and media. We are told, "He has shown you, O mortal, what is good. And what does the LORD require of you? To act justly and to love mercy and to walk humbly with your God" (Mic 6:8 NIV). Campbell and Garner write, "Here we are presented with a call to do three concrete things: to do justice, to love kindness and mercy, and walk humbly with God. Biblical scholar Walter Brueggemann asserts that these are three important dimensions of the life of faith which mutually support one another."[18] We would add that by remembering them we find a partial safeguard to the ever-present contemporary temptation to "shrink faith" to something else such as "believe-ism" without consequences or implications for daily living. It is this Micah-inspired shaping that may deepen and expand both our faith and the God in whom we trust. Eternal vigilance is called for to avoid shrinking faith in shrinking Gods.

Necessity Is Still the Mother of Invention

At the height of the world-wide coronavirus crisis in 2020, Heidi Campbell noted how many churches were mobilizing the technology of virtual reality to provide digital worship for those isolated in their homes. She commented, "Nowadays pastors do not just broadcast to their quarantined flock . . . They expect them to participate too, using apps and social media to make virtual services interactive."[19] Participation is possible in new and hitherto unimagined ways. The online service put together by staff and members in their private homes and coordinated by modern technology by one church in central London (All Souls Church in Langham Place) became so popular that soon millions were participating worldwide. *The Economist* article asks, "When the coronavirus retreats, will digital worship go with it?" Their answer, "Not likely. Life Church, a mega-church based in Oklahoma that helps

18. Campell and Garner, *Networked Theology*, 122.
19. Economist, "Our Father in Cyberspace," 51.

other parishes navigate the online world, says the number of communities using its *Church Online Platform* surged from 25,000 to 47,000 in March [2020] alone."[20] The message: Advances in science, thoughtfully used, have the capacity to enrich our faith in times of trial. In the words of the title of this book, we need to tell a better story of why faith and science belong together.

ADVANCES IN SCIENCE MAY ENLARGE OUR UNDERSTANDING OF GOD

In the intervening years since Phillips wrote *Your God Is Too Small*, advances in scientific knowledge and the fruits of biblical scholarship have changed the views of both scientists and theologians of the relationship between science and Christian faith. *All of this underlines the need to recognize the ever-changing nature of the relationship between what we believe about the nature of the universe we live in, and what we believe about our own mysterious human nature; a relationship that, on the evidence, is clearly seen to be forever changing.* This has alerted us to the need to recognize that the God in whom we believe is far bigger today than the God we could ever have imagined in 1952.[21] The universe God created and is sustaining becomes ever bigger and more amazing with every advance in science. It is of course, possible, to close our eyes to this new knowledge or indeed, as some have done and continue to do, to deny its very existence. Think only of the views of creationists. We shall see in later chapters how "constructive doubt" has the potential to give rise to greater knowledge and deeper faith, both in matters of science and in matters of faith. Reflecting on the contemporary scene, we may illustrate how specific discoveries in diverse areas of science have widespread ramifications, not only for health and human flourishing, but also for a rethink of some long and widely held Christian doctrines. We may illustrate how scientific research on the very basic components of our make-up as well as research on the vastness of the universe continue to challenge our conception of the greatness of the God who created and continues to hold in being everything that exists.

---

20. Economist, "Our Father in Cyberspace," 51.

21. Of course, we do need to qualify what we mean by "bigger" here. For classical theology God is the *infinite source of being* and there is no scope for a *literally* "bigger" view of God than that, no matter how much our understanding of creation grows. However, it is the case that our growing knowledge of the cosmos vastly expands our understand of creation and our wonder at the power and wisdom of the God who causes it to be, sustaining it from moment to moment.

The Challenge of Researching the Very Small

In the year following the publication of Phillips's 1952 book, what was arguably the most important scientific discovery of the twentieth century in biological and medical sciences was published, authored by James Watson and Francis Crick, showing the structure of DNA. No one could then imagine the widespread ramifications of this groundbreaking discovery. For example, on a single day in 2019, the London *Times* contained three different reports of current research with potentially great benefits for humankind. All of them flowed from our understanding of the structure of DNA. An article with the headline "New Test Will Reveal Risk of Getting Breast Cancer," based on a paper in the journal *Genetics in Medicine*, quotes Richard Rupe of Cancer Research UK: "Research like this is hugely exciting because in the future it will enable us to offer much more tailored care which will benefit patients and makes best use of the services that we have available."[22] A few pages later we have the headline, "Your DNA Points to Life Expectancy, Say Scientists."[23] This article reports that a team of researchers at the University of Edinburgh has produced a scoring system to analyze the combined effect of genetic variations that influence lifespan. On the same page there is a report on a study published in *Nature Genetics* which tells us,

> Risky behavior is in the genes of those who love living in the fast lane.... Scientists have found a suite of genetic changes that seem to make people more prone to taking risks—whether in business, with their health or in their personal lives. The variants still only explain a very small proportion of people's risk-taking behavior, but even so the study is by far the largest investigation into how we might inherit propensities to take risks. More than that the findings, also provide a clue as to how the genes might work.... However, the value of the latest research is that by identifying the most significant genetic variants involved, researchers can begin to see how these differences in our DNA translate into differences in how we act. They found that some of the 124 variants that had the biggest effect were expressed in the prefrontal cortex, the part of the brain associated with higher cognitive functions, and a neurochemical such as glutamate that boosts communication between neurons.[24]

---

22. Smyth, "New Test."
23. Horne, "DNA Points to Life Expectancy."
24. Whipple, "Your Attitude."

The purpose of here drawing attention to these randomly chosen reports is to underline further how knowledge of the world we live in, including ourselves, has expanded almost out of all recognition since J. B. Phillips wrote his book *Your God Is Too Small*. The challenge remains, *how can we ensure that our conception of God does full justice to a God who created, and moment by moment holds in being such an amazing creation, including ourselves?*

The Challenge of Researching the Very Large

Were he alive today, I suspect that Phillips would draw attention to the challenges to Christian belief of an ever-expanding universe. When he wrote in 1952, the creation for which the God of the beginning of the twentieth century was responsible was believed to be so much smaller than we now believe it to be. But Phillips would have asked, has our understanding of God grown? It is difficult today to realize that at the beginning of the twentieth century it was thought that the universe was just the Milky Way galaxy. In 1917, Shapley had estimated its radius as roughly 100,000 light years. (A light year, the distance light travels in a year, is about 9 trillion km or 6 trillion miles.) Things began to change in 1924 when Hubble realized that the universe is expanding, and this led to a huge increase in the accepted size of the universe. The year 1952 is before the so-called Hubble constant was revised down by a factor of between 5 and 10 from 550km/s/Mpc. By 1952 there were two competing theories—the steady state theory, which held that the universe is infinite in size, and the big bang theory. For the big bang theory, the age of the universe and its size depends on the expansion rate (the Hubble constant). The accepted value for the Hubble constant in 1952 gives an age of the universe of about 9 billion years and a distance to the edge of the visible universe of about 30 billion light years. By comparison, the accepted values today are 13.8 billion years and 46 billion light years. So, between 1952 and now our understanding of the size of the universe has grown by a factor between 5 and 10, depending on which of two main values of the Hubble constant you accepted in 1952. It is truly awesome to even begin to try and get our minds round the enormity of the universe in which we live—and if some theoreticians are correct then we are only one of many universes. How can we begin to think meaningfully about a God who creates and sustains this awesome universe of which we are such a miniscule part?

The challenge of the quite remarkable advances in our understanding of the universe was further underlined with great and well justified publicity when an international consortium of scientists showed the world on April 10, 2019 the first image of a black hole ever taken. This monumental achievement was made possible, in part, by key leadership from the Harvard-Smithsonian Center for Astrophysics. The telescope producing these remarkable pictures was the Event Horizon Telescope, a global array of radio telescopes involving dozens of institutions and hundreds of scientists. What was especially remarkable was how closely the actual picture resembled the picture constructed by scientists on the basis of their theoretical models of black holes and of so-called Event Horizon mathematical equations. All this illustrates yet again how the scientific enterprise holds out such tremendous potential benefits for all of humankind and its welfare worldwide. *The God who created and continues to create and uphold such an amazing universe simply will not be fitted into many past ways of thinking about God which want to limit him and his activity to a few thousand years.* Such "small Gods" have no place in Christian theology. Catherine Heymans, a professor of astrophysics and European Research Fellow at the University of Edinburgh, as well as first winner of the new Max-Planck-Humboldt Research Award worth €1.5 million to continue her dark energy research, recently commented, "We're really highly insignificant in the grand scheme of things—just one out of seven billion people on planet Earth, orbiting just one star out of 100 billion stars in our Milky Way galaxy, just one galaxy out of 100 billion galaxies in our observable universe."[25]

The announcement of the 2019 recipients of the Nobel Prize in physics added further fuel to the need to be open to the possibility of life elsewhere in the universe. Didier Queloz, one of the joint recipients, discovered the Jupiter-sized planet *51 Pegasi b*, which is quite unlike any previously thought to exist. Rather than being measured in earth years, its orbit lasts four days. At the time of its discovery it was an open question whether other planets existed at all, but the find started an entirely new field, which has now identified 4,118 exoplanets. Commenting on the question of whether other planets might have life, Queloz said, "I can't believe we are the only living entity in the universe. There are just way too many planets, way too many stars, and the chemistry is universal. The chemistry that led to life has to happen elsewhere."[26] Whether life exists in other parts of the universe remains an open question, but no good is done to the cause of Christianity by denying it as a possibility. To follow that path would be to repeat the earlier disputes over the existence of *antipodeans*.

---

25. Edit, "Out of This World."
26. Ritschel, "Aliens Will Likely Be Discovered."

Does an Expanding Universe Have Any Implications for Christian Theology?

It is significant that a recent issue (November 2018) of the highly regarded journal *Theology and Science* is devoted entirely to what they call "astrotheology." The editorial to this issue[27] makes reference to a book just published with the title *Astrotheology: Science and Theology Meet Extraterrestrial Life*. It is edited by Ted Peters, who is also the editor of the journal *Theology and Science*. The titles of some of the contributions to this special issue give the flavor of what is presented there. For example, David Wilkinson's paper is titled "Why Should Theology Take SETI Seriously?" Andrew Davison's paper has the title "Christian Systematic Theology and Life Elsewhere in the Universe: A Study in Suitability." Alexel Nesteruk's paper is called "The Motive of the Incarnation in Christian Theology: Consequences for Modern Cosmology, Extraterrestrial Intelligence, and a Hypothesis of Multiple Incarnations." The challenge to contemporary Christian thinkers is to address these issues in a manner that is accessible to the average pew dweller who is neither a space scientist nor a theologian. It is already evident from the thoughtful contributions listed above that well-informed scientists and theologians are aware of the dangers of knee-jerk reactions and are seeking to reassure Christians worried about the possible implications for their faith if sentient beings exist elsewhere in the universe. However, a short pause and attention to church history can immediately help to put today's concerns with astrotheology into context.

Learning from the Past

One of the questions raised by the possibility of extra-terrestrial beings is whether they are encompassed by the once-for-all sacrificial death of Christ on Calvary. Faced with new challenges to our traditional thinking about the universality of Christ's redeeming love it is all too easy to ignore the deep thinking of great Christians from the past, such as St. Augustine. He struggled with these issues when he thought and wrote about the status of what were labelled the antipodeans: humans living on the other side of the world as understood at that time. *For Augustine and medieval theologians, the possible existence of so-called antipodeans was the equivalent of today's concerns with the possible existence of extraterrestrial people*, even if the antipodeans shared our own planet, since they were imagined to be genetically disconnected from us. As, therefore, today's theologians engage in these new fields

---

27. Peters, "Astrotheology."

of astrotheology it is vitally important to keep in mind that Christianity has been there before. In addition, from at least the Renaissance until the nineteenth century, there was, among Christians and non-Christians alike, a widespread belief in the existence of extraterrestrial inhabitants. It will be important therefore to study the centuries-old Christian literature in the light of contemporary interests and concerns.

The current debates and anxieties of the possible impact of the existence of extraterrestrial intelligent life thus remind us of the ancient and medieval debates about the existence of antipodes and antipodean inhabitants. This debate reached a turning point in the words of Augustine in *City of God*, where he showed himself not very much concerned by the existence of these supposed lands and even non-human inhabitants, but was more concerned with the impact of human-like inhabitants for the common ancestry of humanity. In the face of that issue and the lack of historical/scientific evidence of the existence of antipodeans, he preferred to deny their existence and regard them as a fable.[28] These few lines by Augustine had a huge impact on the medieval debate about the antipodeans, routinely rejected until the end of the fifteenth century.

Medieval theologians discussed the different possibilities *if* they existed. Were they sinners or not? If they were sinners, were they affected by Christ's redemption? Should Christ be incarnate somewhere else and die again? The debate at that time was related to inhabitants on the other side (from the European point of view) of our own planet who were supposed to be unreachable because of the extreme heat of the equator and the uncrossability of the oceans. In this sense, at least, the issues are not so different from some current debates in astrotheology.

Reflecting on changing views of the universe among scientists towards the end of the last century, Owen Gingerich, at the time Professor of Astronomy and the History of Science at Harvard University and a senior astronomer at the Smithsonian Astrophysical Observatory, wrote,

> When the Psalmist asked, "What is man, that thou art mindful of him?" I would say that the statement reflects the overwhelming Majesty of what a creating super intelligence must be, *a very large God indeed*. But I would also turn to another Scripture, Genesis 1:27, "God created man in his own image, male and female created them," and I would answer that as contemplative beings created in the image of God with attributes of creativity, conscience, and self-consciousness, we are central to the purposes of the cosmos. Understanding the cosmos is part of

---

28. Augustine, *City of God*, 16.9.

that purpose. Understanding humankind's role also is part of that purpose. The Book of Nature *and* the Book of Scripture. For me, faith is not blind faith but trust. And I trust that as we learn more about the vast cosmic scope and our place within it, our sense of the spiritual world will never atrophy but will ever expand.[29]

Gingerich's passing references to "faith," "blind faith," and "trust" raise key questions we must address in an age when it is arguable that it is not just "shrinking Gods" we have to confront but also the spectacle of "shrinking faith."

A Return to Scripture

"It is Scripture that brings people to life—the book where they meet Jesus and find him speaking to them."[30] But how we regard Scripture has consequences for how we understand it and seek to live by it. Wright is deeply concerned that not everybody sees things that way. He writes,

> For some, Scripture itself, except for highly select verses and passages, has become as dry and dusty as dogma itself. It is full of problems and puzzles, alternative readings and private theories of interpretation, and seems to them like a black hole that can suck down all the energy of otherwise good Christian people (exegetes and preachers) and give nothing much back in return. For them, what matters is invoking the spirit, worshipping for longer and longer, extended prayer and praise meetings, telling others how wonderful it is to have a living relationship with Jesus. Such people assume (since the background of the tradition is broadly evangelical), that Scripture remains in some sense normative, *but how it exercises that normativity, or how it exercises anything at all, or engages with their life and faith remains unclear.*[31]

When things begin to happen in the way that Wright describes, then *immediately the living God of Scripture very quickly becomes reduced* to dependence upon particular ways of worshipping, particular ways of praying, particular ways of giving praise, and particular ways of witnessing—a variety of "shrunken gods."

---

29. Gingerich, "Astronomical Perspective," 45 (emphasis added).
30. Wright, "Reading Paul," 59.
31. Wright, "Reading Paul," 59 (emphasis added).

Checks and Balances from Science

To illustrate some of his concerns about our readiness to be all too easily trapped in traditional interpretations of particular passages of Scripture, N. T. Wright uses the example of widely and very strongly held views of what Scripture teaches about the second coming of Christ. Reflecting on confused thinking surrounding the so-called "second coming" and what has been labelled the "dogma of delay," Wright notes that, "We cannot in any case think of divinely engineered cosmic catastrophes now that modern science has taught us otherwise. 'The end of the world' is likely to come through the cooling of the sun, not through a miraculous divine intervention."[32] Wright later noted,

> For the "dogma of delay," however, everything else can happily be symbolic, but for some reason "the son of man coming in the clouds" must be literal. . . . But the ancient hope of Israel—which is what all these apocalyptic texts are about—was not for the end of the world, but for the *transformation* of the world; in particular, for the transformation of the actual social and political realities so that justice would be done, wickedness would be routed, and Israel would be free in her own land.[33]

Rather, we must see, as N. T. Wright has argued when discussing the meaning of reference to "the day of the Lord," that, "These will be *transformative events within the ongoing space-time world*, not the destruction of that world and its replacement with a 'purely supernatural' world. All that Paul says about the *parousia* must be seen in this light."[34] An escapist God is yet another shrunken God.

The Hazards of Replacing Scripture with Fantasy and Experience

The challenge for Christians today, as in the past, is how to maintain a close relationship with the biblical revelation of God and his nature and not succumb to the temptation of "making gods" only to fulfil our own immediate wants and needs. The God of the Hebrew-Christian tradition is not a *shrinking God* but an *ever-expanding God* who expects our spirituality to expand in step with every fresh revelation of the might and majesty of his creation. Later chapters of this book will show how the labors of dedicated scientists

---

32. Wright, "Hope Deferred," 41.
33. Wright, "Hope Deferred," 50.
34. Wright, "Hope Deferred," 56 (emphasis in original).

have given us fresh glimpses into how "wonderfully made we are" and how great our God is. The Hebrew-Christian God is at the same time a God who is one who calls to discipleship, who challenges, but at the same time also promises "Come to me, all who labor and are heavy laden, and I will give you rest" (Matt 11:28 ESV).

It is a fine line to tread between welcoming and applauding every effort to share as widely as possible the good news of the gospel of Jesus Christ, as I do, and, at the same time, expressing deep concerns that sadly, today, such sharing, at times, degrades, distorts, and debases the focus of the very message itself. The idea of a "god supermarket" reminds us that this temptation is not new. Forty years ago, Eugene Peterson was already warning his Sunday morning congregations about the dangers and reminding them that "making gods" to serve our needs is not new. He wrote,

> You can buy a religion of promises and wise sayings and interesting answers to big questions for fifteen or twenty dollars. The world is full of such stuff. But what most of us want to know is does it *happen*? Can it *happen here*? And is it *living*? We must ask the stubbornly practical questions when we come to God and to church. I have no patience with a truth that cannot be lived, and I don't want you to have any patience with it either.[35]

These same themes are underlined and illustrated in *A Long Obedience in the Same Direction*. Peterson wrote, continuing his critique of the theme of instant gratification and "short-termism,"

> It is not difficult in such a world to get a person interested in the message of the gospel; *it is terrifically difficult to sustain the interest*. Millions of people in our culture make decisions for Christ, *but there is a dreadful attrition rate*. Many claim to have been born again, the evidence for mature Christian discipleship is slim. In our kind of culture anything, even news about God, can be sold if it is packaged freshly; but when it loses novelty, it goes on the garbage heap. *There is a great market for religious experience in our world*; there is little enthusiasm for the patient acquisition of virtue, little inclination to sign up for a long apprenticeship in what earlier generations of Christians called holiness.[36]

Illustrating today's "shrinking gods" he continues,

---

35. Peterson, *As Kingfishers Catch Fire*, 24 (emphasis in original).
36. Peterson, *Long Obedience*, 16 (emphasis added).

Religion in our time has been captured by the tourist mindset. Religion is understood as a visit to an attractive site to be made when we have adequate leisure. For some it is a weekly jaunt to church; for others, occasional visits to special services. Some, with a bent for religious entertainment and sacred diversion, plan their lives around special events like retreats, rallies, and conferences. We go to see a new personality, to hear a new truth, to get a new experience and so somehow expand our otherwise humdrum lives. The religious life is defined as the latest and the newest: Zen, faith healing, human potential, parapsychology, successful living, choreography in the chancel, Armageddon. We'll try anything—until something else comes along.[37]

Continuing with this theme, he writes,

> Everyone is in a hurry. The persons whom I lead in worship, among whom I counsel, visit, pray, preach, and teach, *want shortcuts*. They want me to help them fill out the form that will get them instant credit (in eternity). They are impatient for results. They have adopted the lifestyle of a tourist and only want the high points. But the pastor is not a tour guide. I have no interest in telling apocryphal religious stories at and around dubiously identified sacred sites. The Christian life cannot mature under such conditions and in such ways.[38]

---

37. Peterson, *Long Obedience*, 16.
38. Peterson, *Long Obedience*, 17.

SECTION II

Stories of Mutual Enrichment

OVERVIEW

Every new conquest achieved by science involved the loss of a domain to religion.[39]

Extinguished theologians lie about the cradle of every science as the strangled snakes beside that of Hercules; and history records that whenever science and orthodoxy have been fairly opposed, the latter has been forced to retire from the lists, bleeding and crushed if not annihilated; scorched, if not slain.[40]

CONFLICTS REAL AND IMAGINED: GAINING HISTORICAL PERSPECTIVE

In the Preface to this book I quoted from a typical email of the kind I receive from time to time, illustrating that today there are honest, thoughtful, and sincere Christian students struggling with apparent conflicts between the tenets of their Christian faith and what they are learning in their university and college lectures about the world in which they live and of which they are a part. Some of the conflicts are unwittingly generated and reinforced by what these Christian students hear from their pastors and church leaders.

39. Boston Cultivator, "Science and Religion."
40. Huxley, "Darwin."

These struggles of thoughtful Christian students are now well documented by numerous surveys by the Pew Research Center and the Barna Group in the USA, and more recently by the work of the BioLogos Organization. Frequently, again as the survey evidence makes clear, there are several recurring foci of these sources of conflict.

One typical "knee-jerk" answer to the question, "What is the relation between science and religion?" is, "There is a conflict." The roots of this widely held response go deep. Certain key historical episodes have prompted the view that there always has been, and continues to be, a conflict between science and religion. In the hands of a good narrator, it is possible to list a succession of clashes—almost always depicted with two contesting sides, and always with the same side (Christianity) shown defending nonsense views that were destroyed by science. The resulting narrative portrays a victorious science forcing a defeated religious enemy to retreat time after time and eventually fade away.

In support of the "science versus Christianity" conflict narrative, four episodes are typically described:

(1) in ancient/patristic times, the debate over the shape of the earth (flat vs. round);

(2) in medieval times, the denial of the antipodeans (humans living on the other side of the earth);

(3) in the early modern era, the debate on the movement of the earth (stationary vs. orbiting the sun);

(4) in contemporary times, the rejection of evolution across species.

In all these cases, we are told that Christianity finally had to abandon its formerly held positions and retreat, recognizing the authority of science over the disputed ground until a new conflict broke out at the new science/Christianity border. However, more careful research of these historical episodes shows a much more complex picture, one that resists these simplistic and neat battleground realignments. This case is set out in detail in a paper by Pablo de Felipe and Malcolm Jeeves.[41]

Other writers, such as Alistair McGrath, Colin Russell, and John Henry, have observed that the "science versus religion" narrative is stale, outdated, and largely discredited. It is sustained not by the weight of evidence, but by endless uncritical repetition, which studiously avoids the new historical scholarship that has undermined its credibility. We can conclude that a "conflict–retreat" portrayal of science–religion relations tells only part of a story that, in fact, is much more complex.

---

41. De Felipe and Jeeves, "Science and Christianity Conflicts."

The popular idea of a conflict, a battle between science and Christianity, in which the latter is in a millennial-old retreat and losing ground to the former, is a modern tale, with a clear anti-Christian axe to grind. This conflict-retreat model, it seems, did not become popular until the final decades of the nineteenth century. Key works to popularize the "conflict model" were the following well-known books: John William Draper, *History of the Conflict between Religion and Science*; John Tyndall, *Address Delivered before the British Association Assembled at Belfast*; Andrew Dickson White, *The Warfare of Science*; and *A History of the Warfare of Science with Theology in Christendom*. Their portrait of the historical science and Christianity relationship fits not only the simple conflict model, but also the conflict-retreat model. For more details on this history, see Colin Russell's article on "The Conflict Metaphor and Its Social Origins."

R. L. Numbers has traced its beginnings, at least as far back as an 1845 article in a US newspaper in which it was stated: "Every new conquest achieved by science, involved the loss of a domain to religion."[42] However, this idea was already implicit in the intellectual milieu of the Enlightenment.[43] The conflict model is an oversimplification, since the history of science and Christianity relations shows a much more complex and richer story.

General overarching historical models of friends and foes are inaccurate. If the idea of conflict as the explanation for science and Christianity relations is inadequate, the use of historical episodes that give *the impression of a historical directionality*—that is, a Christian retreat under the marching of science, here described as a "conflict-retreat" model—*is pure fabrication and manipulation of the evidence*. Pointing to the fact "that one and the same scientific innovation could be given both sacred and secular readings," John H. Brooke has reached the conclusion that "the 'relations between science and religion' cannot be reduced to a simple pattern of religious retreat as the sciences advanced."[44] In fact, one should be more critical and question even the possibility of any generalization, as Brooke himself pointed out years ago: "There is no such thing as *the* relationship between science and religion. It is what different individuals and communities have made of it in a plethora of different contexts."[45] Peter Harrison has also questioned the very use of the words "science" and "religion" in generalizations spanning

---

42. Boston Cultivator, "Science and Religion," 344.
43. Brooke, "Science and Religion."
44. Brooke, "Science and Religion," 746.
45. Brooke, *Science and Religion*, 321.

centuries; these words do not account for the huge intellectual transformations in the meaning of these words and concepts.[46]

A different set of historical episodes gives a very different picture of science and Christianity relations than is usually conveyed with the "traditional" set of historical episodes.[47] Focusing on these alternative episodes paints a much more positive image of Christianity in its relationship to science. However, this did not lead us to propose an "anti-conflict" model, only to provide a corrective to the usual bias and to illustrate that a more complex description should be provided. That is the reason why we cannot accept some of the "apologetic" attempts to deny or minimize the historical debates surrounding the relations of science and Christianity on specific controversial issues. An anti-conflict thesis to advance the cause of Christianity is not acceptable if it requires bending the historical evidence. This sort of thinking can be counted as one of the myths about science and religion, as Noah Efron has pointed out.[48] In the past, historians such as Pierre Duhem,[49] Stanley Jaki,[50] and even Reijer Hooykaas[51] have been criticized for this kind of reasoning. It is true that they emphasized the positive contributions of Christianity to the development of modern science (with some of the historical episodes we noted here in our second set of examples), although it is debatable to what extent their views overstated the limits of both the historical evidence available and sound interpretation. A direct criticism of Jaki's and Hooykaas's historical views on the major influence on Christianity over the development of modern science appeared in the introduction and some chapters of a book edited by David Lindberg and Ronald Numbers titled *God and Nature: Historical Essays on the Encounter between Christianity and Science*. An even harsher criticism of Jaki's views can be found in Lindberg's review of Jaki's *The Savior of Science*.[52] Regarding Hooykaas, it is fair to say that the criticisms he received were mainly for his book, *Religion and the Rise of Modern Science*, which has been labelled as an apologetic in favor of Protestantism (taking into account that he was Protestant himself). However, these criticisms do not mention his work emphasizing the role

---

46. Harrison, *Territories of Science and Religion*.
47. de Felipe and Jeeves, "Science and Christianity Conflicts."
48. Efron, "Christianity Gave Birth."
49. Duhem, *History and Philosophy of Science*.
50. Jaki, *Savior of Science*; Jaki, *Bible and Science*.
51. Hooykaas, *Religion and Modern Science*.
52. Lindberg, "Review."

of Portuguese seafarers in the rise of modern science a century before the Reformation.[53]

Recently, historians have moved away from conflict and anti-conflict models to find the complexity of real life, as noted by David Lindberg[54] and John Brooke.[55] Thus, the story recounted is not one of warfare between science and the church. Nor is it a story of unremitting support and approval. Rather, what we find, as we ought to have suspected, is a relationship exhibiting all of the variety and complexity with which we are familiar in other realms of human endeavor—conflict, compromise, accommodation, dialogue, alienation, the making of common cause, and going of separate ways.

Although historians have studied intensively in the last century the relations between science and Christianity and most have reached a balanced view, popular media have still to discover these complex interactions. A complete account of science and faith relations must make sense of the peaceful events as well as of the conflicts. It is time for a *resetting of the agenda* in the dissemination of the history of science and faith, in particular at popular levels—TV, films, plays, press, educational resources, school textbooks, and others.

As we approach this evidence, I am writing this at a time when we have been warned that in a few weeks we shall face the effects of the peak of the COVID-19 pandemic in Britain. Seldom before has the relevance of science to public policy been invoked so often by national leaders. In their appearances on television, whether it is the President of the USA or the Prime Minister of Britain, they go out of their way to stress that they are following "the best medical and scientific evidence available." For example, Sir Patrick Vallance, the Chief Scientific Adviser in Britain, who had repeatedly emphasized throughout that all his recommendations were based upon "the best available science and scientific modelling" remarked, "We should be prepared to change our minds as the evidence changes. We cannot go in with a fixed plan that is immutable."[56] For understandable reasons, we draw upon the best available scientific and medical evidence to ensure our health and well-being. Why is it then that, at times, some seem reluctant to draw upon the relevant scientific evidence in understanding and interpreting Scripture? And it is not only in the realm of science but in the realm of biblical scholarship and interpretation that we should seek to "draw upon the best available evidence." In the chapters that follow in this section, as

---

53. Hooykaas, *Science in Manueline Style*; Hooykaas, "Rise of Modern Science."
54. Lindberg, "Fate of Science."
55. Brooke, "Historians."
56. Vallance, "Herd Immunity."

we deal with issues of understanding the Bible, we shall seek to draw upon both the best available relevant scientific evidence and the most up-to-date evidence from dedicated biblical scholars. As we approach this evidence, we should indeed be prepared to change our minds as the evidence changes.

Typical and frequently recurring issues concern how, today, we should properly interpret passages of Scripture that give us insights into our human origins, and our human nature. Additionally, as a result of, at times, dramatic claims made from pulpits about miraculous events, honest Christian students are forced to rethink what it is that Scripture actually teaches about miracles, their occurrence, their purpose, and their interpretation. In this section of the book we therefore address some of these recurring issues in detail. We spell out how, with honesty and integrity, awareness of what we have learned from *both* modern science and medicine *and* from the researches of what well-informed biblical scholars are now telling us about how to interpret those parts of Scripture that seem to address these same issues, leads us to a new and greater vision of the God we worship and serve.

4

Human Origins
The Evidence from Science

If theological anthropology is to avoid theoretical isolation from the wider academic world and maintain its relevance for current and future generations, it must listen to the finer details of a broad range of secular accounts of personhood.[1]

Strife over "creation science" continues to meander along, and so continues to exact a high cost in both serious study of nature and serious learning from Scripture.[2]

The story of the empty pew isn't just a work of fiction. It's what is happening throughout this country as the younger generations depart the Christian faith, many unable to identify with a church they feel has rejected science. Like me, you know that the supposed conflict between faith and science is a false narrative, and that those who feel forced to choose can be shown a better way. A way that demonstrates the harmony between science and biblical faith as identified in God's two books: the Bible and the book of nature. As the psalmist tells us, "The heavens declare the glory of God, and the sky above proclaims his handiwork."[3]

---

1. Turner, "Disunity and Disorder," 135.
2. Noll, *Jesus Christ,* 161.
3. Haarsma, "Empty Pew."

LISTENING TO SCIENTISTS

Where Did We Come from and When?

WE ARE STRANGE AND complicated creatures. We share many traits, including cognitive skills and emotions, with other animals, and increasingly learn that the borders between them and us are murky and permeable. Fresh insights into human nature come from the researches of evolutionary biologists, evolutionary psychologists, social psychologists, cognitive neuroscientists, neurologists, geneticists, archaeologists, and anthropologists. How the human mind achieved its present state and complexity remains a mystery. We are still looking for answers to such questions as: How did consciousness arise? How did language develop? How did the potential for ethical decision-making and moral behavior emerge? As we begin to find answers to some of these questions, we must further ask, what is the relationship between these understandings of human nature and understandings of human nature based on the theological concept of humanity being made in the image of God. The understanding of human origins is clearly a multidisciplinary challenge. Diversity of opinion can be a good thing. It may result in a more profound awareness of the complexity of the issues under discussion and of the relevant evidence that needs to be considered.

In response to the need for up-to-date knowledge from a range of disciplines relevant to the puzzles about our origins, in 2015 the deliberations of a group of leading scientists and theologians was published under the title *The Emergence of Personhood: A Quantum Leap*.[4] All the participants recognized and accepted the well-documented and tested claims of the explanatory powers of the neo-Darwinian theory of biological evolution. At the same time, they recognized that there are still unanswered questions to be tackled, as noted in a recent book titled *Darwin's Unfinished Symphony* by Kevin Laland, a colleague of mine at St. Andrews.

That this is a live issue was highlighted further when the journal *Nature* published a commentary provocatively titled, "Does Evolutionary Theory Need a Rethink?" Lead authors Kevin Laland and Tobias Uller argued in their paper that evolutionary theory does indeed need a rethink. But it is an evidence-based rethink, not a hand-waving publicity stunt that is needed. The authors argued that evolutionary theory's decades-old "modern synthesis" of genetics and natural selection had focused too much on the genes an organism is born with, and not enough on the ways organisms develop and interact with their environment to affect adaptation and inheritance. In the past five years, Laland, Uller, and colleagues around the world have

---

4. A volume for which I served as editor.

completed a set of studies designed to put their vision of an extended evolutionary synthesis to the test, carrying out experiments to investigate how non-genetic factors change the way organisms evolve. Full reports of this groundbreaking research have appeared and continue to appear in scientific journals and in a major edited volume.[5]

Their analysis has demonstrated that the modern evolutionary synthesis has indeed been a moving target, particularly as regards the way that developmental mechanisms and socially learned knowledge shape evolutionary innovation. For example, one interesting finding was that developmental plasticity can guide evolution (suggesting that genes may be followers, not leaders, in evolution). The important point is that *science moves on*—and that applies to evolutionary theory as much as to any other theory. The fact that the scientific understanding of biological evolution continues to change should be yet another warning to Christian apologists about the danger of trying to make a particular interpretation of Scripture fit with a particular scientific theory. Such an approach is by its nature doomed to failure. Science moves on, offering fresh glimpses of how humans came to be the way we are today. For a Christian, the new insights will be fresh evidence of God's moment-by-moment upholding at work through the ages.

For a more detailed example illustrating how diverse streams of scientific data have given new insights into human personhood, consider the interdisciplinary consultation reported in *The Emergence of Personhood: A Quantum Leap*.[6] One of the questions the contributors to this volume kept in mind was whether, in understanding the nature and emergence of human personhood, there are gaps in the scientific stories into which reference to God has too readily been made. The contributors reviewed the evidence from paleoarcheology, anthropology, genetics, neurology, sociobiology, evolutionary psychology, neuropsychology, and the cognitive science of religion. All of these disciplines have something to say about human origins and human personhood. They asked, for example, whether evolutionary processes alone led to the gradual development of human characteristics or whether there were, along the way, some "quantum leaps." They were all too well aware that for some people today an apparent gap would present an almost irresistible temptation to fill the gap by reference to God. From a scientific standpoint such a gap could, given time and more research, in principle be filled by, for example, discovering particular genetic mutations or the growing complexity of neural networks in the brain that, together or separately, may have resulted in distinctively human abilities or

---

5. Uller and Laland, *Evolutionary Causation*.
6. Jeeves, ed., *Emergence of Personhood*.

characteristics. The general consensus, amplified below, was that, on balance, the evidence considered endorsed what we might call a gradualist approach. This is important, because in the context of wider debates about the relationship between science and religious beliefs, there has been a constant temptation to look for gaps in the scientific evidence and to fit God into those gaps as an additional explanatory concept.

Donald MacKay, a physicist and brain scientist, wrote,

> There is a quite common approach that we might call "looking for God in the gaps." . . . You explain things scientifically as far as you go, then bring God in to explain what is left. You agree on a kind of division of territory into "the bits of nature that science can explain and God can't touch," and "the bits where science has so far failed and perhaps God must be at work." *And so, of course, God is left with a steadily dwindling territory, liable to devastation by every new discovery in our morning newspaper.* . . . The point is that, however imperfectly a scientist understands the processes he studies, it would be advancing a non-Christian idea of God to suggest God was to be seen at work only in the bits of nature that puzzle the scientists.[7]

In brief, such a "god-of-the-gaps" approach is a recipe for steadily shrinking the God we believe in.

POINTERS FROM RELEVANT DISCIPLINES

Drawing on the chapters in the book *The Emergence of Personhood: A Quantum Leap*, we may get a flavor of how different relevant scientific disciplines can give new insights into how our mysterious human nature came to be the way it is.

From Genetics

Typical Questions

Is our moral sense one more dimension of our biological makeup? Are ethical values a product of biological evolution, or are they given by religious and other cultural traditions. Did Neanderthals have moral values? Did our ancestral species *Homo erectus* and *Homo habilis* evolve a moral sense? Was moral sense directly promoted by natural selection, or did it come about as

---

7. MacKay, *Open Mind*, 34 (emphasis added).

a byproduct of some other attribute, such as rationality, which was a direct target of selection? Alternatively, is the moral sense an outcome of cultural evolution rather than biological evolution?

Pointers from Science

Geneticist Francisco Ayala noted that the distinction between a moral *sense* and moral *norms* is important. He emphasized that we must distinguish between the *capacity for ethics* and the systems or *codes of ethical norms* accepted by humans being biologically determined. He argued that a similar distinction can be made with respect to language. The capacity for language is determined by biological nature, but this is a different question from whether we speak a particular language—and this is not biologically determined.

From Evolutionary Psychology

Typical Questions

Do any substantive differences remain that distinguish us from animals in a way that can properly justify separate treatment in terms of personhood and morality?

Pointers from Science

Evolutionary psychologist Richard Byrne commented, "If a hard and fast cognitive dividing line is ever to be found, my own vote is for human language. . . . As a cognitive psychologist, using the natural behavior of non-human animals to discover precursors to human mental abilities, for me the Holy Grail has always been the evolutionary basis of language."[8] He continues, "Nevertheless, human language did not emerge *de novo*: it was built on cognitive foundations we share with the living apes."[9] The focus of his search is on the natural gestural communication of the bonobo, which he believes deserves special attention because, he says, "that is how my hypothesis of a linguistic dividing line can most easily be tested."[10] Every time someone has sought to identify a feature of human behavior that they believe

---

8. Byrne, "Dividing Line," 24.
9. Byrne, "Dividing Line," 25.
10. Byrne, "Dividing Line," 27.

clearly distinguishes humans from animals, it has seemed only a matter of time before an ingenious research project has demonstrated that, studied in the right way and under the right conditions, these supposedly unique abilities are already there in embryonic form in our nonhuman ancestors. When that happens, another gap has been filled. There have been no clear clues as to how, if it exists, "a quantum leap" in our human lineage may have occurred. It remains unwise to stake human uniqueness on "something" that, given time, may have a perfectly natural explanation.

From Neuroscience

Typical Questions

What do detailed studies of human brains compared with any others in our biological lineage tell us about ourselves?

Pointers from Science

Neuropsychologists Warren Brown and Lynn Paul, acknowledging that the properties of personhood are rooted in physical processes and emergent in our evolutionary trajectory, noted that "comparative neuroanatomy has made it clear that, while humans do not have the largest brains, they have a relatively larger cerebral cortex and, most markedly, a very much larger prefrontal cortex."[11] This enlargement of the prefrontal cortex in humans is primarily the result of increased white matter. Brown and Paul point out that there is a positive linear correlation in the gray-to-white-matter ratio across primate species, and that the human brain falls on this regression line for all non-frontal neocortical areas. But as they also note, "Due to a disproportionate increase in prefrontal white matter, the human prefrontal cortex is well outside of what would be predicted of other species. Thus, the human prefrontal cortex is not simply larger, but more intensely interconnected within itself and with other cortical and subcortical structures of the brain."[12] Brown and Paul believe that some of the core properties of humanness must emerge from complex patterns of physiological interactivity particularly within the brain. This leads them to ask: What happens if, in the course of normal development, or through later damage to the brain, some of these patterns of physiological interactivity are missing or reduced?

---

11. Brown and Paul, "Brain Connectivity," 113.
12. Brown and Paul, "Brain Connectivity," 113.

They explore this hypothetical relationship between connectivity and the emergence of human capacities of personhood by looking at a group of children with abnormalities of cerebral connectivity, specifically children with autism and those with agenesis of the corpus callosum. Their clearly stated hypothesis is that, "if the properties of humanness and personhood are emergent from complex patterns of physiological interactions, then neuropathology that reduces (or alters) the interactivity of brain regions, particularly within the cerebral cortex, will reduce (or alter) the nature of important human characteristics."[13] Using available data, they make a convincing case for the plausibility of their supposition.

Brown and Paul's approach to the emergence of personhood resonates closely with that of professor of neurology Adam Zeman, who specifically focuses on the emergence of subjectivity. With disarming honesty, Zeman refers to our "uniqueness and inwardness" and how they can appear as particularly mysterious elements of our being. For Zeman, "subjectivity is at the heart of human selfhood."[14] However, while subjectivity may appear mysterious, he makes a strong case for ways in which several forms of subjectivity emerged over the course of biological evolution and also matured over the life course of individual human development. These, he believes, go a long way toward explaining the natural origins of subjectivity. Zeman, focusing on the relationship of our physicality to the remarkable cognitive and behavioral achievements that humans exhibit, has no doubt that the origins of subjectivity, one of these features of our nature, were natural and not magical—"at least no more magical than anything else in our magical universe."[15] So, there is no "gap" to be filled here.

From Anthropology and Paleoarchaeology

Typical Questions

What produces our unique cognitive condition? What makes human beings qualitatively different as cognitive entities from every other inhabitant of the planet?

---

13. Brown and Paul, "Brain Connectivity," 105.
14. Zeman, "Origins of Subjectivity," 120.
15. Zeman, "Origins of Subjectivity," 121.

Pointers from Science

Ian Tattersall, curator emeritus and senior scientist in residence in the Division of Anthropology at the American Museum of Natural History, has argued that it is our "unique cognitive condition" that "makes human beings qualitatively different as cognitive entities from every other inhabitant of the planet." In his book *Becoming Human: Evolution and Human Uniqueness*, he writes, "*Homo sapiens* is not simply an improved version of its ancestor—it's a new concept qualitatively distinct from them in highly significant if limited aspects."[16] In his contribution to *The Emergence of Personhood*, having examined the human fossil record carefully, Tattersall observes that "this record is, of course, but a dim mirror of the full behavioral richness of any bygone hominids; *but it nonetheless contains very little indeed to support the gradualist picture.*"[17]

Archaeologist and professor at Cambridge University, Lord Colin Renfrew takes a different view, arguing that "regular but incremental augmentation in the complexity of human society since the end of the last ice age" is a realistic alternative.[18] Renfrew made clear that the essence of his answer is that according to his view, just as we observe "the emergence of personhood in the ontogenetic sense in the birth and development of every human baby, *so we might look for the emergence or multiple emergences of personhood in a succession of ancestral species.*" Starting from the perspective of an archaeologist of prehistory who seeks, in his own words, to "understand the human story on the basis of the material remains that have come down to us from the human past," Renfrew finds "a story that is today becoming clear in outline." Renfrew asked further, how, in the perspective of time, did the emergence of human personhood come about? It is worth quoting his opening statement because it summarizes some very important evidence that we must all consider:

> Ten million years ago there were no humans on earth. There were no people. There were multitudinous living species, including the great apes from which our hominin ancestors evolved. Over those ten million years, as paleontological research has established, a succession of ancestral species, including Australopithecus and Homo erectus, developed, culminating (from our perspective) in the emergence of our own species, *Homo sapiens*, apparently in Africa, more than 100,000 years ago. The out-of-Africa diaspora of *Homo sapiens* seems

---

16. Tattersall, *Becoming Human*, 188.
17. Tattersall, "Human Evolution," 47 (emphasis added).
18. Renfrew, "Personhood."

to have started about 60,000 years ago. These early people were hunter-gatherers, already equipped with quite an elaborate material culture. Some ten thousand years ago, transitions toward a new agricultural economy can be seen in the communities living in different parts of the world, accompanied by a move towards sedentarism. Out of these sedentary communities the first literate societies and the first cities emerged some five or six thousand years ago. This is a phylogenetic story of our species, concisely summarized.[19]

Renfrew asks the key questions: "Where, along this narrative line, does one situate the emergence—or, no doubt in reality, the multiple emergences—of personhood? Where and how did those qualities emerge that we recognize as those of sentient persons, of people imbued with the qualities that we recognize as inherently human?"[20]

For Renfrew, "the criteria for personhood seem difficult to separate from those of being human. The emergence of personhood in the phylogenetic sense initially considered might then well be equated with the emergence of humankind." And in tracing out the emergence of humankind, Renfrew reminds us that "it was the development of DNA analysis, applied to a wide range of living humans, using first mitochondrial DNA and then Y-chromosome analysis, that led to the firm conclusion that the key aspects of human speciation took place in Africa, in the 200,000 years or so prior to around 60,000 bp [before the present time]."[21]

The picture that Renfrew sets out from what he calls the speciation phase (200,000 to 60,000 bp) and the dispersal phase (60,000 to 12,000 bp) raises the question that he describes as the "sapient paradox." He writes: "If our species was established perhaps by 100,000 bp in Africa and certainly by 60,000 bp, why did the new behaviors that we associate with the tectonic phase and that led within a few thousand years to the rise of civilization and of literacy, take so long to emerge?" That, he says, "is a problem that has not yet been clearly answered and is overlooked by most existing accounts of the 'human revolution.'"[22] Reflecting on the trajectory of developments he has outlined of the three phases into which the human evolution can be divided, he asks about *where we can place the emergence of personhood*. For him *it is not easy to identify any kind of a "quantum leap,"* and this might thus lead us to adopt *a gradualist approach*. He goes further, adding that if we were

---

19. Renfrew, "Personhood," 51.
20. Renfrew, "Personhood," 51–52.
21. Renfrew, "Personhood," 57.
22. Renfrew, "Personhood," 59–61.

looking for some kind of an evolutionary leap, then possibly "the ability to talk, to understand and be understood" (echoes here of Byrne's views), which "is an important component of personhood," may have evolved gradually over several million years, as some have argued, or it may have developed more rapidly as an evolutionary leap, as others argue.[23] It remains an open question. Again, one wonders whether discoveries such as the miR-941 gene could contribute to understanding such a leap. If Renfrew is correct, another "gap" has been filled.

Most recently, in 2019, Katerina Harvati and her colleagues at the University of Tübingen report how they have examined a skull fragment held in a museum in Athens.[24] This skull fragment was one of a pair dug up in the 1970s from Apidima, a cave in southern Greece. It was already known that these fragments were parts of human fossils, but until now they had not been dated or properly analyzed. Using techniques of radio isotope dating not available at the time of the original findings Harvati and her colleagues showed that one fossil was 170,000 years old. They report that using computer reconstruction methods it revealed that it was an example of Homo neanderthalensis, Neanderthal man, a species widespread in Europe until 40,000 years ago, when *Homo sapiens* took over. The other fossil, which was the back half of a cranium, turned out to be *Homo sapiens*. It was found to be 210,000 years old and hence the third oldest known example of modern humanity. What is most exciting is that it is the oldest *Homo sapiens* specimen found outside of Africa and Africa is the continent where, on the best available evidence, *Homo sapiens* originated.[25]

How and when *Homo sapiens* spread from Africa to Europe was until recently thought to be simple, but now with accumulating evidence such as that reported by Harvati and her co-workers it is becoming more complex. Genetic data had suggested that most people alive today who are not African or of recent African descent can trace their ancestry to one or a few "out-of-Africa" migrations beginning about 60,000 years ago into Asia and then spreading to Australia, Europe, and the Americas. On their migration some interbred with other human species, now extinct, including Neanderthals. Science does not stand still. And it is not only young people who are confronted with and struggle with these issues. Older people, as they read their daily papers, are made aware of exciting discoveries by paleoarchaeologists that have direct implications for widely held views of human origins. For example, the August 19, 2019 edition of the London *Times* had a full two-page

---

23. Renfrew, "Personhood," 65.
24. Harvati et al., "Apidima Cave Fossils."
25. Harvati et al., "Apidima Cave Fossils."

article by *The Times* Science correspondent Tom Whipple titled "Who Do You Think You Are? Probably a Little Bit Neanderthal." Having read that article, no reader could be in any doubt about how it is *evidence*, not strident protestations, that is influencing our understanding of ourselves, our nature, and where we came from. The author reminds the reader that only a decade ago we thought we had a pretty good idea of human evolutionary history. Briefly, it was that for hundreds of thousands of years our ancestors in Africa had evolved to be clever, resourceful, and world conquering. Eventually about 60,000 years ago they left Africa, spreading around the world, where they met a similar creature to themselves called Neanderthals. Neanderthals did not survive their contact with *Homo sapiens* from Africa. In the words of Tom Whipple, "Today, much of that narrative has crumbled."[26]

The research of Johannes Krause, who conducted detailed DNA testing on the smallest sliver of a finger bone found in the Siberian cave, showed that it didn't look like *Homo sapiens* DNA at all[27] Kraus stated, "I came to the same conclusion: this was indeed some new kind of hominim."[28] The remainder of Whipple's article gives an accessible account of the genus we call humans, which includes *Homo erectus, Homo habilis, Homo rudolfensis, Homo neanderthalis,* and a whole load of other *Homos,* including *Homo sapiens.* Each branch is separate—a distinct species making its distinct way through evolutionary time. But Whipple is not blinded by the science. He noted that when *Homo sapiens* came out of Africa, we had gone from just another human species among many to an unstoppable force. The evidence may one day tell us what our distinctive property was, but it's not yet sufficient. It does seem likely that, while the bodies may have been the same, the brains of those who left Africa on the last migration were very different. Whipple provisionally concluded that "Once *Homo sapiens* started making art, we didn't stop. . . . *Homo sapiens* became quite an exceptional kind of animal, who thought in an exceptional way."[29] This, he says, is something we see in no other species. I would add, or at least not yet. There are many surprises yet awaiting us.

26. Whipple, "Who Do You Think You Are?" n.p.
27. Krause et al., "Mitochondrial DNA Genome."
28. Whipple, "Who Do You Think You Are?" n.p.
29. Whipple, "Who Do You Think You Are?" n.p.

From Cognitive Science

Typical Questions

What cognitive mechanisms must humans have to conceptualize a god and to generate actions for interacting with that god?

Pointers from Science

Higher-order theory of mind appears as a central player in any satisfactory answer. For example, Barrett and Jarvinen identify "a few features of the CSR [cognitive science of religion] account of religion that merit highlighting." Briefly, in their own words: First, these cognitive accounts typically presume strong biological and cognitive continuity with ancestral species and, by extension, with nonhuman primates thought to approximate human ancestors. Second, though conceding the possibility of later exaptation,[30] *cognitive accounts are at their core evolutionary byproduct accounts of religion.* That is, *the cognitive equipment that gives rise to religious expression is presumed to have evolved under selection pressures unrelated to religion or religious entities.* Third, many different cognitive subsystems or "mental tools" cooperate to encourage religious beliefs and practices, and hence belief in gods (or souls, the afterlife, etc.) are byproducts of multiple cognitive adaptations and not just one. Nevertheless, one "mental tool" takes center stage in these accounts: ToM (Theory of Mind).[31] It is noteworthy in the context of this chapter that Barrett and Jarvinen stress evolutionary continuity in the emergence of religion and make no reference to any "gaps to be filled."

The contributors to *The Emergence of Personhood: A Quantum Leap?* concluded that there is no place and no necessity in well-grounded Christian belief to invoke a "god-of-the-gaps." We are not in the business of defending any such shrunken "god-of-the-gaps." Reflecting on all the diverse contributions making a sustained effort to answer the question posed to the contributors to the book, it was clear that a pervasive theme emerged. As those contributors traced out the emergence of personhood over millions of years, there were occasions when it looked as though there might have been a leap, a discontinuity, if not a quantum leap. However, as Ian Tattersall has emphasized and exemplified many times in his book *Palaeontology: A Brief History of Life*, these apparent discontinuities turn out to have a perfectly natural explanation in terms of events that have also occurred in the

---

30. Exaptation describes a shift in the function of a trait during evolution.
31. Barrett and Jarvinen, "Cognitive Evolution," 169 (emphasis added).

earth's history. In one form or another, the gradualist approach advocated by Colin Renfrew in his chapter has been endorsed by many of those seeking an answer to our question. This is important because, in the contexts of wider debates about the relationship between science and religious beliefs, and specifically in this present book, there has been a constant temptation to look for gaps in the scientific evidence and to fit God into those gaps as an additional explanatory concept. There is no place in well-grounded Christian belief for such a conclusion. The Hebrew-Christian God is not a "god-of-the-gaps."

5

Human Origins
The Evidence from Scripture

As readers of Scripture we are committed to being faithful interpreters, and therefore we must do all we can to ascertain that we are reading the text of Scripture without imposing our own worldview or meaning on it.[1]

New insights and new information can emerge at any time. Several hundred years ago, renewed access to the original languages had significant impact on biblical interpretation. In recent decades, the availability of documents from the ancient world has provided a remarkable resource for our reading of the biblical text. We dare not neglect these tools when they can contribute so significantly to our interpretation.[2]

A DIVISIVE CONTEMPORARY ISSUE MAY POINT TO THE GREATNESS OF GOD

WHY INCLUDE A CHAPTER on human origins in a book on shrinking faith in shrinking gods? The answer, questions about our origins are not just an academic issue. They are also pastoral issues, and all too often produce problems for typical religious young persons in the early twenty-first century.

---

1. Walton, "Origins in Genesis," 107.
2. Walton, *Lost World*, 12.

The email I quoted in the Preface illustrates the problem presented by misunderstandings of our biological origins. The student wrote, "Also I hear that our morals can be completely attributed to scientific evolutionary processes. Do you think this is true? If it is does that make them less valuable/precious?" These are real issues for real students. Sadly, when discussing the foundations for our beliefs as Christians, we often find that claims about the reliability of Scripture are confidently made and equally confidently refuted. Often the discussion focuses on what Scripture tells us about ourselves and our origins. In an effort to defend the God in whom we believe, we attribute to him direct "interventions" from time to time in his created order. One obvious time that God must have directly intervened to make us distinguishably different from all other creatures, at a particular time and place, is at our origin as a species. If we believe there are any gaps in our present scientific accounts, then we are immediately tempted to bring in God to fill the gaps. We invoke the "god-of-the-gaps." As already mentioned, this is not just an academic issue. It is also a pastoral issue. Questions about our origins all too often produce problems not only for students, but also for thoughtful pew dwellers who keep up to date with advances in science through well-presented television documentaries.

All too often a student is either told directly, or it is clearly implied, that to be "a true Christian" she must set aside the scientific knowledge about human origins she's been taught in school and college, which, so it is claimed, is incompatible with what is clearly taught in Scripture. The stresses and strains faced by young people today became such a matter of concern to leading Christians in the USA, that Francis Collins, together with fellow scientists and biblical scholars, set up an organization called BioLogos, whose primary aim is to help young people struggling with how to make sense of what they learn from their science lecturers and what some of their pastors tell them they must believe. For example, Deb Haarsma, President of the BioLogos organization, wrote, "In a recent study, nearly half of church-going teenagers agreed that 'The church seems to reject much of what science tells us about the world.'"[3] This underlines the pressing need not to be defensive, but to be ready to give clear and unambiguous answers to difficult questions that may so easily undermine the faith of sincere Christians. *In so doing we must not shrink God in the face of the challenges of scientific progress.*

Evidence for the stresses and strains faced by young people is further underlined by surveys from organizations such as the Pew Research Center and the Barna group, who have systematically sampled the prevailing views of different socio-economic groups in various nations on religion and

---

3. Haarsma, "Kids Ask Tough Questions."

associated topics. For example, a 2011 Barna survey on American Christianity, published under the title "Six Reasons Young Christians Leave the Church," gave wide publicity to the plight of some of today's young people who seem to be leaving their faith behind.[4] The results of this survey were discussed more extensively in a book by David Kinnaman, the lead Barna researcher.[5]

Several of the reasons young Christians say they leave the church are directly relevant to this chapter:

- Churches seem overprotective. As young Christians express the desire for their faith in Christ to connect to the world they live in, they discover that much of their experience of Christianity feels stifling, fear-based, and risk-averse.

- Teens' and twenty-somethings' experience of Christianity is shallow. Some said "church is boring" (31 percent). A quarter said that "faith is not relevant to my career or interests" (24 percent) Another quarter said "the Bible is not taught clearly or often enough" (23 percent). One-fifth who attended a church as a teenager said that "God seems missing from my experience of church" (20 percent).

- Churches come across as antagonistic to science. One of the reasons young adults feel disconnected from church or from faith is the tension they feel between Christianity and science. A third said that "Christians are too confident they know all the answers" (35 percent). A third of young adults with a Christian background felt that "churches are out of step with the scientific world we live in" (29 percent). A quarter embrace the perception that "Christianity is anti-science" (25 percent). The same proportion (23 percent) said they have "been turned off by the creation-versus-evolution debate." Furthermore, the research shows that many science-minded young Christians are struggling to find ways of staying faithful to their beliefs and to their professional calling in science-related industries.

- The church feels unfriendly to those who doubt. Young adults with Christian experience say the church is not a place that allows them to express doubts. They do not feel safe admitting that sometimes Christianity does not make sense. In addition, many feel that the church's response to doubt is trivial. Some of the perceptions in this regard include not being able "to ask my most pressing life questions in church"

---

4. Barna Group, "Six Reasons."
5. Kinnaman, *You Lost Me.*

(36 percent) and having "significant intellectual doubts about my faith" (23 percent).

Discussing the six reasons mentioned in the Barna report, biblical scholar Peter Enns wrote,

> I read through them and I think to myself, "Yup. Yup. Uh huh. That one, too. And that one." These ring utterly true to me from my experience, including being a Christian college professor. . . . I continue to think that parents, churches, and schools need to be aware of these trends and consider ways to address them with less fear of what might happen if they do and more fear of what IS happening if they don't. As one first year student said in class a few years back, "I feel my church did not prepare me for life outside of the church. They were more interested in protecting me from wrong conclusions and making sure I was a 'good Christian' than getting me ready for living in the world." I hear that a lot, and these young people are being done a disservice with predictable consequences. *Christian leaders owe it to their young people to create for them cultures where exploration and interrogation of their faith is seen as part of the journey of faith rather than a problem to be avoided, tamed, or shunned.* Rather than trying to keep young people safely on the beach blanket at any cost by arming them with a naïve faith, leaders should entrust them to God by allowing them to work through the inevitable ambiguities and challenges of faith that we all experience. If not, they will leave and find someplace else to do that, and it likely won't be in a Christian context. To put it another way, rather than simply being "faithful to the past," we owe it our young people to be "faithful to the future," to work out with them what it looks like to have an intelligent, wise, gentle, and viable faith that deeply respects the past while they navigate the present and build a vision for the future.[6]

The BioLogos organization has begun to address some of these clearly expressed concerns of thoughtful young people. One of BioLogos's main aims is to share in a meaningful, positive, and constructive way, how developments in science, particularly relating to topics such as that of human origins, can be constructively related to what biblical scholars today are telling us about the stories of human origins contained in Scripture. The activities of those involved with BioLogos are paralleled by a series of publications, of books and of journal articles, all addressing in one way or another answers

---

6. Enns, "Why Young Christians Leave Church" (emphasis added).

to the question how may we creatively and with honesty relate the knowledge that is being gained by leaders in groups of relevant scientific disciplines which have something to say about the origins and early evidences for humankind, with the stories that the biblical scholars are telling us they are finding to the same questions of human origins within Scripture.

In December 2018, the BioLogos Organization website announced, "Five Wheaton College Professors Release New Book on Theories of Origins."[7] Near the end of their review of the contents of this new book, they write, "In part six we turn to human origins, starting with an exploration of the biblical account of creation of humans. We discuss the scientific evidence relating to human origins as observed in the fossil record, the biology of modern people, including evidence recorded in the genes of humans and some of the fossil forms. Conclusions based on these kinds of evidence are summarized, and the implications of the scientific conclusions are explored in the context of the biblical account, the doctrine of creation, and the image of God in humans." This work of the Wheaton professors is timely and takes up an approach advocated in 1957 by geologist and historian of science by Reijer Hooykaas. He called it *Philosophia Libera*. Hooykaas wrote, "Science is stifled whenever men cherish preconceived ideas which they refuse to submit to test. This happens . . . when the self is exalted as the measure, rather than the humble recipient of truth, . . . when a well-meaning piety exalts secondary standards of authority to a place that belongs only to God."[8]

BEWARE FALSE ASSUMPTIONS AND FAKE NEWS

Whether we are aware of them or not, we all bring with us a set of assumptions about how we are to understand, to interpret, anything and everything that we read. Obviously, we recognize that when the poet tells us, "My love is like a red, red rose,"[9] we know that we should not understand this as a claim by a botanist to have discovered another variety of rosebushes. There is no problem there. However, with other things we read, the situation is not always so clear nor so obvious. We have to think carefully to know whether we are reading factual statements, poetic images, helpful metaphors, or figurative language. Everything we read is contextually embedded and we risk misunderstanding every time we fail to understand the context of what we are reading. This latter point is still sadly not so obvious or so widely shared as we imagine it to be. If it were, then the text of two volumes that I received

---

7. BioLogos, "Five Wheaton College Professors."
8. Hooykaas, *Philosophia Libera*, 5.
9. Burns, "Red, Red Rose."

recently and describe below would never have been written. Knowing of my interest in the relationship between science and Christian faith, a friend presented me with two most beautifully illustrated volumes on the topic. They claimed to trace the history of the earth and of humankind taking account of the Scriptures and of science. The first was entitled *The Time Chart of Biblical History*, with the subtitle *Over 4000 Years in Charts, Maps, Lists, and Chronologies*.[10] The second was entitled *The Time Chart History of the World* with the subtitle *Over 6000 Years of World History Unfolded*.[11] As I began to look into these two superficially impressive volumes, I was disappointed to realize that they were full of lies and misrepresentations: lies about geology and misrepresentations about the status of the theory of evolution. What characterized many of the lies was the assumption that when it comes to answering questions such as how the world works, how humans came into existence, and similar fundamental questions, the approach should be to see how far scientists have progressed at the moment and then *fill in any remaining gaps* in our knowledge by invoking special acts of God. Since science steadily progresses, what this way of thinking means is that we steadily shrink the God in whom we believe—as was pointed out by two other books. The first was written by Ian Plimer, Professor of Geology at Melbourne University, entitled *Telling Lies for God*. The second, by Kenneth Miller, Professor of Biology at Brown University in the USA, is an excellent book about evolution with the title *Only a Theory*.

The specific term "fake news" is only a few years old but throughout history people have circulated false, biased, or imaginary information. Today with the prevalence and the persuasive power of the internet, we face the prospect of the extremely rapid and widespread circulation of fake news about the Bible, which tends to take two forms. Some of the fake news is produced and circulated by believers anxious to demonstrate that the Bible is true. The rest is produced and circulated by critics of Christian faith anxious to do the opposite. Recently Alan Millard, Emeritus Professor of Hebrew and Ancient Semitic Languages at the University of Liverpool in the UK, has documented some of the ways in which such fake news in the realm of religious discourse continues to be widely circulated. Millard writes, "During my own lifetime there have been dramatic headlines claiming that someone has found Noah's Ark. On one such occasion in 1974 the claimant produced a piece of wood he said was part of the Ark, however, when it was subjected to carbon-14 testing the results showed that it was less than 2000 years old

---

10. Edited by Harry Hill.
11. Edited by David Gibbons.

and could not possibly be a candidate."[12] Similar claims from time to time circulate among Bible-believing Christians. Millard asks the pertinent question, "Why do people, especially evangelical Christians, want to find Noah's Ark? They answer, 'If we find Noah's Ark everyone will have to believe the Bible is true.'"[13] If they did find a boat, Millard wonders, how would they know that it had been built by Noah unless it was labelled "Built by Noah and sons"? It might just as easily be the boat of the Babylonian flood hero Atrahasis or the Greek Deucalion. The same researcher who claimed to have found a relic of Noah's Ark also claimed to find the Ark of the Covenant and other equipment from the Temple of Solomon. But his claims suffered the same fate on close scrutiny. Millard wrote, "In fact, he failed to produce a single piece of evidence that independent investigators have been able to substantiate to support any of his 'discoveries.'" Millard wisely concludes, "Ultimately, anyone eager to find Noah's Ark thinking it would prove the Bible true, should recall the words of the One who declared, 'They will not be convinced even if someone rises from the dead'"[14] (Luke 16:31).

The misguided attempt to enlarge the claims for God by "proving" the truth of a particular interpretation of a particular passage of Scripture ended up in dishonoring God and in shrinking him. Millard wrote,

> The conclusion has to be that these are the delusions of a devout Christian who believed he should be able to find anything the Bible described and so "prove the Bible true." Regrettably, they are still circulated in print and on the Internet, misleading many uninformed readers. *They are fake news!* They attract people who want "proof" of biblical reports.[15]

LISTENING TO BIBLICAL SCHOLARS

The previous chapter reviewed the scientific evidence about human origins. But there is, for Christians, another source of relevant information. Its relevance is captured in a recent book chapter entitled "Origins in Genesis: Claims of an Ancient Text in a Modern Scientific World" by Old Testament scholar John Walton of Wheaton College. In his chapter, Walton gives clear guidance to the non-specialist to help in properly interpreting how the early

---

12. Millard, "Is the Bible Fake News?" 4.
13. Millard, "Is the Bible Fake News?" 5.
14. Millard, "Is the Bible Fake News?" 7.
15. Millard, "Is the Bible Fake News?" 7 (emphasis added).

chapters of Genesis should be understood. We may summarize Walton's conclusions in his own words as follows:

- "With regards to origins, scientific consensus sets forth explanations involving big bang cosmology and evolutionary models, evidence that all can be explained by means of natural laws (at least eventually), while those who value biblical explanations contest those claims based on their belief in teaching that God is the Creator and that origins (whether cosmic or human) need to be understood with recourse to God's activity. As we turn our attention to the Bible, however, particularly to the Old Testament where the biblical origins account is located (Genesis 1–2), we ought to begin by asking about the metaphysical categories current in the ancient world in general and among the Israelites in particular. Do they classify phenomena into categories that comport with our distinction between natural and supernatural?"[16]

- "It is common for people today to understand God's creative action in Genesis 2 as entailing the claim that, since he is portrayed as acting, he bypassed natural processes. This traditional perspective presupposes that interests, language, and/or metaphysical concepts of the ancient Israelite author recognize a distinction between natural and supernatural. Ancient Israelites, however, believed that God is always active in numerous and often undetectable ways; they did not have the categories of natural and supernatural. . . . They believed that when they planted a grain of wheat, wheat would grow. But God would be no less involved in that than if barley grew instead. In the same way, we cannot infer from Genesis whether God created humans naturally (through a process capable of scientific description) or supernaturally (beyond the regular and predictable cause-and-effect processes) just because God is identified as taking an active role. They believed God always took an active role."[17]

- "When the Old Testament describes God's extraordinary involvement in the world, it is not to specify a supernatural event that is in defiance of natural, scientifically describable cause and effect. In the ancient world they undoubtedly understood certain phenomena as usual, ordinary, or normal. But they would not have therefore considered them as natural (i.e., scientifically describable; no involvement of God). Generally, the Old Testament identifies phenomena as 'signs

---

16. Walton, "Origins in Genesis," 108.
17. Walton, "Origins in Genesis," 109.

- "and wonders.' These stand as demonstrations both of God's power to deliver his people and of his covenantal love for them."[18]

- "Today, when we make distinctions between natural and supernatural activity in Scripture, not only do we push our modern categories into the Bible, but we also limit God's action. Once we designate some acts as 'special' or 'supernatural,' we imply that other events which can be explained by normal cause-and-effect are not the acts of God. This drifts towards deism (distancing God from the operations of the cosmos) by suggesting the God only acts some of the time."[19]

Applying these principles to the understanding of Genesis 1 and 2, Walton writes,

- "It is very difficult for present-day readers to consider Genesis 1–2 as focused on anything but material origins. The fact that the relevant Hebrew verbs used to convey the creative activity of God are translated by English terms such as 'created,' 'made,' and 'formed' leads a modern reader to think intuitively of material processes."[20]

- "Once we recognize that this is an ancient text, which has little interest or focus on material origins, we can arrive at an understanding of the text that is more in line with the way an Israelite would have perceived it."[21]

- "As modern readers, we have an impoverished understanding of the seven-day account when we fail to understand that it is all about sacred space. Without a clear understanding of day seven, the other six days are meaningless."[22]

- "The text then is not discussing the unique biological origins of the first two humans. It has adopted Adam and Eve as archetypes for communicating the ontological identity of humanity. Their role is not as the first biological examples of the species but as those selected for a specialized assignment in this newly established sacred space."[23]

---

18. Walton, "Origins in Genesis," 110.
19. Walton, "Origins in Genesis," 110.
20. Walton, "Origins in Genesis," 114.
21. Walton, "Origins in Genesis," 114.
22. Walton, "Origins in Genesis," 116.
23. Walton, "Origins in Genesis," 119.

- "The biological origins of human beings was not a concern of the ancient Israelites or any of their neighbors."[24]
- "If the Bible is not claiming that God bypassed scientifically describable processes in the material creation of human beings (since its authors and its intended audience had no such categories), Genesis may not be used to rule out scientific explanations for material human origins (such as evolution)."[25]

COMING TO GRIPS WITH BOTH SCIENCE AND BIBLICAL SCHOLARSHIP

Today we are extremely fortunate in that a number of leading biblical scholars, such as John Walton, Peter Enns, and Ernest Lucas, have done their utmost to share with the non-specialist the fruits of their research so that we may better understand how properly to read and interpret some very familiar passages of Scripture such as those in the early chapters of the book of Genesis.

The Prevailing Cultural Climate Fosters a Belief in Evolution

The impact of the media is ubiquitous. Perhaps most powerful is the effect of television. Almost every week there are documentaries on geology or astronomy or genetics or biology or medicine or psychology. These documentaries contain pervasive direct or indirect references to the evolution of the universe, evolution of plants, and evolution of animals. Documentaries on medicine refer to the evolutionary links between animals and humans, which allow the results of research with animals to be applied beneficially to the solving of human problems. Genetics is referred to frequently with the seemingly very close similarities between animals and humans frequently highlighted. These are often linked to studies of animal behavior, including the cognitive behavior and social behavior of our nonhuman cousins.

There are a number of results of these ubiquitous references to evolution. First, the general population accepts evolution as a given. Children and young people in schools, colleges, and universities are taught and accept evolution as a fact of life. Second, there are high-profile statements by conservative theologians against the concept of evolution. Many of these

---

24. Walton, "Origins in Genesis," 120.
25. Walton, "Origins in Genesis," 120.

reactions are highlighted by atheist scientists anxious to pour scorn on religious beliefs—hence the high profile of Richard Dawkins. Positioned between these views, there are concerns among sincere religious people about whether they can any longer believe in Adam and Eve. For example, a growing number of biblical scholars—including a few from some of the most conservative Christian colleges in America—have argued that Scripture does not, when properly understood, demand belief in a literal Adam and Eve. The public reaction to the work of these scholars was exemplified by the headlines in the widely read journal *Christianity Today*, which proclaimed, "No Adam, No Eve, No Gospel." This reaction is perfectly understandable because there are seemingly clear statements of the apostle Paul in his letters to the Romans and to the Corinthians that, so it is argued and has been long believed, make the gospel dependent upon the reality of a literal Adam and Eve.

How should Christians respond? One unacceptable response was expressed in the title of the book written by Ian Plimer, the geologist mentioned above. As a professing Christian, he expressed his deep concern about some of the things that were being said by some fellow Christians, leading him to title his book, which is an exposé of creationism, *Telling Lies for God*.[26]

Old Testament scholar Peter Enns has underlined the guidance summarized earlier by John Walton. Enns urges us to remember that there are three key facts to keep in mind in understanding these early chapters of Genesis:[27]

1. Recognize that our knowledge of the cultures that surrounded ancient Israel *greatly affects how we now understand the Old Testament*—not only here and there but also what the Old Testament as a whole is designed to do.

2. Because Scripture is a collection of discrete writings from widely diverse times and places and written for diverse purposes, *the significant theological diversity of Scripture we find there should hardly be a surprise.*

3. *How the New Testament authors interpret the Old Testament reflects the Jewish thought world of the time* and that accounts for their creative engagement of the Old Testament. It also helps Christians today understand how the New Testament authors brought together the Israel story and the gospel.

26. Plimer, *Telling Lies for God*.
27. Enns, *Inspiration and Incarnation*.

Enns says that we need to recognize that, "A historical Adam has been the dominant Christian view for two thousand years.... [Nevertheless, to] appeal to this older consensus as a way of keeping the challenge of evolution at bay is not a viable option for readers today. The same argument from consensus was used against Galileo's observation that the earth revolves around the sun, and that old consensus eventually (slowly) failed to persuade. *We should be cautious not to repeat that same mistake.*"[28]

Specifically regarding the creation stories in Genesis, Enns notes,[29]

- "The creation stories are to be understood within this larger framework, as part of a larger theologically driven collection of writings that answers ancient questions of self-definition, not contemporary ones of scientific interest."

- "Christians today misread Genesis when they try to engage it, even minimally, in the scientific arena."

Peter Enns goes on to explore the impact of the new, deeper understanding of the ancient context of Genesis 1 on the evolution question. He reminds us that the foundational principle of interpretation is that the text's meaning is rooted in its historical and literary contexts. Thus, Enns writes, "Exodus is the story of a monolatry not monotheism" and that "to miss this is to miss the theological depth of Exodus." He argues further that the theology of Genesis 1 is clearer when we read it in its ancient literary and religious context. This underlines yet again that "Genesis 1 is not in any way a modern scientific statement but an ancient religious one. It drew on the thought categories available at the time to create a powerful statement within its own context for the uniqueness of Israel's God and his worthiness to be worshipped."[30]

In understanding Paul's Adam, Enns notes that to understand any literature you must ask the right questions, in the right order, and at every stage make clear your presuppositions. Having made clear his presuppositions, Enns examines key passages that, it has been claimed, "require" an historic Adam: Romans 5:15-21 and 1 Corinthians 15:20-58. On these issues, Enns notes, "as a first-century Jew, Paul, along with his contemporaries, assumed various ways of thinking about the world,"[31] and that Paul's understanding of the Adam story is influenced both by the interpretive conventions of Second Temple Judaism in general and by his fully reorienting experience of

---

28. Enns, *Evolution of Adam*, xvi (emphasis added).
29. Enns, *Evolution of Adam*, 33.
30. Enns, *Evolution of Adam*, 45.
31. Enns, *Evolution of Adam*, 81.

the risen Christ. *Paul is not doing straight exegesis of the Adam story.* Rather, he subordinates that story to the present higher reality of the risen Son of God, expressing himself within the hermeneutic or conventions of the time. How does Enns read the Adam story? He writes,

> I read the Adam story not as a universal story to explain human sinfulness at all but as a proto-Israel story. A Wisdom reading of the garden story does not address, and so in no way negates, the universal and inescapable reality of sin and death and the need for a Savior to die and rise. I arrive at this conclusion, however, not from reading the garden story but on the basis of Paul's Christology, which . . . is *what drove Paul to read Adam as he did.* . . . The bottom line for our restricted purpose is this: what Genesis says about Adam and the consequences of his actions does not seem to line up with the universal picture that Paul paints in Romans and one Corinthians—or at least the way in which many Christians have understood Paul after Augustine. . . . But as I hope to show, *I do not think the gospel stands on whether we can read Paul's Adam in the pages of Genesis.*[32]

The Need to Understand Paul as an Ancient Interpreter of the Old Testament

Paul wrote as an ancient man who naturally held widely accepted views on a good number of things. Paul had a cultural context like every other human being. For example, and along with other ancient people, Paul understood the cosmos to be made up of levels, a three-tiered cosmos: heaven above, the earth, and beneath the earth.[33] The fact that biblical authors wrote these things down does not mean they are accurate descriptions of physical reality. Rather, they simply reflect ancient ways of thinking. Paul's conception of what is above him reflects his intellectual world. So does Paul's understanding of humanity as created by God in a discreet act, rather than by a lengthy process involving common descent. The real issue before us is not whether Paul shared these assumptions, but what the implications are for how *we* read Paul, especially his view of Adam.[34] At this point, it is interesting to compare Peter Enns' views with those expressed by a fellow Old Testament scholar in the same ecclesiastical tradition as Enns. Thus, John Walton, a

---

32. Enns, *Evolution of Adam*, 92 (emphasis added).
33. Enns, *Evolution of Adam*, 94.
34. Enns, *Evolution of Adam*, 103.

professor at Wheaton College, has recently offered wise advice about how properly to understand and interpret the ancient documents on which our English Bibles are based. A quotation from Walton's most recent book with Tremper Longman III captures the essence of the view of Scripture that he has enunciated in the past. Longman and Walton write,

> If we are to interpret Scripture to receive the full impact of God's authoritative message, and build the foundation for sound theology, we have to begin by leaving our cultural river behind, with all our modern issues and perspectives, to understand the cultural river of the ancient intermediaries. The communicators that we encounter in the Old Testament are not aware of our cultural river—including all of its scientific aspect; they neither address our cultural river nor anticipate it. We cannot therefore assume any of the constants or currents of our cultural river are addressed in Scripture. . . . Consequently we are obliged to respect the text by recognizing the sort of text it is and the nature of the message it offers. In that regard, we have long recognized that the Bible is not a scientific textbook addressing issues from our modern advantage point. That is, God's intention is not to teach about the scientific aspects of events or phenomena. He does reveal his work in the world, but he doesn't reveal how the world works.[35]

Finally, we may compare the views of Peter Enns and John Walton, both from the USA, with the views of Ernest Lucas, an Old Testament scholar resident in the UK. Ernest Lucas, before becoming an Old Testament scholar, spent the early years of his career in scientific research. When delivering the Fliedner lectures in Spain in 2016, Ernest Lucas very helpfully identified key questions that should be borne in mind when interpreting any text, including a biblical one.[36] His five questions were:

1. What kind of language is being used?
2. What kind of literature is it?
3. What is the intended audience?
4. What is the purpose of the text?
5. What information from outside the Bible might be helpful in interpreting this text?

---

35. Longman and Walton, *Lost World of the Flood*, 7–8.
36. Lucas, "Relevance of Genesis."

Lucas encouraged his audience to remember that failing to take into account these questions we are in danger of replacing the authority of the Bible by the authority of our assumptions. As a result, we all too easily twist and abuse the Bible. Lucas reminded his audience that Howard Van Till (quoted in our opening chapter) had long ago warned of these dangers when he wrote, "Twentieth-century Western culture seems to me particularly inept at understanding and using figurative or symbolic literature. We are so accustomed to straightforward, matter-of-fact prose that we expect nearly all writing to be of that form. . . . [S]cientific writing has made an illegitimate claim of superiority over artistic literature."[37]

Taken together, all three authors (Enns, Walton, and Lucas) warn us that if we fail to take into account the kind of questions that I listed earlier as a means of trying to understand the human form in which God's word comes to us and simply assume that we know what kind of literature it is and how it should be read, we are in danger of replacing the authority of the Bible by the authority of our assumptions. As a result, we will twist and abuse the Bible. It is a strange phenomenon that there is one thing on which both the "new atheists" and some fundamentalist Christians are agreed. This is that Genesis 1–3 should be read as a scientific account of the origin of the cosmos and of humans. When read this way it is clearly at odds with modern science. This leads the new atheists to reject the biblical account as a piece of outmoded pre-scientific speculation. It also leads the fundamentalist Christians to reject modern scientific theories of origins, claiming that they are the result of atheistic, materialistic presuppositions, which distort the understanding of the evidence.

TAKING STOCK

Even when we listen to the advice and guidance offered by biblical scholars such as Enns, Walton, and Lucas, all of whom share many of the same assumptions, we need to recognize that problems still remain in rightly understanding the early chapters of the book of Genesis and their relevance to issues such as understanding human origins. A recent remarkably comprehensive review of both the scientific and the biblical literature is given in Luke Janssen's book *Standing on the Shoulders of Giants: Genesis and Human Origins*.[38] Janssen would be the last to claim that his account of the origin of humans is the last word. (In 2019, for instance, a paper in *Nature* by Vanessa

---

37. Van Till, *Fourth Day*, 11.
38. Janssen, *Genesis and Human Origins*.

Hayes and a group of researchers at Garvan Institute in Sydney, Australia presented yet another intriguing piece of evidence about human origins.)[39]

By 1980 Alan Wilson of the University of California had established fairly firmly that *Homo sapiens* began as an African species. He developed what became known as the "mitochondrial Eve hypothesis" by looking at a special type of DNA passed, unmixed by sexual reproduction, from a mother to her children. Wilson's research showed that the family trees of present-day human mitogenomes, their branches caused by mutations over the millennia, converge in a way that makes clear that their common ancestor lived in Africa. Hence the nickname "mitochondrial Eve." What is true of Eve was also true of Adam. Part of the DNA on the Y chromosome, which is passed unmixed from father to son, can be used to draw up a similar tree, also rooted in Africa. What is new about this discovery is that it matches up with recent research on climatic changes in the part of Africa where "mitochondrial Eve" is believed to have lived.[40] The story will continue to develop. One thing is clear: it would be foolish in the extreme to try to match up a particular theory about "mitochondrial Eve" with a particular understanding of the early chapters of Genesis.

Equally well-informed scientists and biblical scholars may all review the same evidence but nevertheless at the end of the day differ on issues such as, for example, whether there was ever an original pair matching the Genesis story of Adam and Eve. In a recent paper jointly authored by a group of scientists from different disciplines and guided by biblical scholar Ernest Lucas, two different views were offered, both of which on current evidence seemed plausible.[41] One of them refers to the direct intervention of God at a point in time to select a pair, Adam and Eve, and in some way to make them in the image of God, and this, as such, implies an intervention by God. The other view maintains that God in his wisdom right from the beginning of the story guided the emergence of humans so that through all the physical and biological processes which he was moment-by-moment sustaining and upholding, humans would emerge who had a capacity for a personal relationship with their Creator. It is this capacity for personal relationship with their Creator that many theologians regard as one of the defining characteristics of what it means to be made in the image of God.

---

39. Chan et al., "Human Origins."
40. See Janssen, *Genesis and Human Origins*.
41. Lucas et al., "Bible, Science, and Human Origins."

6

Human Nature
The Evidence from Science

Scientific theories of human nature may be discomforting or unsatisfying but they are not illegitimate.... With deference to the sensibilities of religious people, the idea that man was created in the image of God can surely be put aside.[1]

If we look for insights into human nature to guide the future of religion, we find more such insights in the novels of Dostoevsky than in the journals of cognitive science.[2]

IN THE PREFACE I quoted an email from a student seeking honestly to relate his faith with his understanding of science. The student wrote,

> Dear Dr. Jeeves,
>
> I am a Christian having trouble believing in a soul, afterlife, or higher power. A lot of people in your particular field are atheists. Does their atheism make you question your faith? Why or why not? Do you feel the mind is reducible to the brain? If consciousness was confined to the brain would that eliminate the idea of a soul/afterlife? Can you give me a few scientific/logical

---

1. Nature, "Evolution and the Brain," 753.
2. Dyson, "Complementarity," 53.

(preferably scientific) reasons to believe in an afterlife? If you respond to this I greatly appreciate it.

Embedded within this brief and disarmingly honest email from a thoughtful student are a number of profound questions. They are questions that arise in the minds of many thoughtful pew dwellers. What, for example, is the relation between the mind and the soul? And how do these relate to the brain? If my consciousness and what makes me "me" depends upon the intact working of my brain, what happens to "me" when I die? Is it legitimate and does it make sense to look to science to give us assurance that there is anything after this present life? These are issues that not only puzzle thoughtful students but also concern pastors who are aware of some of the wider implications for some traditional Christian beliefs of advances in relevant sciences, which they and their congregation read of in the press every day. In this chapter I shall summarize as concisely as possible the nature and implications of the evidence about the relation of brain and mind circulating today in the scientific marketplace. I shall also spell out why I believe such scientific knowledge should be welcomed as giving new insights into our mysterious human nature, and how, properly understood, it poses not a threat to our faith but an encouragement.

The answers we give to questions raised by these issues have the potential either to shrink or expand our understanding of God. Either we shrink God to a "gap-filling" God or we expand to a truly upholding God. This is a theme recently highlighted by Deborah Haarsma and Lauren Haarsma. They suggest that when we are confronted by the challenges of science to some of our most deeply held religious beliefs, we all too easily resort to a god-of-the-gaps approach. They wrote, "Unfortunately, this approach almost always reduces to looking for God only in the gaps in our current scientific understanding, implying that scientific explanations for things in the natural world eliminate the need for God. . . . Science is a great way to learn truths about the history and operation of the natural world, but there are many questions it cannot answer."[3]

This approach of looking for God only in the gaps of science is evident in many of the models created down the centuries to help in our thinking about human nature. The emergence of successive models underlines the fact that any model, however refined, is never fully adequate for the task. Our understanding of nature is subject to continual development—as is our understanding of God. This certainly applies to models of human nature. This chapter offers an overview of *current* scientific thinking about our mysterious human nature. But the scene will continue to change as, we are

---

3. Haarsma and Haarsma, "Christ and the Cosmos," 226.

reminded by the President of the Royal Society of London and Nobel Laureate Venki Ramakrishnan, who wrote, "The court of science never passes a final judgement but constantly re-evaluates the evidence to arrive at our current understanding.... The evidence will win out in the end. Science... is not perfect, but science is still our best bet for understanding the world around us and for improving our lives."[4]

The past half century has witnessed remarkable advances in our understanding of the brain. The last decade of the twentieth century, labelled "The Decade of the Brain" by the United States Senate, resulted in increased funding for brain research of all kinds. By the turn of the twenty-first century, researchers saw the possibility of actually seeing which areas of the brain are most active when volunteers were doing all sorts of tasks, such as looking at art, listening to music, showing maternal love, meditating, *and* praying. Everything seemed well set for yet further rapid advances in the study of mind and brain leading some scientists to suggest that the first decade of the present century should be called "The Decade of the Mind and Brain." Very soon with the widespread use of smart phones and similar devices it became customary to talk about the software and the hardware of such devices. This way of thinking about the relationship between mind (the software) and brain (the hardware) seemed to make good sense. It served further to underline the unity of the device being used and by implication the unity of the human person. It made sense to see mind and brain as two essential aspects of the one unity, the human person.

But what about the soul? Is the soul the same as the mind? If not, how does it differ? For two millennia a pervasive theme of dogmatic and systematic theology, when focusing on theological anthropology and the doctrine of humanity, emphasized that humankind alone is created "in the divine image" or "in the image of God." This refers, of course, to the book of Genesis where we read, "So God created mankind in his own image, in the image of God he created them; male and female he created them" (Gen 1:27 NIV). On this view, it was held that a straightforward answer to the question of *what makes us human and distinguishes us from the rest of creation* was that, since God is a spiritual being, he endowed us also with spirituality, giving us an immortal soul. That, however, turns out to be too simple. As we shall see in the next chapter, any reference to the writings of biblical scholars and theologians who have traced out the understanding of the concept of soul over more than two millennia demonstrates the wide variety of views that have been taken over that period.

4. Ramakrishnan, "Scientific Insight," 26.

THE NATURE OF THE SOUL

The nature of the soul and of the human person continues to be intensively studied by theologians, philosophers, biblical scholars, and scientists. For example, Michael Welker, Professor of Systematic Theology and Executive Director of the Research Center for International and Interdisciplinary Theology (FIIT) at Heidelberg University, organized a series of meetings bringing together twenty international scholars, biblical researchers, theologians, philosophers, lawyers, and scientists, inviting them all to reflect on the characteristics of a human person. Along with the other participants in those meetings, I witnessed lively debate and discussions. These discussions were subsequently brought together by Welker in a book titled *The Depth of the Human Person: A Multidisciplinary Approach.*

Welker's introductory chapter gives a brief overview and an insight into the ways in which different academic disciplines may have something to say about the human person. For example, "The physicist and theologian John Polkinghorne argues that science and theology should help each other in dealing with the vexing complexity of the human person. . . . A *reconceptualization of the soul is required*, which could allow us to develop a dual-aspect, energy/information scientific description of anthropological complexity."[5] Welker continues, "With these ideas, John Polkinghorne *does not want to argue for in an intrinsic immortality of the soul*: 'As far as naturalistic thinking is concerned, the pattern carried by the body will dissolve with the body's decay. Yet it is a perfectly coherent Christian hope that the faithful God will not allow that pattern to be lost but will preserve it in the divine memory.'"[6]

Welker, echoing the views reviewed in the next chapter, notes that,

> The Old Testament scholar Andreas Schule draws attention to the fact that worldviews matter, when it comes to anthropological concepts such as "body," "soul," and "spirit." However, a simple juxtaposition of an ancient (religious) worldview and a modern (scientific) worldview will not be helpful at all. He describes an important change of worldviews already reflected by the anthropological discourse of the Old Testament. This change is connected with the shift of anthropological concentration from the soul *(nefesh)* to the spirit *(ruach)*. . . . Only the view that the soul can be rescued by God's saving work but not a created immortality is shared by the other biblical traditions.[7]

---

5. Welker, *Depth of the Human Person*, 3 (emphasis added).
6. Welker, *Depth of the Human Person*, 3 (emphasis added).
7. Welker, *Depth of the Human Person*, 6.

These views of Andreas Schule are reinforced by those of New Testament scholar Gerd Theissen. Welker notes that "Theissen shows that Paul is not trapped into a static dualistic anthropology, but rather develops a transformative anthropology and cosmology."[8] Approaching biblical anthropology from a different perspective, systematic theologian Gunther Thomas concentrates on the challenges that flow from "intensive experiences of finiteness" associated with illness and frailty encountered especially in the later phases of life—challenges that most anthropologies are unable to address. He argues for the development of a theological framework that allows us to move beyond the affirmation of "intellectualism and moral self-determination."[9] These views of Gunter Thomas foreshadow some of the accounts given in a later chapter of this book where the nature of religious faith is put under the microscope and where we see how the capacity for such faith is dependent upon the neural intactness of the human person.

One thing is abundantly clear. Understanding the human person is very much a "work in progress." Be very wary of someone who claims that his or her perspective is "the accepted view" that you must believe. To make such a declaration is to expose a failure to understand the mystery of what it means to be fully human. It is in that spirit that the remainder of this chapter should be read.

MIND, SOUL, AND BODILY LOCALIZATION

The early Greeks regarded the soul as the essence of a person's being and the source of all life. For them the soul was contained in several parts of the body, including the heart and the liver, but that part of the soul that controlled mental functions was generally thought to be located in the head. It was Galen, an anatomist of Greek origin, who did the most to advance the very early scientific understanding of the soul's mental functions. He performed experiments on animals as well as observing head injuries, and he made a strong case for connecting mental functions specifically with the brain. Stuart Zola-Morgan divided the history of ideas about the localization of brain function into three eras.[10] The first era we have just referred to, the second era stretched from the second century to the eighteenth century. During these years debate centered on whether mental functions were localized in the "gaps in the brain" (the fluid-filled ventricular system) or in the brain tissue itself. The mediaeval church exerted a strong influence

8. Welker, *Depth of the Human Person*, 6.
9. Welker, *Depth of the Human Person*, 11.
10. Zola-Morgan, "Localization of Brain Function."

on this debate by taking the position that ethereal spirits and ideas flowed through the empty spaces of the brain. By the fifteenth and sixteenth centuries, Vesalius and others began to question this idea. In the following century, Thomas Willis, who coined the term neurology, paved the way for the detailed study of brain tissue. In his book *The Anatomy of the Brain*,[11] he argued for a distinction between the immortal "rational soul" that he believed was unique to humans and the "corporeal soul" shared by humans and other animals. Making this distinction allowed Willis to pursue his researches and avoid clashing with contemporary ecclesiastical authority. Having publicly acknowledged a distinctly human "immortal soul" he was free to adopt a psychophysiological approach to the "animal soul" embodied in the brain tissue. The third era is from the nineteenth century to the present time. During this period the debate centered on how mental activities are organized in the brain. One early view claimed that particular mental functions were carried out by specific parts of the brain. An alternative view argued that large parts of the brain are involved in all mental activities—with no specific functions located within particular parts the brain. Gradually the view that there were specialized mental faculties, each with a material substrate in a particular region of the brain became dominant.

In the second half of the twentieth century, three previously unrelated areas of scientific endeavor began to converge. These were experimental psychology, comparative neuropsychology, and brain imaging techniques. Thus, for example, some researchers used single cell recording techniques to study the neural underpinnings of perception in awake and alert monkeys.[12] At the same time, there were exciting developments in brain imaging techniques, notably positron emission tomography (PET scans), nuclear magnetic resonance (MRI scans), and functional nuclear magnetic resonance imaging (fMRI scans). These new methods made possible the monitoring of brain activity while people with intact brains were performing specific mental tasks.

Over the past fifty years there were occasional reports in the neurological literature of patients who, having suffered strokes, said that they could no longer recognize individual human faces, including their own. They could recognize objects, animals, or houses, but not faces. With the advent of brain scanning techniques, it became possible to identify the specific areas of the brain that, when damaged, seemed to result in problems with face processing. For example, a patient consulted a neurologist when he found himself unable to recognize faces. It was not that his visual perception

---

11. Willis, *Cerebri Anatome*.
12. Perrett et al., "Neurons Responsive to Faces."

generally was impaired. He could recognize houses, birds, cows, motor cars, cups, saucers, but not faces. It seemed that the inability to recognize faces was very specific and followed damage to the posterior occipital lobes of the brain, frequently on the right side. Even more surprising were other published reports of patients who could no longer recognize other specific perceptual categories—in one case birds, in another case cars. Another example is a farmer who became unable to identify one cow from another, having previously been able to recognize them individually. A similar case has been described of a very competent ornithologist, who seemed to know the name of every bird, but following the onset of his illness was no longer able to name any bird, even though he would have done it promptly before the onset of his illness. Detailed studies of cases such as these have now helped us to identify those parts the brain that need to be intact if this ability to recognize faces is to continue normally.

Such cases pose challenging questions for anyone claiming that the mind/soul is an immaterial something inside each of us untouched by our material make up. For example, how is it that this immaterial mind/soul which is used in human perception is affected when there is localized damage to the brain? There is now accumulating evidence that illustrates habitual regular use of specific mental abilities can mold or change the structure of the brain. For example, using modern brain imaging techniques, Eleanor Maguire and her colleagues studied the brains of London taxi drivers. It is well known that licensed London taxi drivers are renowned for their extensive and detailed navigation experience and skills. Maguire studied structural magnetic resonance images (MRIs) of their brains and compared them with those of matched control participants who did not drive taxis. They discovered that the posterior hippocampi of the London taxi drivers were significantly larger than those of the control participants. The hippocampal volume also correlated with the amount of time spent as a taxi driver. The researchers concluded, "It seems that there is a capacity for local plastic changes in the structure of the healthy adult human brain in response to environmental demands."[13] Thus, when the hippocampus is used extensively, there are measurable changes in its shape and size, suggesting that a hippocampus capable of good navigational skills is not predetermined exclusively by genes. Even more persuasive is the fact that some of the same taxi drivers showed a reduction in hippocampal size when they retired, when they were no longer exercising their navigational skills to the same extent.[14]

13. Maguire et al., "Navigation-Related Structural Change," 4398.
14. Woollett et al., "Talent in the Taxi."

Results of studies such as these, and many others well documented in the literature, pose serious questions for any wishing to defend the view that each of us possesses an immaterial part of us called the mind/soul untouched by changes in our body and events in the world. All the evidence, accumulating all the time, points convincingly in the opposite direction. Despite this we continue to witness from time to time attempts, using selective case studies, to defend the notion that each of us possesses an immortal soul. One such attempt, which gained wide publicity through the widely read Christian journal *Christianity Today*, is described below. We believe that the conclusions reached about this case should be challenged since they ignore much of the evidence already available from medical science research.

DEFENDING THE SOUL

In September 2018, the science section of *Christianity Today* contained an article titled "More Than Material Minds." It was written by Michael Egnor, and opens with these words, "As a Christian and a neuroscientist, I keep learning that to be human is to have a soul."[15] In this fascinating article, Egnor describes how he watched CAT scans display on a screen, revealing a picture of the head of "Katie," a young baby with serious brain abnormalities. Because the baby grew up to be a child with nearly normal cognitive abilities, Egnor takes this case, along with some other famous examples from the history of neuroscience, as evidence that the mind and personality cannot reside within the physical brain tissue, thus necessitating the existence of a non-material soul. Michael Egnor appears to be well qualified to argue this point. He is a neurosurgeon and Professor of Neurological Surgery and Pediatrics at New York's Stony Brook University, so we are wise to consider what he has to say.

Egnor's defense of the soul clearly resonates with many Christians, but it is not the only perspective on these issues. In our response to Egnor's article, my colleague and co-author Thomas Ludwig pointed out that Egnor does a real service by highlighting the important role of conscious experience and conscious agency ("free will") in our understanding of what it means to be human. However, we don't agree with Egnor's conclusions about the necessity of an immaterial soul, because we don't believe that his examples support those conclusions. As academic neuroscientists and serious Christians, we believe that Egnor's examples actually point to a different way of thinking about mind, brain, and soul—one that reflects better biblical

15. Egnor, "More than Material Minds," n.p.

descriptions of human nature. Specifically, there is an alternative interpretation of the data presented by Egnor. The following few points regarding the researchers referred to by Egnor indicate and illustrate our concerns.

From Nobel Laureate Roger Sperry and Michael Gazzaniga

Egnor claims that a split-brain patient's intellect remains undivided, yet his example of visual half-field presentation shows that a split-brain patient's left hemisphere cannot reason about information presented only to the right hemisphere. Surely if the soul/mind transcends brain tissue, it would have access to all the information stored anywhere in the brain.

From pioneering brain surgeon Wilder Penfield

Egnor claims that Penfield's electrical probes could produce sensory experiences or muscle movements, but not complex thoughts. This is correct, but Egnor fails to note that Penfield stimulated individual small locations on the surface of the cortex. Complex thoughts such as the ones Egnor calls "intellectual seizures" involve coordinated activity of many brain areas. Actual seizures of the non-convulsive type ("absence seizures"), which involve surges of electrical activity across large areas of the brain, completely inhibit conscious experience and reasoning until the activity subsides. Surely an immaterial soul/mind could continue to function during an absence seizure of the brain tissue.

From neuroscientist Benjamin Libet

Egnor correctly reports that Libet found a consistent electrical waveform (the "readiness potential") building up prior to a person's conscious decision to make a small hand movement, which Libet takes as evidence that "the brain" makes a decision before "the person" is consciously aware of that decision. We agree with Egnor's rejection of Libet's conclusion. As Donald MacKay has shown, the readiness potential consistently occurs in a Libet-type task whether or not the person actually decides to move! Libet's research does not prove that free will is an illusion, but Libet's failure to find an electrical signal corresponding to "free won't" is not relevant to the argument. Any veto of a planned movement would involve many areas of the pre-frontal cortex relatively far away from the electrodes measuring motor cortex activity.

From the case of the patient Katie

Egnor argues that Katie's deficient brain (only one-third of the normal brain tissue area) could not possibly support normal intellectual functions; therefore, the soul must not reside in or be tied to physical brain tissue. This conclusion doesn't follow from the evidence. What would happen to Katie's soul or intellect or free will if we removed the remaining one-third of the brain tissue? Rather than providing evidence for an immaterial soul/mind, Katie's intellectual ability is testimony to brain plasticity after damage during prenatal development or early childhood.

From studies of dualism

Egnor's article promotes a dualistic mind–brain or soul–body distinction that has only weak support from Scripture. The careful studies of biblical scholars such as Patrick Miller (Princeton), Lawson Stone (Asbury), Bill Arnold (Asbury), Joel Green (Fuller), and N. T. Wright (St. Andrews) have provided a different perspective. As we recently wrote,

> Over the past century, biblical scholars also began to move away from a dualistic anthropology in order to recover a more holistic Hebrew view of the human person. The rejection of Platonic dualism provides an opportunity for theologians and psychologists to work together in engaging the neuroscience findings that support a fundamental mind–brain and mind–body unity of the human person. In our view, the most helpful way to move forward is to recognize the mysterious duality of our mental life and physical body, while accepting our essential psychobiological unity as whole, complete persons.[16]

While Egnor's article raises important issues that have not yet been settled in neuroscience or in biblical theology, there is an alternative view that we believe is both a more biblically-based interpretation and one that more accurately reflects the proper understanding of the neuroscience evidence. This alternative view is described in more detail in my Boyle Lecture.[17]

---

16. Jeeves and Ludwig, *Psychological Science and Christian Faith*, 231.
17. Jeeves, "Psychologizing and Neurologizing about Religion."

THE SOUL AND BEING MADE IN THE IMAGE OF GOD

What are the distinguishing features of humans? A detailed discussion of this question has been provided recently by another leading biblical scholar, Anthony Thiselton, in his contributions to a book devoted to understanding the emergence of personhood.[18] Thiselton made a sustained attempt to do justice to the contributions of the scientists contributing to the book while applying the main brushstrokes of the picture of humankind offered from a theological approach. In his chapter, Thiselton repeatedly and very helpfully cross-referenced the contributions of the scientists. After a very detailed exposition of what is meant by claims that have been made that humans are made in the image and likeness of God, an exposition that covered reflections over the past two millennia and before, as well as more recent trends, Thiselton looked again at the three key aspects of what it means to be made in the image of God—relationality, representation, and vocation, or attainment—in the light of some of the contributions from the scientists in earlier chapters of the book. He wrote:

> Justin Barrett's account of continuity within a relational framework also coheres well with Paul Ricoeur's sense of self against Hume.... His appeals to a theory of mind remain entirely relevant. C. A. Campbell has pointed out that on the basis of Hume's theory of the self as near successive perceptions, we might perceive the striking of a clock ten times as the tenfold repetition of its striking one o'clock; where continuity of a stable mind would interpret this as striking ten o'clock! Barrett's emphasis on potential qualities rather than actual ones also coheres with our emphasis on location and attainment.... Francisco Ayala's account of the moral and ethical also offers close resonance with my references to Ricoeur. Roy Baumeister and Warren Brown have indicated, with Barrett and this chapter, that the self does not denote an isolated individual. The importance of relationality in communion is not limited to theology alone. Baumeister devotes a section of his chapter to the question: "Solitary Selves?" He asserts: "The selfhood of a thoroughly solitary being would be quite limited." He adds: "Identity is thus not inside the person but in the social matrix."[19]

In closing his chapter, Thiselton made meaningful links with evolutionary psychologist Richard Byrne's account of the possible ways in which language may have emerged. He noted that Byrne affirms that "Language

---

18. Thiselton, "Image and Likeness of God."
19. Thiselton, "Image and Likeness of God," 196.

is regarded, at least in most intellectual traditions, as the quintessential human attribute," and comments, "If a human person is not the individualist ego postulated by Descartes, what allows the self to interact with others in personhood is *language,* or other forms of communication, as Richard Byrne argues."[20] Thus, the three key aspects of what it means to made in the image of God, namely relationality, representation, and vocation, or attainment *make no reference to the implantation of an immortal soul.* And, as the other contributors to the book referred to made clear, these aspects can be traced as emerging as part of evolving creation, all a result of God's divine upholding. *No need to fill in a gap as an afterthought. A truly great God, not a shrinking, occasional gap-filling God.*

In the same edited book, theologian Alan Torrance took up some of Thiselton's themes, reminding us that,

> The roots of the concept of the "personal" lie within the Judeo-Christian tradition, for which personal existence needs to be understood in the light of God's establishing a relationship with the human animal. For the fathers of the Christian church, this found its focus in God's transformative engagement with humanity and the creation of a "new humanity" through the kinship that the Eternal established with humanity in time—in the person of Jesus Christ. . . . Personal existence is both given with—and, ultimately, subject to—the communion that God establishes and sustains through concrete historical, personal communion with human creatures. This is a communion that is transformative and creative of what needs to be conceived in dialogue with evolutionary science, not as an old but as a new humanity. . . . That new form of existence was defined in terms of the categories of participation *(koinonein)* and *agape,* the two concepts that "personalism" has used to define human existence to the extent that it can be described as "personal."[21]

Dualism, Monism, and Socially Embedded Spirituality: An Ongoing Debate

The focus of our discussions in this chapter and the next one has been on how recent developments in biblical scholarship, in psychology, and in neuroscience have prompted a rethink of some widely held and long-established beliefs about body, mind, and soul. We shall see that for centuries the

---

20. Thiselton, "Image and Likeness of God," 199.
21. Torrance, "Retrieving the Person," 218.

debates were about the relative claims of various forms of dualism versus monism. We have also seen how, more recently, the writings of both Old Testament and New Testament scholars have prompted a rethink of belief in some form of traditional body–soul dualism.

The science continues to move on. In a 2019 paper, David Muthukumar has critiqued and traced out the helpfulness and shortcomings, as he sees it, of various past ways of constructively thinking, in a Christian context, about our psychobiological unity.[22] He spells out the earlier views of the present writer advocating dual-aspect monism.[23] He follows this with an account of the views put forward by Nancey Murphy and Warren Brown in their book *Did My Neurons Make Me Do It? Philosophical and Neurobiological Perspectives on Moral Responsibility and Free Will*—advocating what they call "non-reductive physicalism."

Muthukumar goes on to indicate the helpfulness of Philip Clayton's critique of non-reductive physicalism by reminding us of the importance of human agency. He finally puts forward his own view, which seeks to take full account of what he describes as "the socially embedded identity of self." In expressing his own perspective, he refers to the views of Warren Brown and Brad Strawn, who have claimed that, "Human nature is emergent from more than just a complex brain, but from entire body systems involved in behavioral interactions with the world and their consequences in ongoing sensory feedback about the outcomes of such actions."[24]

Drawing upon the work of Michelle Maiese[25] and Shaun Gallagher,[26] Muthukumar argues for the importance of recognizing the socially embedded identity of self. In doing this he draws attention to the importance of bodily sensations and kinesthesis. He also seeks to link his ideas with the functions of mirror neurons. These ideas are certainly important new pointers, since it would seem that his emphasis on the importance of "level of bodily sensations, in particular kinesthesis, or sensory experience of one's own movement"[27] immediately opens up the possibility, in principle at least, of empirical testing on that very small number of people in whom for a variety of reasons these bodily sensations and experience of one's own movements are diminished or absent through injury or disease. What this means

---

22. Muthukumar, "Embodied and Socially Embedded 'Self.'"

23. See Brown and Jeeves, "Portraits of Human Nature"; Jeeves, "Changing Portraits of Human Nature"; Jeeves and Brown, *Neuroscience, Psychology, and Religion*.

24. Brown and Strawn, "Beyond the Isolated Self," 74.

25. Maiese, *Embodiment, Emotion, and Cognition*.

26. Gallagher, *Body Shapes the Mind*.

27. Muthukumar, "Embodied and Socially Embedded 'Self,'" 120.

is that yet again it is possible to put forward potentially ground-breaking views while remembering that when they are sufficiently clearly spelled-out they may be open to empirical testing. Our understanding will continue to move forward through advances in science, which in turn may prompt theologians to rethink hitherto settled views of human nature.

This is yet another reminder that, as science and biblical scholarship advance, there will, from time to time, remain gaps in our knowledge. But we must resist the temptation, so often fallen to in the past, of invoking some aspect of God, his nature, and his activity, to fill these gaps. They will surely in due course be filled and then once more we shall have shrunk our understanding of the God "who upholds all things by the word of his power" (Heb 1:3 KJV).

7

Human Nature
The Evidence from Scripture

> When people examine other people, they are examining individuals who exist in actual or potential solidarity with Jesus Christ.... But the solidarity itself offers a powerful Christian resource for taking up serious study of the human person and the human personality.[1]

GAINING HISTORICAL PERSPECTIVE

THE PERVASIVE AND PERSISTENT influences of Greek thinkers such as Plato is evident throughout the following centuries. However, to focus primarily or exclusively on the dominance of Greek influences on later Western thinking is to ignore the continuing influences of earlier empires such as the Babylonians, Assyrians, and Persians. They, together with Greek and Roman influences, reshaped both Judaism and the development of Christianity. Taking note of these influences makes good sense in the light of the discussions about human origins in the previous chapter. We noted how the emerging consensus is that *Homo sapiens* left Africa about 70,000 years ago. As they did so, their journey took them through what is sometimes called the Levantine corridor, a narrow stretch of land connecting Africa to Eurasia. As Luke Janssen has recently spelled out in detail, this relatively

---

1. Noll, *Jesus Christ*, 38.

small patch of land that we now call the Near East or the Middle East is one of the oldest incubators of human philosophical and theological thinking.[2]

The Persistence of Pervasive Dualism in Thinking about Human Nature

The notion that humans possess a soul was typical of the thinking of major figures from the past, ranging from Plato, Galen, Origen, Nemesius, and Augustine (who held a modified Platonic view) up to Descartes in the seventeenth century. Until relatively recently in the Western world, the dominant cultural ideas about human nature have been a combination of Christianity and Platonic philosophy. Plato's conception of disembodied, immaterial, and immortal souls found its way into much Christian thinking, despite Paul's teaching of the resurrection of the body in a new form (1 Cor 15).

But this is not the only way of understanding the notion of soul. Aristotle, Plato's great successor in the fourth century BCE, believed that the human soul should not be understood as an ethereal entity that can survive on its own, but as a way of living and functioning, even in plants and animals. The human kind of soul is our distinctive cluster of faculties including perception, emotion, reasoning, and rational action. "It is surely better not to say that the soul pities, learns, or thinks," wrote Aristotle, "but the man does these with his soul."[3] Thought of in this way, it does not make sense to talk of a soul or mind existing without a body, for if there is no body then there can be no way that a person is living and functioning. However, Aristotle also suggested there is something different about the human intellect, our faculty for purely theoretical thought, which perhaps can exist separately from the body "as the everlasting can from the perishable."[4]

Some of Aristotle's Islamic and Christian successors were happy to exploit this apparent backtracking in his philosophy of mind. In the late Middle Ages (the thirteenth century), Thomas Aquinas made an impressive synthesis of Christian and Aristotelian ideas, which has since become Catholic orthodoxy. Though strongly influenced by Aristotle, he retained an element of Platonism by arguing that the soul has a separate existence in the interval between death and resurrection.[5] This compromise position

---

2. Janssen, *Genesis and Human Origins*.
3. Aristotle, *De Anima*, 408b15.
4. Aristotle, *De Anima*, 413b26.
5. Thomas, *Summa Theologica* 76.a1.6, where Aquinas states that the intellective principle of the soul remains in existence even when it is not united to the body, after the body has been corrupted by death.

may help solve the problem of maintaining continuity and personal identity, but at the cost of incurring whatever problems are associated with Platonic/Cartesian dualism of body and soul.

Strongly dualistic views are found in the writings of some of the Protestant Reformation leaders, such as John Calvin. They persist in a minority of philosophers, but the contemporary philosophical tendency is towards identity of mind and brain, or at least to a dualism of aspects or properties of the living person. For more detail of these themes, see *Thirteen Theories of Human Nature*.[6]

Within mainline Catholic and Protestant traditions there have been and continue to be strong affirmations of belief in an immaterial and immortal soul as distinct from the physical body. For example, the official Catechism of the Catholic Church states, "The church teaches that every spiritual soul is created immediately by God—it is not 'produced' by the parents—and also that it is immortal: it does not perish when it separates from the body at death, and it will be reunited with the body at the final Resurrection."[7] John Calvin wrote something similar:

> Moreover, there can be no question that man consists of a body and a soul; meaning by soul, an immortal though created essence, which is his nobler part. Sometimes he is called a spirit. . . . And Christ, in commending his spirit to the Father (Luke 23:46), and Stephen his to Christ (Acts 7:59), simply mean that when the soul is freed from the prison-house of the body, God becomes its perpetual keeper.[8]

These clearly stated claims from both Catholic and Reformation traditions still resonate strongly with the beliefs of millions of Christians. This dualistic perspective survives today despite, as we shall see, the fruits of the work of dedicated biblical scholars pointing to the need to rethink what so-called classical texts teach about humans and human nature.

Dualistic views are also an intrinsic part of the beliefs circulating widely among "new agers." New age spirituality feeds off both the waning of communal religion and the advance of science. According to such views, you are a soul who inhabits a body and thus you are able to travel out of the body, read others' minds, and glimpse the future. Your soul may have inhabited another being and may again be incarnated in someone to come. At your body's death you will meet a gentle being of light (which, it is claimed, has already been experienced by those near-death survivors

---

6. Stevenson et al., *Thirteen Theories*, 87–90; 103–5; 123; 128–31; 134–36; 156–66.
7. Catholic Church, "Image of God," 1.2.1.6.366.
8. Calvin, *Institutes of the Christian Religion*, 1.15.2.

whose spirits temporarily vacated their bodies). Dualism is thus a crucial component of such beliefs. Such views are not a thing of the past. A series of books by surgeons and physicians who have studied so-called near-death experiences have claimed to adduce new evidence for the separate existence of the soul. It departs the body, so it is claimed, during a near-death experience and returns on resuscitation. But these views do not go unchallenged. For example, in October 2019 in a blog with the title "Cardiac Arrest and the Conscious Experience of Death," David Myers summarized the views of Sam Parnia, Director of Critical-Care Resuscitation Research Science at New York University's Medical Centre. Parnia claimed to bring forward additional evidence for the existence of the soul. Myers wrote, "Parnia is persuaded by his accumulation of credible-seeming accounts of resuscitated patients recalling actual happenings during their brain-inactive time. . . . My skepticism arises from three lines of research: the failure of parapsychology experiments to confirm out-of-body travel with remote viewing, the mountain of cognitive neuroscience evidence linking brain and mind, and scientific observations showing that brain oxygen deprivation and hallucinogenic drugs can cause similar mystical experiences (complete with the tunnel, beam of light, and life review)."[9]

As Myers makes clear, there are many unanswered questions to be posed concerning this so-called new evidence. Most importantly, Myers makes the suggestion that the open-minded way to tackle this topic would be for Sam Parnia to cooperate with a distinguished neuroscientist who would expect a null result in an "adversarial collaboration" in which the hypotheses are preregistered with the Open Science Framework. We await with interest further developments. The point is that the way to tackle these issues is not by shouting louder at each other from a distance but by open-minded constructive collaboration.

TOWARDS A HEBREW-CHRISTIAN VIEW OF HUMAN NATURE

One of the "thought models" we carry around with us, though seldom made explicit, is what we believe about our human nature. Do we have a body, mind, and soul—the so-called tripartite model of a person? Today this model is being seriously challenged. Keith Ward, retired Regius Professor of Divinity at Oxford, argues that we need to recognize the great difference between official doctrines on the human soul and popular understandings of it. Ward accepts that the idea that the soul, as a part of the human person,

9. Myers, "Cardiac Arrest."

which can be disconnected from the body without any harm to the personality, is a widely held view in some of Plato's dialogues. It is also a view found in the writings of some of the most influential early Christian writers such as Augustine, who was heavily influenced by Plato. Such Christians believed that the soul is a spiritual substance distinct from the body. However, Ward claims that this is a misunderstanding of Christianity.[10] He asserts that the Christian tradition, like the Jewish and Muslim traditions, starts at a very different place. The soul is not a separate entity additional to the body. Ward has argued that the Hebrew and Aristotelian view of humans recognizes that humans are fully and properly material objects and he believes that their distinctiveness lies in their mental abstract thinking and responsibly free acting.

Michel Welker, Professor of Theology at Heidelberg, has argued that there is an emerging consensus about how the soul is to be understood in contemporary discussions of human nature. For example, Welker comments, "Like almost all of the biblical authors, Paul does not ascribe any special salvific power to the 'soul.' It just stands for the mind–body unity, for the whole person ('a village of two hundred souls')."[11]

Old Testament scholar Andreas Schule comments, "What makes the rendering of the 'soul' problematic is the fact that this term could suggest that the [Hebrew] *nephesh* is in fact something immortal, something capable of existing apart from the physical body. The idea of an immortal soul, however, is entirely absent from the Hebrew transmission of the Old Testament."[12]

Despite these warnings from theologians and biblical scholars, body–soul dualism remains a widely held belief, not only among Christians but also in most other religious traditions. It is so deeply rooted in human culture that some, including developmental psychologist Paul Bloom, believe that young children are "natural-born dualists," biologically predisposed to perceive the world in dualistic terms.[13] In spite of the popularity of dualism, the evidence from contemporary biblical scholarship supported by the results of extensive studies by neuroscientists on mind–brain relations offers fresh insights that encourage us to consider reinterpreting some of the ancient biblical texts and returning to a more holistic view of the human person. For centuries, the words "soul" and "mind" were used interchangeably. Within the Christian context, the traditional proof text for the existence and

10. Ward, *More Than Matter?*
11. Welker, *Depth of the Human Person*, 2.
12. Schule, "'Soul' and 'Spirit,'" 12 (emphasis added).
13. Bloom, *Descartes' Baby*.

importance of the soul is found at the beginning of the Bible: "And the LORD God formed man of the dust of the ground, and breathed into his nostrils the breath of life; and man became a living soul" (Gen 2:7 KJV). This, for centuries, led to the view that the soul departs the body at death, lives in the spiritual domain, and is reunited with the body at the resurrection of the dead on the last day.

For two millennia a pervasive theme of dogmatic and systematic theology, when focusing on theological anthropology and the doctrine of humanity, emphasized that humankind alone is created "in the divine image" or "in the image of God." On this view, it was held that a straightforward answer to the question of what makes us human and distinguishes us from the rest of creation was that, since God is a spiritual being, he endowed us also with spirituality, *giving us an immortal soul*. That, however, turns out to be too simple. Any reference to the writings of biblical scholars and theologians who have traced out the understanding of the concept of soul over more than two millennia demonstrates the wide variety of views that have been taken over that period.

Because the soul was thought to be the most important and most distinctive part of the person, it became vital to defend the status of the soul when defining what it means to be human. However, such a view is widely challenged today not by skeptical unbelieving scientists, but by biblical scholars, who see human uniqueness arising not from our possession of an immortal soul representing the "image of God," but rather from our calling to enter into the personal relationship offered to us by our Creator. Thus, Vladimir Lossky writes, "Creation in the image and likeness of God implies the idea of participation in the divine Being, of communion with God."[14] Anthony Thiselton, one of today's leading biblical scholars and an expert on hermeneutics, claims that "to be made in, or called to, the image of God is to represent God."[15] Another biblical scholar, N. T. Wright, has written, "I have been arguing for some time: that image of God was not in Genesis 1 intended to refer to some characteristic or special ability or trait of humans but rather a vocation. The vocation in question is that humans were designed by the Creator to have a special role in his governance of the world. Eventually it comes round to using the royal priesthood language which I think is absolutely central."[16]

Finally, awareness that we are created "in the image and likeness of God" should bring deep reassurance about our value in God's sight and how

---

14. Lossky, *Mystical Theology*, 118.
15. Thiselton, *Thiselton Companion*, 477.
16. Wright, personal communication.

our actions can move us closer to or further from God's likeness. James Bryan Smith writes, "When I realize I am made in God's image, I understand I am sacred and valuable. When I understand that I cannot alter this image by any foolish, sinful ways, I am grateful to God. When I accept that by my actions I am either moving closer to or further from God's likeness, I take sin seriously."[17]

Listening to Biblical Scholars and Philosophers of Religion

Other biblical scholars have echoed Andreas Schule's views, described above. For example, Lawson Stone has written,

> To summarize: the term *nephesh* in Genesis 2:7 refers not to a part of Adam's nature, nor to some possession such as a transcendent personal spiritual hypostasis termed a "soul" that lives forever and distinguishes humanity from the animals. Rather, *nephesh hayyah* denotes Adam as a living creature like the animals created in Genesis 1 and 2. It underscores Adam's linkage with the animal creation, not his difference from it.[18]

Some who wish to challenge the clear conclusions of Lawson Stone sometimes attempt to do so by appealing to a passage in the Old Testament Scriptures where Samuel appears at Endor. Writing on this point, Old Testament scholar Bill Arnold said, "a *prima facie* reading of 1 Samuel 28:3–19 may result in the conviction that Samuel's 'soul' was present at Endor, and that this text therefore has troubling implications for the monist anthropology under consideration in recent discussion."[19] After a thorough and detailed consideration of this passage Arnold offers his conclusions:

> First—a warning—a superficial reading of 1 Samuel 28 may lead today's Christians to interpretations that appear to refute a monist anthropology. But as we have seen, believers from earliest times had disagreed about this difficult text, and no consensus can possibly emerge from 1 Samuel 28 defending a traditional dualism. Moreover, those interpretations of 1 Samuel 28:3–19 that assume a physicalist approach are closer to the Israelite *Weltanschauung*, and the implications of this for the emerging Christian monism should be explored further. . . . Second, we should give closer attention to the Bible's phenomenological

---

17. Smith, *Magnificent Story*, 76.
18. Stone, "Soul," 56.
19. Arnold, "Soul-Searching Questions," 75.

language with reference the nature of human beings. We do so quite naturally and logically with regard to cosmology when reading the Bible. So for example, we know that the earth does not have "four corners" and we understand the "rising" and "setting" sun as a reflection of the ancient pre-scientific worldview rather than as a technical cosmological description for our times. Likewise, we make the necessary intellectual adjustments when we read of earth's flat disc-shaped structure and the existence of Sheol below the surface of the earth.[20]

Writing in this way, Arnold echoes and reinforces the views on biblical interpretation of John Walton spelled out in the previous chapter. Arnold continues,

Something similar has to be done when we read the phenomenological language of the Bible's anthropology. When the text makes reference to the process of human thought, there is a conspicuous absence of "brain" language, and perhaps it is instructive to point out that biblical Hebrew has no word for "brain." It appears that none of the ancients understood how the brain functioned, or even anything about its use. Yet biblical Hebrew has many terms describing human personhood, including words conventionally rendered "spirit" and "soul" (*ruach, nephesh*), and terms for internal organs as the seat of emotions, such as "heart," "liver," and "kidneys" *(lev/levav, kaved, kelayot,* etc.). But all philological and literary contextual data from the Hebrew Scriptures related to Christian anthropology are notoriously difficult to interpret. Recent studies have admitted the Hebrew Bible's purely physical perception of human personhood, *acknowledging the impossibility of developing a Christian dualist anthropology on the basis of these data.*[21]

Attempts to defend traditional views of the soul have also been called into question by New Testament scholars such as Joel Green. Referring to advances in science, he has written,

Not least within the Christian tradition such neurobiological findings will be disturbing, since personal identity has long been tied to the existence of an ontological entity known as the soul, separate from the body, and identified with the person's genuine "self." An understanding of the human person derived from the neurosciences impinges immediately on Christian theology on

---

20. Arnold, "Soul-Searching Questions," 82.
21. Arnold, "Soul-Searching Questions," 82.

two points. First, from the neuroscientific perspective, it is now unnecessary to postulate a second, metaphysical entity, such as a soul or spirit, to account for human capacities and distinctives. Second, at the level of molecular biology, any meaningful distinction between human beings and other animals is impossible to maintain. These conclusions raise unsettling questions: in the absence of a soul, what is it that makes us authentically human? If not the soul, then who or what is a proper subject of the human being, the "I" or self? To speak in more traditional terms, what does it mean any longer to affirm that we are bearers of "the divine image"? Without a second, metaphysical entity, such as a soul or spirit, to account for human capacities and distinctives, do we not leave our humanity to be explained exclusively and exhaustively—indeed reductively—with recourse to genetics or neuroscience?[22]

After a detailed and extensive discussion of the issues surrounding the biblical understanding of the soul, Green helpfully concludes,

> If the possession of a "soul" is not the distinguishing mark of the human person, that which separates human beings from the rest of creation, what is? Unlike other members of creation, animate and inanimate, humanity is created by God "in his own image" (cf. Gen 1:26–27). Again, at this point Genesis does not define humanity in essentialist terms but in relational—more specifically identifying the human person as Yahweh's partner, and with emphasis on the communal, intersexual character of personhood, the quality of care the human family is to exercise with regard to creation as God's representative, the importance of the human modelling of the personal character of God, and the irrefutable vocation of humans to reflect in their relationships God's own character. *The distinguishing mark of human existence when compared with other creatures is thus the whole of human existence and not some part of the individual.*[23]

Thus, what makes us human is not the insertion—by a shrunken "gap-filling" God—of something labelled a "soul," but *the whole person's relationship with her Creator, Redeemer, and Sustainer.*

Of direct relevance to the topic of this book, we find in current debates about the soul the emergence of other "smaller gods," more "gods-of-the-gaps." A key feature of our interpretation is the recognition that the Hebrew-Christian God is one who, from the very beginning of his creative acts,

---

22. Green, "To Be Human," 180.
23. Green, "To Be Human," 196.

created humans as he intended. He created them so that he could proclaim "it is very good" (Gen 1:31). *There was no need to keep returning to insert a "soul" into every one of his new creatures at conception.* His divine plan to create us in his image was perfect. And creating us "in his image" did not require inserting a soul.

In addition to biblical scholars and scientists, philosophers of religion such as Diogenes Allen, Stuart Professor of Philosophy at Princeton Theological Seminary, have written helpfully about contrasting views of personhood. According to Allen,

> There are two major traditional views of people. Although they overlap in some respects and have often been more or less conflated or assumed to be equivalent, they are, in fact, distinct. These two views are the Cartesian view and the biblical view. According to Descartes, who espoused what has become known as the Cartesian view, people are a union of two different substances. Descartes used the notion of substance in a precise way, to mean something that can exist independently of all else, except God. According to Descartes, the mind and body are two separate substances, and, thus, bodies can exist without minds, and minds can exist without bodies. So even though people are in fact a union of mind and body, they are essentially mind, and they could exist (should God will it) without a body. "Body" for Descartes is not something alive in and of itself, but is simply a lump of stuff. It is stripped of all property save extension, shape, and being moved. *All* the qualities of a person such as sensation, emotion, and will are properties of mind and are part of our self-identity. . . . This view was dubbed by the late Oxford philosopher Gilbert Ryle as "the ghost in the machine."[24]

According to Allen,

> The biblical view of people is not the same as the Cartesian, as can be seen by consideration of the notion of the soul. For Descartes, soul is identical with mind. But we find in the Bible that this is not the case. In Genesis 2:7 we read, "the LORD God formed man from the dust of the ground, and breathed into his nostrils the breath of life; and the man became a living being" (NRSV). The basis of humankind was a fragile, corporeal material, but by the breath of God it was transformed and became (in the Hebrew) *nephesh*. The earth in the shape of man was not supplied with *nephesh*, but it was *transformed into a nephesh*. Earth in the shape of a man was changed *and became a nephesh*,

---

24. Allen, "Persons in Perspective," 165.

a living soul. According to Descartes's notion of body, the body of a person is no different in itself from that a non-living body. It is still a machine, but one inhabited by a mind or soul. But in the Bible, a living person is one intimate being, not a Cartesian juxtaposition of body and mind (or soul). Thus, in the Bible, we do not *have* a soul; we *are* souls, that is, living beings.[25]

The "God-Shrinking" Power of Pervasive Dualism

N. T. Wright has given a specific example of one of the ways in which a contemporary shrunken God can manifest itself in the form of what he calls "Superman theology." Emphasizing the way in which paying attention to the story of Israel enables us to understand what the New Testament writers are saying, for example, about the cross, applies also to our understanding of Christology itself. Wright argues,

> Christology, for instance, has, in my view, suffered in the Western tradition because people simply put a checkmark in the "Jesus as divine" box without really stopping to think which God they are talking about, what it means within the biblical narrative to say such a thing, and how this integrates properly, not merely accidentally, as it were, with the other box that people usually check, the "Jesus is human" box. The signs that all is not well include, on the one hand, a kind of Superman theology when Jesus is "the man from outside" coming with miraculous, "supernatural" power to "zap" everything that is wrong, *all conceived within a strictly dualistic view* that ends, not surprisingly, in his followers being miraculously "raptured" up to join him in "heaven," and, on the other hand, an official acknowledgement that Jesus was human, which nevertheless leads to no engagement whatsoever with the question of what it meant to be Jesus of Nazareth, to live and think as a first-century Jew longing for God's kingdom, to be possessed of a deep and radical vocation and to construe that in terms and stories available to a first-century Jew, and so on.[26]

Wright continues,

> The mention of the "rapture" points to a further example of how not to connect the dots. For many Christians, the question "Do

---

25. Allen, "Persons in Perspective," 166 (emphasis in the original).
26. Wright, "Reading Paul," 59 (emphasis added).

you believe in the second coming?" means, quite simply, "Do you believe in a dispensationalist rapture doctrine?" and indeed there are some who would love to believe in the genuine New Testament doctrine of the second coming who feel obliged not to put a check mark in the box because they cannot and will not swallow the rapture. . . . Rapture theology is what you get, in other words, when you take the doctrine "He will come again with glory to judge the living and the dead, and of his kingdom there will be no end" and put it, first, within a heaven and earth dualism in which the only point of human existence on earth is to work out how to leave it with a ticket to the right destination, and, second, within a very localised nineteenth-century reading of one particular set of texts, especially 1 Thessalonians 4:17, which flesh out, within that larger (wrong) story, what the "second coming" might look like.[27]

Human Nature: An Emerging Consensus

Any attempt to pull together the many and diverse threads of thinking about human nature extending back many millennia will inevitably face the charge of oversimplification. But the attempt must be made if only to see where we have got to at the beginning of the twenty-first century and what are the major challenges that face us today as we continue to think about human nature. There seems to be a wide consensus that, shaped by ancient Sumerian, Akkadian, Egyptian, and Greek mythology, Christian theology, with firm foundations in Hebrew theology and Greek philosophy, built up a series of pictures or thought models of human nature. Ancient Near Eastern thinkers, including those who authored the Hebrew Scriptures, were fairly unanimous about the origins of the human body. It was fashion by a divine action on non-living clay or dirt, often combined with some divine element such as saliva or breath. However, they seem to have little interest in, and even less to say about, the immaterial aspect of human experience. For a millennium there seemed to be very little development in the concepts of mind, soul, and spirit, only variations on a common theme. But then there was a radical change over the next thousand years. Greek philosophers and theologians dominated attempts at explanations and descriptions of the immaterial aspects of human nature. Many different schemes were developed about how to think about human mind, soul, and spirit. Patristic theology in broad terms believed that humans comprise a soul/spirit, a creation from

---

27. Wright, "Reading Paul," 68–69.

God that is immortal and that is housed within a fleshly body also divinely created. This is tainted by sin and mortal. There was also the widely held belief that our soul/spirit is destined one day for a union with God in heaven and that this takes place by divine action.

Then, as science developed, challenges arose to the different aspects of Christian thinking. Attempts were made to do away altogether with any reference to the immaterial and to find purely naturalistic explanations. As the previous chapter sketched out, the result is that this perspective is widely accepted. Nevertheless, today, it seems that both philosophers and scientists are lining up with theologians in recognition that there remains something about us more than the material. This immaterial component, consciousness or whatever it is called, still awaits explanation. There is a gap in our knowledge and the knee-jerk reaction is to jump in and fill this gap with some reference to or assertion about the activity of God. In the meantime, debates about a whole range of recent models of human nature continue. On offer in the marketplace there are various forms of dualism (emergent dualism, holistic dualism, naturalistic dualism, integrated dualism, Thomistic dualism), and over against these views there are the varieties of monism (dual-aspect monism, non-reductive physicalism, eliminative materialism, and so on). Some of the best minds in science and philosophy are already grappling with the so-called problem of consciousness. Rapid developments in fields such as artificial intelligence will accelerate such research and debate. Watch this space. If you are a Christian with the gifts and skills to make a contribution be sure you are there to make your contribution. We need Christian participants in the laboratories down where the action is, not uninformed spectators up in the stands.

Taking Stock: How Science and Faith Mutually Enrich Our Understanding of Human Nature

In the previous chapter we focused on what we have been able to learn about our mysterious human nature from advances in science. Many of these advances have come from research in neuropsychology, neuroscience, and neurology. In this chapter we have focused on what we can learn about our mysterious human nature from Scripture.

After these two chapters were written, an extremely important and timely book has been published by Cambridge University Press, edited by Alasdair Coles, a professor of neurology at Cambridge, and Joanna Collicutt, a neuropsychologist at Oxford. This book brings together contributions from neurologists, neuroscientists, philosophers, psychiatrists, and general physicians, as well as contributions from a variety of faith traditions, including Christianity, Islam, Judaism, and a variety of Eastern religions. It makes sense to pause and note how some of the salient points made by the contributors (gathered below) support the themes of these two chapters:

1. It is important to remember that "the terms 'religion' and 'spirituality' are slippery, and variably understood." Coles and Collicutt note that "our preference is to favour 'religion,' as it encompasses individual and communal behaviour, practice, and belief, as well as subjective experience."[28]

2. In an introductory general discussion of science and religion, Joanna Collicutt emphasizes that "a dualistic model of the human person is not inherent to Christian theology; in fact, it is at odds with it. It had developed because the church had uncritically hitched its wagon to an earlier unsatisfactory science and metaphysics. The new science of neurology (and the other emerging branches of modern science) prompted theologians to return to first principles, to re-appropriate the embodied and integrated models of the human person found in the Hebrew Bible, and re-examine many of their assumptions in ways that proved to be creative and fruitful."[29]

3. Stuart Judge, Reader in Physiology at the University of Oxford, argues that any claims about the selective relationship of parts of the brain to religious experience should be subjected to the normal procedures followed in scientific research. Referring to the work of Persinger, Judge noted, "The claim (by Persinger) was that these (the very weak magnetic fields overlying the temporal lobes) induced a 'sensed presence.' Granquist et al. (2005) studied 89 subjects using Persinger's apparatus in a double-blind design in which on half the trials the stimulator was not activated, and found no effect of stimulation. Such effects as were found correlated with suggestibility of subjects."[30] Judge's conclusions are supported by Alistair Coles, who writes, "Michael Persinger's attempts to show that healthy students and pre-adolescents with religious experiences score higher on his own non-validated scale of 'temporal lobe symptomatology' (Persinger 1984, 1991) can safely be ignored."[31]

---

28. Coles and Collicutt, *Neurology and Religion*, xi.
29. Coles and Collicutt, *Neurology and Religion*, 6.
30. Coles and Collicutt, *Neurology and Religion*, 18.
31. Coles and Collicutt, *Neurology and Religion*, 98.

4. Referring to widespread discussions of the so-called "God module" in the brain, neuropsychologist Warren Brown notes, "It is not likely that a 'God module' exists such that there is an area of the brain that is involved in religiousness, and only religiousness. Neural systems that are activated during events or activities with extremely high levels of personal significance may be activated in contexts other than a particular person's religious life, but the neural process itself would nevertheless be general and only the current content religiously specific. Thus, we should find a great deal of overlap between neurological disorders of religiousness and disorders of other aspects of a patient's life."[32]

5. A chapter by Pennycook, Tranel, Warner, and Asp titled "Beyond Reasonable Doubt: Cognitive and Neuropsychological Implications of Religious Disbelief." This chapter highlights the dangers of trying to link religiosity and religious belief with specific areas of the brain. They conclude their comprehensive review, "Our theoretical and empirical work challenges the legitimacy of neuropsychological models that argue the prefrontal cortex is critical for religiosity and religious belief (e.g. Morimoto 2004).... However, the specific contribution of the prefrontal cortex's sub-regions (likely in conjunction with other brain regions) to religious doubt is still a matter for debate."[33] Clearly further work remains to be done.

6. Another timely cautionary remark is given by Julian Hughes, Professor of Geropsychiatry at the University of Bristol, who notes, "In summary, from the scanty evidence available, although we have noted an intriguing connection between the temporal (and frontal) lobes and hyper-religiosity, it is not enough to have temporal lobe dysfunction to make the person religious. Most religious people, after all, do not have cognitive dysfunction; and, it would seem, the mere presence of temporal lobe atrophy is not enough to cause hyper-religiosity, otherwise this would be a much more conspicuous sign of dementia."[34]

7. One of the most timely and salutary contributions to this volume is the chapter on "Near Death and Out of Body Experiences" by Michael Marsh, an Oxford medical graduate and theologian. Marsh notes, "Surely it is more sensible . . . to conclude that ND/OBE experiences occur, and are remembered, during those final moments while subjects are rapidly regaining conscious awareness. Therefore NDE are

---

32. Coles and Collicutt, *Neurology and Religion*, 32.
33. Coles and Collicutt, *Neurology and Religion*, 126.
34. Coles and Collicutt, *Neurology and Religion*, 153.

more than likely to be brain-generated phenomena, and not trips to 'Heaven,' 'Hell,' or other imagined cosmic spaces, neither events generated by external agencies."[35]

---

35. Coles and Collicutt, *Neurology and Religion*, 234.

8

Miracles of Nature
Divine Upholder or Occasional Gap Filler?

But they inherit and operate within the deeply damaged vision of the creator and the Cosmos they get from Deism and which shares its worst features with Epicureanism: that some things happen naturally, while other things happen only because God makes them happen.[1]

The trouble is that even conservative scholars who have tried to defend the Bible against this kind of attack have regularly done so within the same split-level world, so that those who have defended the miraculous, who have wanted to speak of God's action in the world, have done so in terms of invasion—of a God who is normally outside the processes of the created order reaching in, doing a few tricks, and then going away again. And that picture has very little to do with the God of the Bible.[2]

MIRACLES ARE NOT RELIGIOUS MAGIC: A VERY CONTEMPORARY ISSUE

WHY WRITE ABOUT MIRACLES in a book on shrinking faith in shrinking gods? For at least two reasons. First, to question the wisdom and biblical

---

1. Wright, *Surprised by Scripture*, 14.
2. Wright, *Surprised by Scripture*, 14.

warrant for the claims of some Christians who believe they can "prove their faith" by referring to as many dramatic/strange/miraculous events as possible—what Alan Millard described, as we saw in an earlier chapter, as a modern example of "fake news." Such an approach unwittingly reduces the moment by moment Creator and Upholder of all things to the occasional divine intervener. Second, to challenge the portrayal of Christian faith by some critics of Christianity who focus on miracles as part of their case against the Christian faith. For example, Richard Dawkins wrote, "The Virgin Birth, the Resurrection, the raising of Lazarus, even the Old Testament miracles, all are freely used for religious propaganda, and they are very effective with an audience of unsophisticates and children. Every one of these miracles amounts to a violation of the normal running of the natural world."[3]

Graham Twelftree, in his recent edited volume *The Nature Miracles of Jesus*, raises the central question: "How are twenty-first-century readers to interpret such stories that seem incredible?"[4] Research in comparative religion demonstrates that our presuppositions about the world influence how we interpret both ordinary events such as thunderstorms and unusual "miraculous" events. As we consider the miracles reported in Scripture, we must remember that the presuppositions of Hebrew culture were different from those in Greek culture, even more different from the various ancient cultures of Africa, India, and China, and vastly different from the Enlightenment worldview that provides the lenses through which Christians today interpret those miraculous events.

As N. T. Wright continues to remind us, we are all too easily trapped within ways of thinking about both science and Scripture that are relics of the past rather than examples of contemporary thinking. Specifically, Wright refers to contemporary discourse that uses the word *miracle* and the word *supernatural*. He writes, "Now a central part of my problem with this whole discourse is that the very word *miracle* itself, in the way we now hear it in post-Enlightenment Europe and America, is bound to be fatally damaged by the implicit Epicureanism of our latent worldview. So too with the word *supernatural*, which was used well before the Enlightenment but since then has taken on resonances of the same worldview."[5] Wright continues his discussion of contemporary views widely held amongst Christians, "But they inherit and operate within the deeply damaged vision of the creator and the cosmos they get from deism and which shares its worst features with Epicureanism: that some things happen naturally, while other

---

3. Dawkins, "Snake Oil," 235.
4. Twelftree, *The Nature Miracles of Jesus*, 225.
5. Wright, *Surprised by Scripture*, 13–14.

things happen only because God makes them happen."⁶ N. T. Wright uses an example to illustrate his point. He refers to the occasion when an aircraft took off from LaGuardia airport and almost immediately ran into a flock of geese. The pilot remarkably landed the plane safely on the Hudson River. Wright comments,

> Lots of people said it was a miracle, and I wouldn't for a moment say that God was not involved in that whole process. But the reason the plane landed safely was that Sullenberger (the pilot) had been flying planes and gliders, and teaching others to do so, for thirty years. His character had been formed so that all those complex thoughts and actions were second nature. The danger in using the word *miracle*, in other words, is that we assume the zero-sum either/or. *Either* God did it *or* the pilot did it. And it is an assumption, shared by most post-Enlightenment Christians and secularists alike, which needs to be challenged in the name of a genuinely biblical worldview.⁷

For Wright, the dominant Enlightenment worldview continues to influence thinking even amongst those he describes as "conservative scholars." Thus, he comments,

> The trouble is that even conservative scholars who have tried to defend the Bible against this kind of attack have regularly done so within the same split-level world, so that those who have defended the miraculous, who have wanted to speak of God's action in the world, have done so in terms of invasion—of a God who is normally outside the processes of the created order reaching in, doing a few tricks, and then going away again. And that picture has very little to do with the God of the Bible. Such would be defenders of the Bible have, in any case, usually not wanted to get too close to the idea of God becoming King on earth as in heaven, which is the main theme of all four gospels.⁸

In the context of the title and argument of this book about "shrunken gods" it is relevant and interesting that in developing his arguments on this theme Wright comments,

> As a result, the great narrative the Bible offers has been shrunk, by generations of devout preachers and teachers, to the much smaller narrative of "me and God getting it together," as though

---

6. Wright, *Surprised by Scripture*, 14.
7. Wright, *Surprised by Scripture*, 14.
8. Wright, *Surprised by Scripture*, 136–37.

the whole thing—creation, Abraham, Moses, David, the early church, not least the Gospels themselves—were simply a gigantic set of apparently authoritative teachings about how unbelievers come to faith, how sinners get saved, how people's lives get turned around. Of course, the Bible includes plenty about all of that, but it includes it within the much larger narrative of creator and cosmos, covenant God and covenant people—the single narrative that, according to all four Gospels, reaches its climax with Jesus.[9]

Later, Wright, discussing the effects and implications of erroneous and limited perspectives that he believes are today still widely held, comments, "Perhaps it is time to allow other perspectives to come into the frame, since the meaning we have made of our dismembered world has obviously reflected the gods we secretly worship rather than the God in whose image we are made."[10] Yet another example of false and shrunken gods so widely available in the religious marketplace today. All of which brings into sharp focus the question posed by Wright, "In the twentieth century as in the first, we are precipitated into the vital question 'Which God are we talking about anyway?'"[11]

Magic or Faith?

Philip Yancey is widely regarded as one of the most perceptive, reliable, and knowledgeable evaluators of the religious scene in North America. His book *Prayer: Does It Make Any Difference?* contains a chapter titled "Magic or Faith?" which alerts us to the dangers of magical thinking. Yancey wrote,

> In earlier years I found myself surrounded by people who viewed God as a genie in a bottle who granted their every wish (though I observed it was inconsistent deliverance, as in Hebrews 11, rescuing some from peril while allowing others to be sawn in two). The successes were often trumpeted from the housetops, while the failures were quickly buried in the backyard for no one to see. . . . I saw in hospice that the rain fell on the just and the unjust and that some Christians were delivered for God's purposes and others lost their lives and went to heaven giving glory to God. . . . I rebelled against an interpretation of life that had God rushing around the world answering prayers to clear

---

9. Wright, *Surprised by Scripture*, 138–39.
10. Wright, *Surprised by Scripture*, 160.
11. Wright, *Surprised by Scripture*, 168.

away parking places for Christians too tardy for appointments. I heard many of these people praying that God would magically intervene and help poor sick people—never sensing they might be the answer to those prayers. It seemed more a belief in magic than in God.[12]

The front cover of the April 2019 edition of the *The Psychologist*, the monthly bulletin of the British Psychological Society, has the words "Experiencing the Impossible" with the subtitle "Gustav Kuhn considers the science of magic, and what it reveals about the human mind." In the middle of the page there is a picture of a conjurer with a pack of cards and a light shining down on a human skull. The opening words of the inside article by Gustav Kuhn are an important reminder of the danger of confusing miracles with magic. It reads, "Magic is one of the oldest forms of entertainment, and for thousands of years conjurers have used sleight of hand (such as the 'cups and balls') and other forms of deception to manipulate your conscious experience."[13] He notes that one of the pioneers of psychology, Alfred Binet, deviser of one the first and most widely used tests of intelligence, had a keen interest in studying magic. Today psychologists such as Gustav Kuhn use cutting-edge eye-tracking technologies to investigate how magicians misdirect our attention, and this kind of work informs us about why people fail to see things right in front of their eyes. The relevance of such work today is that we are continually exposed to false information and it is often difficult to distinguish between, for example, real and fake news. The article notes further,

> Throughout history magicians have pushed the boundaries of what we believe to be possible. Ancient Egyptian priests used conjuring tricks to create the illusion of communicating with deities; Victorian spiritualists staged seances that fueled beliefs in the spiritual underworld, and more recently, magicians have helped perpetuate beliefs in psychic powers.[14]

This article is an excerpt from Kuhn's book *Experiencing the Impossible: The Science of Magic*. One simple take-home message from the book is that, as Christians committed to truth, we must always be on our guard against putting the label "miracle" on events or phenomena that are no more than magic.

---

12. Yancey, *Prayer*, 214.
13. Kuhn, "Experiencing the Impossible," 32.
14. Kuhn, "Experiencing the Impossible," 34.

The temptation to shrink the Hebrew-Christian God of "miracles" to pagan gods of "magic" is alive and well. Part of the reason for this is the pious language in which some modern, supposedly miraculous events, are described. There are references to magic in Scripture. Its use seems to be universal and may be either "black" or "white." "Black magic" attempts to produce evil results, curses and spells and suchlike, and often takes the form of witchcraft. "White magic" attempts to undo the curses and spells and to use occult forces for one's own good and the good of others. Frequently the magician tries to compel a god or demon or spirit to work for him and he follows a particular pattern of occult practices to do this. Both the Old and New Testaments refer to magic, to magicians, and to wisemen. Magic and sorcery are always condemned in Scripture since magic is a rival to true religion. True religion centers in the personal experience of the one true God with an attempt to live a life that is conformable to his will. The pagan world certainly regarded private miracles as magic (Acts 8:9–11), but the Bible never treats divine miracles as superior magic. There is no use of incantations or invocations of spirits or spells. Moses did not silence Pharaoh's magicians by being a better magician but acted solely as the agent of God, behaving when and how God instructed him. His rod was not the conjuror's magic wand, but the symbol of God's designation. It was "the rod of God" (Exod 4:20). Magic was widely practiced both in Egyptian and Assyrian Babylonian cultures and, unsurprisingly, also permeated Hebrew culture from time to time.

The connection between miracles and magic comes up again in the life of Jesus, as described in Richard Horsley's 2014 book *Jesus and Magic: Freeing the Gospel Stories from Modern Misconceptions*. Horsley writes in his introduction, "To Enlightenment reason it was clear that the healings and exorcisms—like multiplying food, walking on water, and raising the dead—did not happen by natural causes but must have involved supernatural causes (God). That is, they were 'miracles,' perhaps even with elements of 'magic.'"[15]

According to Horsley, if we are to free the Gospel stories from modern misconceptions, we must examine the way that ancient people understood healing and exorcism.[16] With this central question in mind, Horsley attempts "a critical review of the scholarly constructs of miracle and magic that have come to focus and even control investigation and interpretation of (stories of) Jesus's healing and exorcism."[17]

---

15. Horsley, *Jesus and Magic*, vii.
16. Horsley, *Jesus and Magic*, viii.
17. Horsley, *Jesus and Magic*, x.

The conclusions that Horsley draws are relevant to the discussion of miracles here. He writes:

> The concepts of miracle and magic under which the healing and exorcism stories of Jesus had been classified and interpreted are the products of Enlightenment Reason shaped by (natural and social) scientific perspectives. The concept of miracle and especially the concept of magic were also influenced by colonial and Orientalist attitudes. Interpretation of Jesus and the field of New Testament studies in general somehow became stuck in these modern constructs. Most books in the recent wave of scholarly interpretation of the historical Jesus give little or no attention to "miracle stories"; this neglect applies to the healings and exorcism of Jesus as well. But the most influential scholars who have devoted considerable attention to the healing and exorcism stories have simply perpetuated the modern constructs in which New Testament studies have been stuck for at least the last half century or more. . . . A survey of ancient Judean, Hellenistic, Jewish and Greco-Roman sources, however, finds no evidence for a concept that corresponds to the modern concept of miracle. The Judean and Hellenistic elite who produced the texts that are extant simply did not make a distinction between nature and the supernatural, a distinction that became standard in modern Enlightenment thinking.[18]

In contrast, the Bible makes clear distinctions between magic and miracles. A lot of the confusion has been caused by failing to observe that Scripture does not sharply distinguish between God's constant sovereign providence and his particular acts. In Scripture, belief in miracles is set in the context of a worldview that regards the whole of creation as continually dependent upon the sustaining activity of God and subject to his sovereign will (see for example Col 1:16–17). In Scripture, we find three aspects of God's divine activity underlined—*wonder*, *power*, and *significance*. They are all found present, not only in special acts, but also in the whole created order (Rom 1:20). So we find that when the psalmist celebrates the mighty acts of God he moves seamlessly from the creation to the deliverance from Egypt (for example Ps 135:6–12). What we find is that when the biblical writers refer to the mighty acts of God they can't be supposed to be distinguishing them from the course of nature by their particular causation since they think of *all* events as caused by God's sovereign power. This means that the discovery, as we shall see later, of possible natural causal connections

---

18. Horsley, *Jesus and Magic*, 163.

between the plagues of Egypt, a repetition of the blocking of the Jordan, or increased knowledge of psychosomatic medicine, cannot of themselves contradict the biblical assertion that the deliverance from Egypt, the entry into Canaan, and the healing works of Christ were mighty acts of God. As one writer has put it, "Wonder working for the crowds or the sceptics was inconsistent with Jesus mission. It was in this sense that Jesus could not do it in Nazareth."[19]

DO MIRACLES SHRINK GOD OR EXPAND OUR UNDERSTANDING OF GOD?

It is seldom realized, in thinking about God's relation to his creation, just how easy it is, unthinkingly, to "shrink" the God in whom we believe. Intuitively, one might think that to speak of a God of miracles would be to enlarge our idea of God. And so, in an important sense, it should be. However, when bringing together belief *both* in the lawfulness of the natural order *and* in miracles a number of questions are immediately raised. Such as, whether belief in the lawfulness of nature *leaves room* for God to *intervene* in the natural order; or whether God *uses* natural laws in order to bring about his creative purposes; or whether we should regard miracles as God's *interventions* in the otherwise orderly working of creation. Many will recognize ways in which *these questions are so often solemnly asked and often firmly answered one way or the other*. But a little thought helps us to see that ideas such as *leaving room* for God, or God *using* natural laws, or God *intervening*, all stem from a way of thinking about the relation of God to his creation that is intrinsically inadequate. It is inadequate and it "shrinks" God. Indeed, these ways of thinking are not merely inadequate, they are also misleading.

An essential feature of any model we have of God's relation to his creation, whether implicit or explicit, is that, according to the Bible, *nothing continues to exist apart from God's moment-by-moment activity*. It therefore becomes meaningless to ask whether the laws of nature *leave room* for God's involvement. How could they *leave room* for God's activity, since God's activity is *present all the time*? Or again, how could God *intervene* and suspend the laws from time to time, since he is there all the time, holding everything in existence? In what sense could God *use natural laws*, since natural laws are our way of summarizing our experience of the regular occurrence of events in the creation that God holds in being all the time? The expressions *leaving room, intervening,* and *using* assume and condone a radical misconception of God and of his relation as Creator to the created order. It

19. Cressey, "Miracles."

is a radical misconception that immediately *shrinks* our understanding of God. The biblical view of God requires that the whole pattern of space–time events is not only conceived but also held in being moment-by-moment by God; it is thus incorrect to term "miraculous" events as interventions. They are in fact no more and no less dependent upon God's activity than daily occurrences, which we so readily take for granted, like boiling a kettle, riding a bicycle, even if we use shorthand language to summarize our experience in terms of what we call natural laws. In recent years there have been developed some extremely helpful ways of thinking about the relation of God to his creation, including ourselves, which draw upon developments in modern technology. Following the lead given by Donald MacKay, we shall think, for example, about God as the electronic artist. For the moment we need to keep in mind that since all events are dependent upon God's continuing activity, the term "miracle" is best reserved for those events that reverse our normal expectations or observations, retaining the word "providence" to cover the daily gifts and our day-to-day existence, which we constantly receive at God's hands.

Denis Alexander, Director Emeritus of the Faraday Centre for the study of Science and Religion at Cambridge, writes, "It is rational for a person to believe in miracles within the biblical understanding of the term, while at the same time encouraging critical assessment of miraculous claims that are poorly supported by evidence."[20] Alexander reminds us that, "nearly all the founders of modern science, such as Descartes, Boyle and Newton, who introduced the idea of 'laws of science' believed in the biblical miracles, just as many scientists do so today."[21] Alexander argues that miraculous events in the Bible should be seen as "a sign of God's special grace in a particular historical-religious context."[22]

HELP FROM BIBLICAL SCHOLARS

It is at this point that we pick up once again a theme repeated often in this book, that in understanding issues at the interface of science and Christian faith it is just as important for those of us who are scientists to do our utmost to understand and benefit from advances in biblical scholarship, as it is for the biblical scholars to attempt as far as possible to keep abreast of advances in relevant sciences. The understanding of miracles is a very good example of this principle. Biblical scholars have reminded us that the Hebrew and

---

20. Alexander, "Miracles and Science," 94.
21. Alexander, "Miracles and Science," 98.
22. Alexander, "Miracles and Science," 98.

Greek texts of the Old and New Testament respectively, at different times bring out different nuances to the words "wonders" or "miraculous." For example, Denis Alexander claims, "The Greek word *teras* and its Hebrew equivalent *mopheth,* translated as wonders, are used in the texts to draw attention to events which are so remarkable that they should be remembered. The term focuses much more on the amazement produced in the witnesses than on the specific purpose of the event."[23]

Another Greek word is also used, *dynamis*. From this we derive our word dynamite, so it is not surprising that in Scripture it is frequently translated as "acts of power or mighty works." The emphasis in the Bible is that miracles are the result of the operation of the power, the *dynamis* of God, who is seen as the source of all power. Whereas the word *teras* underlines the impact the miracle has on the observer, *dynamis* points to its cause. There is also a third word that is critical in understanding how the Bible views miracles. It is the word usually translated "sign," *ot* in Hebrew and *semeion* in Greek. So, for example, the plagues described in Exodus chapters 3 to 10 are described as a "sign." We also find that "sign" is the main word used in John's Gospel when referring to the miracles of Jesus. The intention of a *semeion* is to reveal aspects of who God is and especially of his character of power and love.

The words *teras, dynamis,* and *semeion* are not the only ones used in the New Testament to refer to miracles, but they are the most commonly used, and are frequently used at the same time. Certainly, the Bible makes no attempt to distinguish miracles that have what we today call natural causes from those that do not. This is because in the Bible we are taught that God is the ultimate and ongoing cause of everything that exists. That applies to events in the normal workings of daily life (as for example, Ps 104:14–24) or in the remarkable events like the crossing of the Red Sea. The Bible does not focus upon the relation of the event we call a miracle to the natural order, but rather upon the impression that the event made upon the minds of those who witnessed it (for example, Mark 3:11 and Exod 14:31). We find also that the relation that the miraculous events bear to the wider purposes of God's revelation of his will is emphasized in Scripture. *The biblical miracles, therefore, direct our attention to the impression that the event makes upon those who witness it, rather than to theoretical questions, such as whether the cause of a miracle is regular but still unknown to us, or whether it is in some way contrary to our normal expectations.*

An examination of the Bible soon convinces us that to label an event miraculous does *not* imply that there are no natural causes for that event.

---

23. Alexander, "Miracles and Science," 126.

Indeed, on some occasions we are invited to notice a natural cause that was responsible for the event. The crossing of the Red Sea is especially instructive in this regard, since the cause of the rolling back of the water is stated in Exodus 14:21 to be *a strong east wind*. This aspect of the occurrence of miracles has encouraged some people to regard such miracles as nothing more than divine coincidences. It does, however, remain the case that it is only against the backdrop of what we have already come to expect of the regular workings of creation that we can perceive the unusual events to which we attach particular significance and regard as miracles. *Miracles are certainly not invasions by God into an otherwise natural working of creation, for this would deny that in some sense God is there already.* Neither are they merely natural, if by this we imply that God is not active in the whole stream of events moment-by-moment. They are, rather, special acts of God, and seen to be such—albeit acts in which the secondary means that are responsible for the event are neither more nor less given by God than any other day-to-day occurrence.

A second pervading feature of some miracles is the way in which they are seen as mighty acts of divine power. As Clark Pinnock wrote, "The mighty acts of Jesus were performed by one who is himself called the power of God, and these works are entirely appropriate actions to be performed by one was both man and God. As some have put it, they serve for him as credentials in the midst of an unbelieving generation."[24] Another all-pervading characteristic of miracles is their importance as signs, tokens, or pledges of an age yet to come; this is true in both the Old and New Testaments. Indeed, some would regard this as a key aspect of miracles. Thus, the healing miracles are seen as a temporary rolling back of the claims of death, which will one day be abolished. All three of these features of miracles are present in the healing recorded in the third chapter of the Acts of the Apostles. We are told that those who observe the miracle were "filled with wonder and amazement"; the apostles made it clear that this mighty act of divine power was, as they put it, "not by our own power," but by the power of Christ; and finally we may see this as a sign and pledge of an age yet to come, when all disease and sickness will be done away with.

One final aspect of miracles is noteworthy in the context of this book. It is sometimes not realized how relatively scarce miracles are within the biblical narrative as a whole. Put another way, if we were today writing a narrative with the express intention of impressing upon our readers the otherworldliness of the events that were portrayed, and the claims that were made from these, we should be sorely tempted to ensure that our narrative

---

24. Jeeves, *Scientific Enterprise*, 30.

was well stocked with miraculous events throughout. When we consider the thousands of years covered by the biblical narrative, we find that this is not the case. The miraculous events tend to concentrate around three major periods of the total biblical record, namely the events of the exodus of Israel from Egypt, the time of the prophets of the ninth century BCE, and the apostolic era recorded in the New Testament. Such outstanding biblical characters as Jeremiah and David have no miraculous acts attributed to them.

Sir Colin Humphreys has shared his reflections on some of the miracles of Scripture.[25] He suggests that it is possible to distinguish three types of miracles:

- Miracles of timing. These are events that break no scientific laws and a clear scientific mechanism is at work. Many biblical miracles are like this, for example, the crossing of the Jordan (due to an earthquake-induced mudslide) or the star of Bethlehem (a comet), the crossing of the Red Sea (a strong east wind), the sun stopping shining (a solar eclipse) at the time of Joshua, the rolling away of the stone at the resurrection (an earthquake, as Matthew records). The miracle was in the timing.
- Miracles where a physical law is broken. Examples are the healing miracles of Jesus.
- Miracles which are unique. Physical laws are broken. There is one unique miracle like this—the resurrection of Jesus.

As we watch the events, in nature and in the lives of individuals, emerge and develop, some of them will be very striking and cause us to stop and think. If we were watching these events on our televisions in a play they would indeed, at times, seem "unique," but for the creator, producer, and presenter of the whole show *they would have been part of the story in his mind from the very beginning*. Such is the Creator and Upholder of all things, in whom, as Christians, we believe.

THE RESURRECTION OF JESUS CHRIST

Anyone reflecting on what I have written about how to understand miracles of nature as recorded in Scripture may wonder how I understand the bodily resurrection of Christ as recorded in Scripture and in the great creeds of the Christian church. Specifically, how does belief in bodily resurrection fit with current knowledge in biology and physics? Given the ongoing discussions

25. Humphreys, *Miracles of Exodus*.

of this question by distinguished theologians such as N. T. Wright,[26] any short answer to this question will run the risk of superficiality, but I will attempt to summarize a few important points.

We should begin by noting that the Bible makes no attempt to distinguish between miracles that have what we might call "natural explanations" and those that do not. In the biblical understanding of creation, God is the ultimate and ongoing cause of everything that exists and everything that happens, whether in the normal daily routine of the created order (as for example in Ps 104:14–24) or in remarkable events like the crossing of the Red Sea. Thus, the act of restoring the dead Jesus to life is an action of God the creator. We should also keep in mind the helpful reflections of Colin Humphreys concerning the need to distinguish between the different types of miracles as recorded in Scripture. Some break no physical laws, but the timing of the events makes them miraculous, while others break a physical law temporarily, with the normal order of the universe restored soon afterwards. In contrast to these types of miracles, the resurrection of Jesus stands as absolutely unique, because it breaks physical laws in a way that is permanent.

If God is the creator of everything, then it is rational to believe that, if God so chooses, he may at times act in ways that are quite different from our normal expectations. The resurrection of Jesus is a one-off event—something that lies beyond science and the scientific understanding of physical reality. The resurrection must be interpreted within the overall theological framework of the whole of New Testament teaching. It is the context and meaning of the whole narrative that renders the miracle plausible.

The bodily resurrection of Christ, an event that is central to Christian faith, illustrates some key features of the biblical understanding of miracles. First, the particular religious and historical context is essential to understanding the miraculous nature of the event. Just as there were many weddings taking place in Palestine with wine drinking in progress, there were no doubt many empty tombs in Jerusalem. It is the historical situation and the religious context that mark the events of the wedding at Cana as special, and the same is true of the empty tomb on Easter morning. On that week in Jerusalem, only one tomb had been sealed with a large stone and guarded by soldiers. Only one tomb was occupied by someone newly crucified because of his claim to be the Son of God. The religious and historical context allowed the interpretation of the empty tomb as a special sign of God's grace and a miracle that shaped the theological understanding of the first Christians.

---

26. Wright, *Resurrection*; Wright, *Surprised by Hope*.

A second point is that belief in any purported historical event depends on reliable witnesses and circumstantial evidence. Scholars have debated the number and identities of the eyewitnesses to the crucifixion, the empty tomb, and the resurrected Jesus, but clearly some individuals claimed to have seen all three, and their lives were transformed in a way that lasted for decades. The circumstantial evidence for the resurrection is strengthened immeasurably by the fact that the early followers of Christ were so convinced that they had encountered the risen Christ that they staked their lives on it. They believed that they would participate in the resurrection miracle—a New Testament event that had been foreshadowed in the Old Testament (for example, in Isa 26:19; Ezek 37:1-14; Pss 16:10-11; 17:15; and Job 19:25-27).

The testimony to the resurrection of Jesus and the hope of participating in a bodily resurrection were passed down across the early centuries of Christianity. Both the Apostles Creed and the Nicene Creed address the question of what happens after death. They speak not of the natural immortality of the body nor the survival of the soul after death, but of the resurrection of the dead body and of the everlasting life of that body in the world to come. It is evident that the model for the coming resurrection of the people of God is the resurrection of Jesus himself. In 1 Cor 15, where Paul refers to the believers who had seen the Lord and had "fallen asleep," Paul emphasizes the centrality of the resurrection of Jesus. "If Christ has not been raised, our preaching is useless and so is your faith" (1 Cor 15:14 NIV). It is only because Christ is risen that the believer has any hope of resurrection.

OVERVIEW OF MIRACLES IN SCRIPTURE

For the ancient Israelites, miracles involve God displaying his power to control natural events like earthquakes. For example, it is an important theme underlined in the words of Psalm 77, which reads,

> You are the God who performs miracles;
> You display your power among the peoples . . .
> Your thunder was heard in the whirlwind,
> your lightning lit up the world,
> the earth trembled and quaked.
> Your path led through the sea,
> your way through the mighty waters,
> though your footprints were not seen.
> You lead your people like a flock
> by the hand of Moses and Aaron. (Ps 77:14, 18-20 NIV)

This quotation specifically links miracles with thunder, lightning, and earthquakes, which belong to God.

Another feature of the God of the Old Testament is that he is frequently revealed as a healer, both in his words and actions. Quotations from Old Testament Scripture reveal how his healing work changes both physical and material well-being (for example, 2 Kgs 4:32–35, 5:14: Job 42:12–13; Ps 103:3). At the same time, the Old Testament writers concede that powers other than God can produce "signs and wonders." Such miracles are seen as inferior (Exod 7:10–12). Reports and rumors of miracles are not as rare as one might imagine in a century dominated by daily reports of advances in all branches of science. Verification of miracles is a much rarer event. A recent report on the occurrence of miracles through appealing to St. Charbel in Lebanon presents a dramatic picture:

> Miracles are on the rise in Lebanon. So says Father Louis Matar, the Maronite priest who keeps a tally of such things. St Charbel, the closest thing Lebanon has to a patron saint, gets most of the credit. He has notched up 26,000 miracles since his death in 1898, when villagers said light beamed out of his tomb. After slowing down at the start of this century, he has regained his form. "We're seeing more miracles in these past two years than we have in the past decade," says Father Matar.[27]

The report notes perceptively, "Studies suggest that people often turn to religion in the face of hardship. Some Lebanese may be seeking help from St Charbel to cope with the slow burning economic crisis, staggering inequality and the threat of renewed war with Israel."[28] Paul Tabor, an anthropologist at the Lebanese American University, commented, "People are at best totally dependent on their sectarian leaders and at worst left out in the cold. *It is this precariousness that is driving many into the arms of saints and gods.*"[29] It was ever thus.

MIRACLES AND "GODS-OF-THE-GAPS"

Any discussion of miracles must be set in the wider context of the question of whether it is reasonable for people living in the twenty-first century to believe both in the lawfulness of the natural order and in miracles. Not infrequently such questions are often formulated by asking whether

---

27. Economist, "Miracles in Lebanon."
28. Economist, "Miracles in Lebanon."
29. Economist, "Miracles in Lebanon," (emphasis added).

nature leaves room for God to intervene in the natural order; whether God uses natural laws in order to bring about his creative purposes; whether we should regard miracles as God's interventions in the otherwise orderly working of creation. The reader will recognize ways in which these questions have in the past been solemnly asked and firmly answered one way or the other. A detailed and helpful dialogue on these underlying questions has recently been made available by the publication of the book *It Keeps Me Seeking*. The three authors are two professors of physics at Oxford and a professor of philosophy from Princeton.[30] Some of the questions touched on in this chapter are explored in much more depth in their book. It is not uncommon for preachers, using today's multimedia, when promoting their particular "gods on offer" in the religious marketplace, to appeal to reports of present-day healing miracles to substantiate the case for the God they are offering. Talk of "God intervening" or of "leaving room for God to act" is frequent. But is there biblical warrant for such language? Since such "gods on offer" are by their very nature "diminished gods" and "gods-of-the-gaps," we need to scrutinize them carefully. Are miracles being reduced to magic?

A salient feature of the picture that the Bible presents of God's relation to his creation is to underline that nothing continues to exist, or continues in being, apart from God's moment-by-moment activity. That being so it becomes meaningless to ask whether the laws of nature *leave room* for God's involvement. How could they *leave room* for God's activity since God's activity is present all the time? Or again, how could God intervene and suspend the laws from time to time, since he is there all the time, holding everything in existence? In what sense could God *use* natural laws, since natural laws are one way of summarizing our experience of the regular accounts of events in the creation that God holds in being all the time? The terms "leaving room," "intervening," and "using" convey a radical misconception of God in relation to the created order. The biblical view requires a pattern of space-time events not only conceived by God but held in being moment-by-moment. It is incorrect to claim that miraculous events are *interventions*. They are in fact no more and no less dependent upon God's activity than day-to-day accounts that we certainly take for granted, such as boiling a kettle, riding a bicycle, taking a pain killer for a headache, even if we use shorthand language to summarize our experience in terms of what we call natural laws. As Briggs and his friends remind us concerning the miracle stories of the Bible.

> The problem is that the authors of those stories didn't themselves have a precise definition of the miraculous, and so their

30. By Andrew Briggs et al.

intention couldn't possibly have been to assert that a miracle—in this precise sense—did occur. No, the biblical authors don't generally speak directly about metaphysical issues, and they aren't aiming at scientific precision. They tell us that certain events happened, and the significance of those events. They don't say anything about whether those events have some sort of naturalistic explanation.[31]

EXPLAINING AND EXPLAINING AWAY

In the epilogue to his 2003 book, Colin Humphreys makes clear that he is extremely keen to underline the difference between explaining and explaining away. Thus, he writes,

> We have followed Moses and the Israelites on an epic journey from Egypt to Mount Sinai, where the Ten Commandments were given and a nation was born—surely one of the most significant journeys in history. We've used a combination of modern science and ancient texts to throw light upon the miracles recorded in the biblical account of the Exodus, and we've shown that many, if not all, of these miracles have natural explanations. However, I've emphasized that they are still miracles: miracles of timing. Some of the miracles have very specific explanations, for example, the crossing of the Red Sea, which enables the exact geographical location to be so specified. These key marker sites greatly help in the reconstruction of the Exodus route, and a new route is proposed in this book.[32]

He later writes, "Any one of these events occurring at the right time could be ascribed to lucky chance. When the whole sequence of events happens at just the right moment, then *it is either incredibly lucky chance or else there is a God who works in, with, and through natural events to guide the affairs and the destinies of individuals and nations.* Which belief is correct: Chance or God? I'm not going to answer that question for you; you must answer it for yourself."[33]

There are, of course, other detailed narratives, especially in the Old Testament, that underline God's providential care for his people and for his creation. For example, the biblical account of Joseph's life (Gen 37–50) is

---

31. Briggs et al., *It Keeps Me Seeking*, 264.
32. Humphreys, *Miracles of Exodus*, 335.
33. Humphreys, *Miracles of Exodus*, 339–40 (emphasis added).

both compelling and graphically presented in great detail in the Old Testament. Related to some of the natural occurrences in Egypt discussed above, we may note the frequent occurrence of famines in Egypt and the surrounding region and Joseph's conviction that they were not outside of God's control. Indeed, Joseph maintained unambiguously that both the good years and the famine years were under the sovereignty of God (Gen 41:32). In one place, to emphasize God's sovereignty, Joseph explained that, "God has revealed to Pharaoh what he is about to do" (Gen 41:25 NIV). Moreover, it is clear from the text that Joseph was convinced that it was not just the natural processes that caused the famine that were under God's sovereignty. Joseph makes a point of saying that the whole sorry episode of human sinfulness shown by the way his brothers sold him into slavery was indeed used in God's providence for God's purposes. It is remarkable how gracious Joseph managed to be when he finally revealed himself to his brothers and reiterated three times that everything that happened to him was used for good by God. To make the same point twice is to emphasize it strongly; to make it three times is to put it beyond any possibility of doubt. Thus, Joseph said: "Now do not be distressed or angry with yourselves because you sold me here, for God sent me before you to preserve life. For the famine has been in the land these two years, and there are yet five years in which there will be neither plowing nor harvest. And God sent me before you to preserve for you a remnant on earth, and to keep alive for you many survivors. So it was not you who sent me here, but God." (Gen 45:4–8 ESV).

Another relevant example from the Old Testament Scriptures, in the context of this book, which has been exposing various of the "false gods" promoted in the religious marketplace today is the remarkable story narrated in the book of Job. The theology of Job's friends was that Job's suffering must be a direct result of his behavior towards God, therefore he must have done something wrong. Their arguments take several different forms but one of the more subtle sides of their argument is the false gospel that the righteous are rewarded materially. So Eliphaz says "Submit to God and be at peace with him; in this way prosperity will come to you" (Job 22:21 NIV). Could this be considered a very early form of today's prosperity gospel? What is new under the sun? In June 2019, Michael Brice-Saddler wrote a piece on the web headed "A wealthy televangelist explains his fleet of private jets: 'It's a biblical thing.'" In it he noted that "Like many televangelists, [Kenneth] Copeland preaches the 'prosperity gospel,' which stems from the belief that faith, often in the form of donations to preachers and ministries, will garner riches down the line."[34]

34. Brice-Saddler, "Wealthy Televangelist."

9

Miracles of Nature
Illustrative Examples

We are inclined strongly against gap arguments, but for quite different reasons than those of the typical naturalist critic. We think that gap arguments are bad because there are certain rules of good thinking—rules that were written on our hearts by our Creator. But note that our critique of gap arguments suggests another way of perceiving and responding to God: good reasoning finds its root and support in the character of God: hence, it is God's being that ultimately explains why we are able to perceive that gap arguments are bad![1]

HELP FROM SCIENTISTS

IN RECENT YEARS A series of papers published in top-flight scientific journals such as *Nature* and *The Quarterly Journal of the Royal Astronomical Society* have demonstrated how, by drawing on advances in both biblical scholarship and in science, specifically advances in astronomy, it is possible better to understand some "miraculous events" reported in Scripture. For example, in understanding the Star of Bethlehem a deeper understanding by biblical scholars of who the Magi were, puts those events firmly into a proper cultural and historical context which together assist in better understanding how, at that time, unusual celestial events would be interpreted. By way of illustration we shall consider three such papers which appeared in

1. Briggs et al., *It Keeps Me Seeking*, 160.

scientific journals all authored or co-authored by Sir Colin Humphreys FRS. It is important to note that when the papers referred to are being considered for publication in these prestigious scientific journals *the referees are solely concerned with the scientific accuracy of what is being reported.* These papers could have appeared in one of the several excellent contemporary journals discussing science and Christian belief. If that had happened the charge would have been made that the referees would be predisposed to accept the papers since they appeared to be favorable towards Christian faith. This is not the case here. *These papers were refereed by hardheaded scientists strictly on their scientific accuracy and merit.*

The Star of Bethlehem

The second chapter of the Gospel of Matthew records, "Wise men from the east came to Jerusalem saying, 'Where is he has who has been born king of the Jews? For we saw his star when it rose and have come to worship him'" (Matt 2:2 ESV). Later, "After listening to the king, they went on their way. And behold, the star that they had seen when it rose went before them until it came to rest over the place where the child was. When they saw the star, they rejoiced exceedingly with great joy" (Matt 2:9–10 ESV).

In his paper in the *Quarterly Journal of the Royal Astronomical Society* published in 1991 under the title "The Star of Bethlehem—a Comet in 5 BC—and the Date of the Birth of Christ," Humphreys notes that, "There are four key questions arising from the account in Matthew's Gospel, and other ancient literature, of the star of Bethlehem: (1) who were the Magi? (2) is there a known astronomical phenomenon which fits the account? (3) what induced the Magi to embark on their journey? and (4) can astronomy be used to solve the long-standing problem of the date of the birth of Christ?"[2] Humphreys's paper attempts to answer these questions. In the context of our present discussions and to illustrate its relevance to an understanding of miracles in Scripture the paper shows how by taking into account several specific characteristics of the Star of Bethlehem as recorded in Matthew's Gospel, as well as significant and substantial evidence of astronomical events about that time, all but one of the astronomical objects suggested in that literature as the star Bethlehem can be ruled out. Noting the accounts of Dio Cassius, of Josephus, and of Matthew, Humphreys concludes that the only astronomical object to appear to be sufficiently low-lying and to be capable of satisfying the descriptions of these three is the star of Bethlehem.

2. Humphreys, "Star of Bethlehem," 405. The most detailed study of the biblical and scientific data on the star of Bethlehem is now Nicoll, *The Great Christ Comet.*

In Humphreys's view, "Thus a comet uniquely fits the description in Matthew that the star was new, it travelled slowly through the star field from the east to the south, it went ahead of the Magi, and 'stood over' Bethlehem, the place where the child was born."[3]

The remainder of the details of this important paper which makes detailed references to carefully kept Chinese astronomical records and other sources of information around that time, *leaves little doubt that there is a "natural explanation" for these remarkable events*. But, and this is the important point, this "natural explanation" in fact makes the whole event far more surprising and compelling since it means that it was not a sudden "trick of a cosmic magician" *but that before the foundation of the earth these remarkable coincidences were built into the total story of creation long before humans appeared*. To underline the point, glimpses into the "natural explanation" reinforces and makes even more amazing and wonderful events such as the Star of Bethlehem. No "god-of the-gaps" here, but a moment-by-moment sustaining God.

The Sun Stood Still

The book of Joshua in the Old Testament records that, "The sun stopped in the midst of heaven and did not hurry to set for about a whole day" (Josh 10:13 ESV). Together with his colleague Graeme Waddington, Humphreys has researched what they refer to as "a puzzling event in the Bible." Their paper begins,

> A puzzling event in *The Bible* that mentions both the moon and the sun can be interpreted as describing a solar eclipse. We have dated it to 30 October 1207 BC, making it possibly the oldest datable solar eclipse recorded. This enables us to refine the dates of certain Egyptian pharaohs, including Ramesses the Great. It also suggests that the expressions currently used for calculating changes in the earth's rate of rotation can be reliably extended back 500 years, from 700 BC to 1200 BC.[4]

Once again, drawing upon expertise in astronomical science as well as detailed research into the evidence from preserved clay tablets, these authors note,

> Modern English translations of this passage, such as the NRSV quoted above, have all followed the King James Authorized

---

3. Humphreys, "Star of Bethlehem," 393.
4. Humphreys and Waddington, "Solar Eclipse," 5.39.

Version (AV) of The Bible, translated in 1611, and assumed that the Hebrew text means that the sun and moon stopped moving. However, a plausible alternative meaning is that the sun and moon stopped doing what they normally do: they stopped shining. In other words, the text is referring to a solar eclipse, when the sun stops shining. As a solar eclipse can only occur when the moon is directly between the earth and the sun, the moon itself is not visible and so it is not reflecting sunlight to the earth—like the sun, it has "stopped shining" as well.[5]

Their paper concludes,

> A reinterpretation of a puzzling passage in the Old Testament book of Joshua suggests that a solar eclipse was being reported. Calculations show that this event could be the annular solar eclipse of 30 October 1207 BC. If accepted, this appears to be the oldest solar eclipse recorded. When combined with Egyptian records, this eclipse enables us to hone the most accurate dates available for the reign of the famous Egyptian pharaoh Ramesses the Great to be 1276–1210 BC ±1 year.[6]

Once again, this "natural explanation" reinforces and makes even more amazing this timing of a providential act of God on behalf of his chosen people. Again, not a celestial magician, but an ever-present upholding God from the foundation of the world.

But, and it is an important "but," we must be always aware that there are advances in biblical scholarship that are directly relevant to better understanding some enduring puzzles about biblical interpretation. The Joshua accounts of the sun and the moon in Joshua 10:12–15 are one such instance. In October 2013, John Walton, Professor of Old Testament at Wheaton College, posted an article with the title, "Biblical Credibility and Joshua 10: What Does the Text Really Claim?" Walton wrote,

> This account ranks as one of the most frequently invoked passages for how the credibility of the Bible fails in the world of science. For those who insist that we must take the text literally, the issue concerns the inerrancy of the Bible and the ability of God to do whatever he chooses. While those who take God seriously would not deny that God can do whatever he chooses to do, we recognize that we must also ask what it is the text claims. . . . *We must read the Bible as an ancient text, not as a modern one.*[7]

---

5. Humphreys and Waddington, "Solar Eclipse," 5.40.
6. Humphreys and Waddington, "Solar Eclipse," 5.42.
7. Walton, "Biblical Credibility," n.p. (emphasis added).

He notes further that even those who insist that we read the text literally also note that we have to make adjustments to the geocentric views of the ancient world. Walton further notes that in doing that they are, however, no longer taking the text literally. He writes, "If we are going to adjust our interpretations to ancient thinking, we had better do a thorough job of it." Walton goes on to argue, taking into account the relevant evidence, properly to understand this text requires one to see the way it is embedded in widely held views of propitious omens for many actions. From this perspective, "Certainly a reading of the text in light of omens is more likely for an ancient text than a reading in light of physics." Walton concludes., "Joshua's knowledge of the Amorites' dependence on omens may have led him to ask the Lord for one that he knew would deflate their morale—for the opposition to occur on an unpropitious day."[8]

In May 2016, Mark Chavalas, Professor of History at the University of Wisconsin-Lacrosse, reopened consideration of how this puzzling passage in the book of Joshua 10:12–15 may properly be interpreted. His research focused on Neo-Assyrian omen tablets housed in the British Museum. Notice again that this is evidence-based exposition and exegesis. Chavalas, setting out and developing John Walton's view, wrote,

> The lyric poetry of Joshua 10:12 states that the sun halted in Gibeon, and the moon in Aijalon. This signifies that the sun was in the east, and the moon in the west, meaning it was morning, not evening. Thus, Joshua was certainly not asking for more sunlight (after all, the day had just begun). Furthermore, the event was considered unique, not because of any astronomical abnormalities, but because God listened to the voice of a man and fought for Israel (v. 14). . . . The phraseology in Joshua 10:12–13 sounds suspiciously like the vocabulary used in Mesopotamia celestial omen texts. . . . Many of the technical phrases in these omens concern the "stopping" and "waiting" of the heavenly bodies. From the standpoint of the viewer on earth, the sun and moon "stopped and waited" for each other (that is, they were seen together, a bad omen for the fifteenth day after a full moon). The phraseology is not unlike Matthew 2:9, which states that the Christmas Star stood over Bethlehem (this makes sense from the standpoint of a traveler, of course).[9]

Chavalas continued,

---

8. Walton, "Biblical Credibility," n.p.
9. Chavalas, "Does the Bible Claim."

Celestial omen observation was not just prevalent in Mesopotamia but northwest in Syria at the sites of Ugarit, Mari, and Emar (all in regions with significant Amorite connections). The biblical text and Joshua's poetic statement about God's favoring Israel with the motion of the sun and moon were part of a broader ancient Near Eastern tradition of asking for divine help on the battlefield. But this context also helps answer an easily anticipated question: why would a follower of the God of Israel ask for an omen, a practice that was considered divination and regarded as a capital crime? The answer is that the Bible recasts the omen. Joshua was not asking for a celestial phenomenon for himself, or even for Israel, but probably for the enemy; he must have known what it meant for them to have the sun and moon aligned on the fifteenth day, presumably the day of battle. If they received a bad omen, it would have significantly lowered their expectations of victory, to say the least! . . . Jews and Christians believe that God can do whatever He pleases, including violating natural laws (e.g. causing the sun and moon to stop in their tracks). One does not have *to manufacture a miracle where the biblical text does not call for it. To be correctly understood, the Bible must be read in its historical and literary contexts; only then can we mortals respond in awe.*[10]

These accounts by biblical scholars and historians do not deny or repudiate the account given by Colin Humphreys. Instead, they underline yet again the need to be up to date *both* with what scientists are saying *and* what biblical scholars are writing before making dogmatic pronouncements about what puzzling texts in Scripture must mean.

MORE LESSONS FROM MIRACLES IN THE OLD TESTAMENT

Given the several millennia covered by biblical history, the total occurrence of miracles in the biblical narratives is surprisingly rare. There are, however, some periods in which the reporting of miracles is frequent. The first is during the exodus and the second such period is during the life of Christ upon earth. We are fortunate, that, relatively recently, a detailed study of the miracles of the exodus has been undertaken and published.[11] Our purpose in looking at these two periods now is to see what we can discover about any enduring expectations we should have about the nature and frequency

10. Chavalas, "Does the Bible Claim" (emphasis added).
11. Humphreys, *Miracles of Exodus*.

of the occurrence of miracles today. At the same time, a close study of the miracles as undertaken by Colin Humphreys will help us to be clear about what the biblical record teaches us about the origin and nature of these miracles at the time that they occurred.

The Miracles of Exodus

Down the centuries, many have speculated about the nature and veracity of the striking events occurring during the exodus. One of Britain's most distinguished scientists, Sir Colin Humphreys, a Fellow of the Royal Society and formerly a research director at Cambridge, dedicated a period of years to a detailed on-site study entitled *The Miracles of Exodus*. Very aware of the dangers of a "mere scientist" moving into this highly contested set of issues, throughout his investigations he carefully consulted with two of his colleagues at Cambridge, the Regius Professor of Hebrew and the Professor of Egyptology to help him in his task. Humphreys's book brings together knowledge from science, history, geography, archaeology, ancient languages, and the Bible in order better to understand what really happened at the exodus. The book of Exodus begins by narrating the predicament of the Israelites in Egypt. As slaves they were helping to build cities under a cruel and oppressive Pharaoh. Moses was born and his mother laid him in a basket among the reeds on the bank of the Nile since at that time the Egyptians were killing the Hebrew male infants. Miraculously, Moses survived. Taken care of by Pharaoh's daughter Moses grew up in a privileged environment. One day, however, he saw an Egyptian slave master beating a Hebrew slave and, in his anger, Moses killed the Egyptian. Fearing for his life he fled to the land of Midian, a land at that time outside of Egyptian control.

When he was living in Midian, we are told that Moses visited Mount Sinai and witnessed an amazing sight. A bush that was burning with flames but nevertheless it was not consumed as expected. It just went on burning. It was at this fiery bush we are told that Moses heard the voice of God telling him that he was to lead the Israelites out of Egypt, to bring them to Mount Sinai, and then to lead them on to the promised land of Canaan. With these orders clear, Moses returned to Egypt. He went to Pharaoh and asked him to let the Hebrew slaves leave the land. Pharaoh refused. The narrative then tells us that God sent ten plagues of increasing severity upon the Egyptians until finally Pharaoh yielded and allowed the Israelites to leave. It is narrated that in their journey a pillar of cloud by day and a pillar of fire by night went in front of the Israelites to guide them to Mount Sinai. But Pharaoh changed his mind. He sent his army to pursue them and trapped them at the Red

Sea. The text reports that, remarkably, a very strong wind drove back the sea enabling the Israelites to cross. It further notes that Pharaoh's army following the fleeing Israelites was swept away by the incoming sea and drowned. Free at last the Israelites continue their journey to Mount Sinai. It was along this journey that a number of extraordinary events occurred. Moses turned bitter water into sweet; a mysterious substance called manna provided for the Israelites to eat; a large number of quail provided another source of food; Moses produced water when the Israelites were thirsty, but it was water from a rock. At last, the Israelites reach Mount Sinai only to be greeted by an awesome sight: fire and smoke were being emitted and a sound like a trumpet blast confronted them. Sadly, here also, despite all their blessings the Israelites still rebelled and built an idol to worship: a golden calf. The narrative continues recording how after the building of the ark of the covenant and of the portable Tabernacle at Mount Sinai the Israelites travelled onwards through various deserts entering the promised land by crossing the River Jordan. But here a further remarkable miracle occurred. When they reached the river, it was in full flood but suddenly, and miraculously, it stopped flowing as they stood at the water's edge enabling them to walk across the dry riverbed to the other side. The Israelites had reached the promised land and after an extraordinary journey the nation was born.

Such a succinct account of a remarkable series of events immediately raises the question, how can we, as people of the twenty-first century, who, through advances in science, understand the natural history of the migration of quails or the movement of tectonic plates that move the earth, leading to the sudden blocking of rivers or the sudden flooding of countries, understand this remarkable series of reported events that go against our natural expectations of how the world and the creatures within it behave.

Crossing the River Jordan

Humphreys's very readable and extremely well illustrated book is written as if he is a twenty-first-century Hercule Poirot studying not a crime, but a series of highly unusual events. To illustrate his typical approach, we may take the way he investigated the remarkable drying up of the River Jordan to allow the people of Israel to cross into the promised land right at the end of the exodus journey. We shall also then, very briefly, indicate the results of his similar investigations of the other miracles of the book of Exodus. The reader is referred for the details of these to his book. Humphreys records,

> On my one-week vacation to Israel and Egypt in the spring of 2001, to revisit some of the route of the Exodus, I was browsing

in a bookshop in Eilat and I picked up a book by Leen and Kathleen Ritmeyer called *From Sinai to Jerusalem: The Wandering of the Ark*. In this book the authors reproduce a rare photograph from the nineteenth century showing the River Jordan overflowing its banks in the springtime, and with permission I reproduce this photograph here. So, this was the river in flood that the Israelites needed to cross. Picture the scene! Imagine you were there. Isn't it amazing to be able to reconstruct ancient events in detail as we have in this chapter? And not just any ancient events: events that changed the course of history.[12]

The biblical account of the crossing of the River Jordan as recorded in the book of Joshua reads as follows, "Now the Jordan is at flood stage all during harvest. Yet as soon as the priests who carried the ark reached the Jordan and their feet touched the water's edge, the water from upstream stopped flowing. It piled up in a heap a great distance away, at a town called Adam in the vicinity of Zarethan, while the water flowing down to the Sea of the Arabah (that is, the Dead Sea) was completely cut off. So the people crossed over opposite Jericho" (Josh 3:15–16 NIV). Noting that if you look at a modern map of the state of Jordan there is no town called Adam, Humphreys asks, is it possible to locate the ancient town of Adam after three thousand years? He consulted his Hebrew experts and the net result from their knowledge and his personal studies resulted in Humphreys's discovery that on modern maps of the state of Jordan, a town appears on the eastern side of the river Jordan called Damiya. It is about seventeen miles north of where the River Jordan passes closest to Jericho. He discovered that not only that, but in the 1989 Bartholomew world travel map of Israel with Jordan the same town is actually marked *Damiya (Adamah)*. This he concludes strongly suggests that the ancient town of Adam is modern Damiya. Later scholars agree with this, which is why the Bartholomew map stated it quite clearly. His next move is to turn to science for the critical evidence. He discovered that on July 11, 1927 a well-documented earthquake shook the town of Jericho, causing cracks in the buildings and panic in the local population. The earthquake was detected in seismological stations as far as apart as, Europe, South Africa, North America, and Russia. It measured a magnitude of about 6.5 on the Richter scale—a large earthquake. He turned next to one of the world's leading geophysicists, Amos Nur, Wayne Loel Professor of Earth Sciences and Professor of Geophysics at Stanford University. He discovered that Nur had made a detailed study of the 1927 earthquake

---

12. Humphreys, *Miracles of Exodus*, 26.

and found that it was due to slippage along a geological fault called the Jericho fault, which runs approximately north-south under the Jordan River.

About this 1927 earthquake Nur had written: "During the 1927 earthquake, several ground cracks appeared, together with an outpouring of groundwater. This soil liquefaction phenomenon has been well observed in earthquakes elsewhere. During the earthquake, mudslides occurred along the Jordan near Damiya, about 30 km (about 18 miles) north of Jericho; these temporarily stop the rivers flow.[13]" The place that Nur spells as Damiya is, on the maps, spelled as Damia. The important thing is they are the same place. Humphreys goes on to narrate how Nur then researched historical records and found that the River Jordan had been temporarily stopped on a number of occasions, all because of mudslides induced by an earthquake. The earliest historical record of this that Nur found occurred in 1160. Nur thus recognized the relevance of these earthquakes to the passage in the book of Joshua we referred to earlier. Nur wrote, "Adam is now Damia, the site of the 1927 mudslides which cut off the flow of the Jordan. Such cut-offs, lasting typically 1 to 2 days have been recorded in 1906, 1834, 1546, 1534, 1267, and 1160. The stoppage of the Jordan is so typical of earthquakes in this region that little doubt can be left as to the reality of such events in Joshua's time."[14]

Humphreys goes on, "We therefore have a scientific explanation of the crossing of the Jordan in terms of a natural mechanism: an earthquake induced mudslide behind which the waters of the Jordan piled up until they broke through, typically 1 to 2 days later. While the river Jordan was temporarily stopped, the Israelites were able to cross over. I believe this enables us to identify Adam, the place of the earthquake induced mudslide, with modern Damiya beyond reasonable doubt."[15] Humphreys further notes that most ancient civilizations believed in gods but that in some respects the God of ancient Israel was different. The God of Israel was one whom they believed controlled all the forces of nature. He further notes that if we look at the biblical description of another major miracle of the exodus, namely, the crossing of the Red Sea, we discover that the Israelites undoubtedly regarded this as one of the greatest miracles that happened to them. But the Bible is explicit that this miracle was caused by a natural mechanism, a strong east wind, and the Bible also says that this wind was the agent of the hand of God (here represented by the hand of Moses stretched out over the sea).

13. Humphreys, *Miracles of Exodus*, 20.
14. Humphreys, *Miracles of Exodus*, 20.
15. Humphreys, *Miracles of Exodus*, 21–22.

Humphreys also calls attention to the timing of the Israelites's crossing of the Jordan. They had been wandering in the wilderness forty years and they were now opposite Jericho at the Jordan River. The river was all that separated them from the promised land. Just as the Israelites gathered on the banks of the Jordan, the earthquake-induced stoppage of the river occurred. For the ancient Israelites, this event thus fitted an important pattern: miracles of God that involve God displaying his power to control natural events such as earthquakes. Psalm 77 specifically links miracles with thunder, lightning, and earthquakes, all of which belong to God. Humphreys comments,

> In other words, the ancient Israelites view of miracles did not normally involve directly seeing the footprints of God, left behind like a celestial visiting card saying "God was here" after a miraculous event. *The miracles of God, for the ancient Israelites, instead involve God displaying his power through natural events like earthquakes occurring at the right time.*[16]

Humphreys goes on to document in detail the results of his scientific and exegetical detective work as he studies the miracles of Exodus. For now, I shall briefly describe Humphrey's conclusions about two of the miracles and indicate how, in the purposes and economy of God, and in the timing of God, there was in each case a perfectly natural explanation. But the explanations do not make the events any less miraculous. Thus, we may continue to expect that the God of Scripture who "upholds all things by the word of his power" (Heb 1:3 KJV), will work in similar ways in the present and the future.

The Burning Bush

Scripture records, "Now Moses was tending the flock of Jethro his father-in-law, the priest of Midian, and he led the flock to the far side of the desert and came to Horeb, the mountain of God. There the angel of the LORD appeared to him in flames of fire from within the bush. Moses saw that although the bush was on fire it did not burn up. Moses thought, "I will go over and see this strange sight—why the bush does not burn up" (Exod 3:3 NIV). Using the detailed sources available from biblical scholars, together with more recent writings, such as the work of T. E. Lawrence in his famous book *The Seven Pillars of Wisdom*,[17] Humphreys locates the most likely place referred

---

16. Humphreys, *Miracles of Exodus*, 24 (emphasis added).
17. Lawrence, *Seven Pillars of Wisdom*.

to as east or southeast. The question is what kept the bush burning without being consumed? Further details and further sleuthing pointed to the simplest solution being that the location of the burning Bush may well have been in a volcanic region to the east or southeast. If this is correct, then the burning bush is located over a volcanic vent or escaping natural gas. Hence it continues to burn but the bush is not consumed. Humphreys concludes, "*Without further information it is not possible to say whether natural gas or the volcanic vent mechanism is more likely to be correct, but both are certainly possible natural explanations of the burning bush.*"[18]

Turning Bitter Water Sweet

Scripture records, "When they came to Marah, they could not drink its water because it was bitter. (That is why the place is called Marah.) So the people grumbled against Moses, saying, 'What are we to drink?' Then Moses cried out to the LORD, and the LORD showed him a piece of wood. He threw it into the water, and the water became fit to drink" (Exod 15:23–25 ESV). Humphreys's detective work suggests to him that "Moses didn't invent Marah, meaning a 'bitter place'; rather that the place was already called bitter by the local Midianites and the Israelites called it by the Hebrew word for bitter."[19] Humphreys offers two possible interpretations of how throwing a piece wood into water, believed to be salty water, could produce sweet tasting water. One of these explanations is based on detailed local knowledge of the area of the likely route of the exodus. His first suggested explanation is based on the knowledge that the wood of the a*cacia seyel* tree was burned locally as producing "the best kind of charcoal fuel." That being so, he writes "Hence it is not unlikely that there was some burned acacia wood, covered with a layer of charcoal, lying about in the ancient Marah, and I suggest it was this wood that Moses threw into the salty water at Marah to purify it." His alternative explanation draws on the practice in some parts of the world where certain trees are known to be used as water purifiers without being burned. He gives the example of Sri Lanka, "where wood from the so-called kumbuk tree *(terminalia arjuna)* is used to line the inner walls of wells because it purifies and desalinizes water. . . . Thus there is a tentative scientific explanation for how Moses sweetened the water with a piece of wood."[20]

---

18. Humphreys, *Miracles of Exodus*, 81 (emphasis added).
19. Humphreys, *Miracles of Exodus*, 268.
20. Humphreys, *Miracles of Exodus*, 273.

10

Miracles of Health and Healing
Scriptural and Scientific Insights

> More than half the spontaneous prayers I hear in church pertain to the sick. In the broader picture of prayer, that gives the same imbalance as a pastor preaching from the book of Job every Sunday. At the same time, it also shows how instinctively we turn to prayer when illness strikes.[1]

TODAY, "SHRUNKEN GODS" ARE preached and promoted with, at times, an almost exclusive emphasis on the health benefits of faith and, in some cases, of promises of miraculous healings. In his book on prayer, Philip Yancey, referring to the large accumulation of letters he had received from people asking him about prayer and sickness, wrote, "Yet the stack of letters from my filing cabinet convinces me that we can do . . . harm by holding out false hope of physical healing." And referring to letters he received from parents of children with Down's syndrome or Huntington's chorea, he adds, "But I know of no miraculous healings of those conditions, and to offer false hope would be even more cruel."[2]

It is important to note that the anecdotal evidence cited by Yancey resonates strongly with the experience of many Christians who, either themselves or through some family members or close friends, face serious illness. The nature and occurrence of reported unexpected healings among

---

1. Yancey, *Prayer*, 240.
2. Yancey, *Prayer*, 241.

religious people is a lively issue for biblical scholars, theologians, and scientists. This is illustrated by the publication of two volumes of collected essays edited by Fraser Watts[3] and Sarah Coakley.[4] These volumes make clear that there is a pressing need for "semantic hygiene" if we are to understand what is being claimed in contemporary reports of religious or spiritual healing.

Some writers, including Sarah Coakley, use the term "spiritual healing." Other contributors use "faith cures," as in Heather Curtis's chapter[5] or "biblical healings," as in Beverly Gaventa's chapter.[6] Still others, mainly in Roman Catholic traditions, refer simply to "miraculous cures or Marian healings," as in Emma Anderson's chapter.[7] A selection of quotes from Sarah Coakley's opening chapter to her collected essays, to which she gave the title "Spiritual Healing, Science, and Meaning," highlights the need for semantic clarification. She writes, "The term spiritual healing . . . may simply refer, first, to any healing that is not strictly physical, that is, which relates to the psychic, or non-somatic, or spiritual elements of the self. On this definition, it is the locus of the healing that is being described as spiritual."[8] She continues, "A second rendition of spiritual healing, in contrast, refers to a healing that is effected directly by God (or by other purported spiritual forces), or by God assisted by human others, secondarily and cooperatively. On this definition it is the source of the healing event that is being described as spiritual (that is, God or the divine)."[9] Coakley notes, "A final point of semantic clarification that needs to be made at the opening of this book refers to our other key term, healing. For this, too, is a multivalent notion; and perhaps the first and most important point of clarification here is that the healing may not necessarily connote a physical cure (although, of course, it can)."[10]

Biblical scholar and theologian Beverly Gaventa begins her chapter "Healing, Meaning, and Discernment in the Biblical Text" by asking the question, "What is the meaning of healing in the Bible?" She helpfully reminds us that,

> Contemporary readers of the Bible often find themselves both drawn to and mystified by accounts of spiritual healings and see them as miracles in which God or some agent of God performs

3. Watts, *Spiritual Healing*.
4. Coakley, *Spiritual Healing*.
5. Curtis, "Healing, Belief, and Interpretation."
6. Gaventa, "Healing, Meaning, and Discernment."
7. Anderson, "Healing and Ecclesial Response."
8. Coakley, *Spiritual Healing*, 3.
9. Coakley, *Spiritual Healing*, 4.
10. Coakley, *Spiritual Healing*, 6.

a special act that cures an afflicted individual of some disease or debilitating condition. . . . Many biblical accounts of spiritual healing give the impression, at least at first glance, of being straightforward. Jesus encounters a leper who asks for healing and receives it (Mark 1:40–44; Matt 8:1–4; Luke 5:12–16). A woman who has suffered from a crippling condition for 18 years is restored to health when Jesus pronounces her healed and lays hands on her (Luke 13:10–17). With the words, "Lazarus, come out," Jesus restores life to a man who's been dead for four days (John 11:1–44).[11]

Gaventa makes a further important point that,

> It is important to understand that biblical perspectives on healing are far more complex than is apparent in the account of any single incident. In biblical literature, spiritual healing is a richly textured phenomenon. The Gospels relate many situations in which Jesus performs healings, including the healing of paralysis, leprosy, haemorrhage, blindness, and even death itself. Indeed, one dominant thread in the Gospels' presentation of Jesus is that of a healer.[12]

After reviewing some of the accounts in the Old Testament Scriptures of God's healing power, Gaventa states,

> These varying stories come together in the identification of God as the healer of Israel. The declaration that "I am the LORD who heals you" (Exod 15:26) is frequently reaffirmed in the Old Testament. . . . The identification of God as the healer of Israel was taken up in the New Testament in descriptions of Jesus as a healer. . . . The Fourth Gospel intensifies this identification by labelling Jesus's healings (and other miracles, see John 2:1–12) as "signs" that reveal Jesus's "glory" (for example John 4:54; 6:2; 9:16; 20:30). . . . Overwhelmingly in the Gospels, the question is not the contemporary one of whether a healing is real, but where it comes from: Whose power accomplished the healing, and what does it signify?[13]

At the end of her chapter Gaventa helpfully concludes,

> We began with a simple story in Mark 1, in which Jesus heals Peter's mother-in-law of a fever, a story that could, if taken out of

---

11. Gaventa, "Healing, Meaning, and Discernment," 29.
12. Gaventa, "Healing, Meaning, and Discernment," 30.
13. Gaventa, "Healing, Meaning, and Discernment," 33–34.

its larger literary and canonical setting, reinforce contemporary notions of miracles as isolated events in which an individual is instantly rescued from an illness or debilitating condition. Certainly, miraculous and unexpected events can occur in the biblical narrative. *Yet we have seen that healing in the Bible, properly understood, is anything but an isolated and extrinsic phenomenon.* It is, rather, integral or related to the larger biblical story of God's creation and restoration of humankind. As such, it takes place in the context of human communities of nurture and faith. And it requires discernment and interpretation within and beyond those communities.[14]

It is of particular importance that the sentence in italics in the previous paragraph is kept in mind throughout the remainder of this chapter. That is because all too often so-called "healing miracles" are seen as "isolated and extrinsic events." In the twentieth and twenty-first centuries psychologists, neuroscientists, and physicians have noted the changing associations between religion and health. This is documented within the Coakley book in a chapter by Howard Fields titled "Meaning in the Neural Investigation of Pain"[15] and my own chapter titled "The Brain and Cognitive Processes in Healing."[16] Such contributions are important, but it is equally important to note that church historians of the past twenty centuries also have had something to teach us. Their contributions remind us that those who write claiming a blanket positive and beneficial association between religion, health, and prosperity must have very short memories.

Such a view contrasts strongly with true discipleship, which involves, at times, persecution and suffering. Within the Hebrew-Christian tradition persecution has been a recurring feature of the Christian life for more than two millennia. This must never be forgotten—especially today when some strident Christian media outlets promote dramatic claims about by-product benefits of religious commitment and the religious life. One wonders whether some of those writing about the relationship between religion and health in the twenty-first century are suffering from an attack of almost total amnesia. Some televangelists present the Christian message as a means of ensuring better health and prosperity in the present and in the foreseeable future. This approach is breathtaking in its excessive claims and oversimplicity. To be fair, some preachers could point to a considerable body of

---

14. Gaventa, "Healing, Meaning, and Discernment," 39 (emphasis added).
15. Fields, "Neural Investigation of Pain."
16. Jeeves, "Brain and Cognitive Processes."

research by psychologists and others demonstrating an association between religion and health. More of that below.

Try telling survivors and relatives of those Jews who, because of their faith, faced mass extermination in the mid-twentieth century. Try telling those familiar with the life and death of Dietrich Bonhoeffer that firm Christian faith and true discipleship always carried with it great benefits to health and prosperity in this present life. Try telling some of the Coptic Christians in the Middle East today being killed for their commitment to their Lord, that Christian faith always carries with it health and prosperity in this present life. With that very important proviso, we shall briefly summarize the sorts of evidence that have accumulated to indicate a link between religion, spirituality, and health. An important question will be whether these should be seen as natural biproducts of a devout religious life or whether they are being "sold" in an attempt to gain converts to a particular religious group. *If the latter is happening, then we are once again confronting a "shrunken God"* and not the Hebrew-Christian God of the Scriptures who calls to discipleship of the kind embodied by Christians such as Bonhoeffer and whose deep faith and commitment led not to health and prosperity but to a martyr's death.

HEALING: A CENTRAL PART OF CHRIST'S MINISTRY

In the world of the New Testament, healing is an integral part of the mission to the needy. Nearly one third of the Gospel passages are taken up reporting incidents and debates surrounding Jesus Christ's healings. In the history of the Christian church, healing has always been a vital strand within the church's pastoral care. This particular Christian ministry to the sick and needy has influenced, promoted, and increased medical care in wider society. Historians and biblical scholars have noted that the healings of Jesus, by word and by touch, contrasts strongly with the spells, conjurations, and miracles of punishment cast by the physicians of ancient Greece. From the sixth century onwards, sadly, superstition permeated the church so much that by the twelfth century healing was sought almost entirely through the relics of the saints. In 1163, the Council of Tours went so far as to prohibit certain clergy from even studying medicine.[17] This rift between Christianity and medical practice continued and deepened during the following centuries. By 1551 with the Council of Trent the shift had been completed away from the ministry of healing by limiting the age-old right of anointing the sick to that of extreme unction, reserved for those in danger of death. For

---

17. Mitchell, "Anatomy and Surgery," 315.

John Calvin, at the time of Reformation, the gifts of the Spirit, including healing, were seen only as temporary "to make the preaching of the gospel wonderful." Luther, although early in his career holding a similar view, later seems to have become more open to the possibility of the miraculous in the face of the recovery from the point of death of his friend Melanchthon (1497 to 1560). In subsequent centuries there were reported occasional outbreaks of spectacular healings. For example, John Wesley not only wrote *Primitive Physick*, a treatise on medical practice,[18] but he also documented a number of miracles of healing.

While a significant proportion of miracles recorded in the New Testament deal with healings, the same does not apply in the corpus of the Old Testament documents. In the Old Testament the occurrence of reported miracles, considering the long span of years covered by those documents, is relatively scarce. There are, however, certain periods of the Old Testament history when there was a series of quite dramatic miracles reported. The events of the exodus discussed in the previous chapter are one such well-known example. In their case, the majority of the miracles are reports of striking and unusual events associated with the natural order, such as plagues, flooding, or the mysterious provision of food in the midst of this famine.

Quantitative Studies of Spirituality and Health

Harold Koenig, Professor of Psychiatry and Behavioral Sciences at Duke University Medical Center in the USA, has recently reviewed the advances over the past ten years in the rapidly maturing field of spirituality and health.[19] Koenig notes that while in the USA the National Institutes of Health (NIH) remains unfriendly to studies of spirituality and health, substantial research progress has been made:

- As of the year 2010, more than 3,300 quantitative studies on religion, spirituality, and health had been conducted.

- Research in the years since 2010, using better scientific design and more rigorous statistical analysis, has confirmed the main results of the earlier studies.

Typical of such recent studies are those by psychologist Lisa Miller and her colleagues at Columbia University using MRI (magnetic resonance

18. Wesley, *Primitive Physick*.
19. Koenig, "Religion, Spirituality, and Health."

imaging). Scans of the brains of people at high risk for depression showed significant reduction in cortical thickness in areas related to depressive symptoms. Interestingly, this cortical thinning was present only in those for whom religion/spirituality was not important or only somewhat important. In contrast, *those for whom religion/spirituality was very important had significantly thicker cortex in these areas,* which "may confer resilience to the development of depressive illness in individuals at high familiar risk for major depression."[20]

Koenig further notes these findings suggested that religious involvement may actually change the structure of the brain among those predisposed to depressive illness, making them less vulnerable to depression. Another very large-scale study conducted by the Harvard School of Public Health involving 48,984 women found that religious attendance prevented the development of depression, and depression prevented religious attendance, suggesting that effects were bidirectional in nature and adding complexity to this relationship.[21]

Noting that earlier research into suicide rates indicated that three quarters of such early research has shown that more religious individuals were less likely to commit suicide, attempt suicide, or have positive attitudes towards suicide,[22] Koenig writes,

> In 2016, investigators at the Harvard School of Public Health analyzed data from a 14-year prospective study of 89,708 women, showing that women who attended religious services at least weekly were *84 percent less likely to commit suicide* than women who never attended, with more than a fivefold reduction in suicide incidence rate from seven per 100,000 person-years to only one per 100,000 person-years.[23]

After briefly discussing the relationship of religious commitment to physical health Koenig concluded, "Thus, there is little doubt today that religious involvement is related to better mental health, better health behaviors, better physical health, and greater longevity. There are plausible mechanisms to explain why these associations exist, and it is time for these research findings to become integrated into patient care."[24]

Some of these reported associations between quality of life, spirituality, and religious commitment have become sufficiently well established

---

20. Miller et al., "Neuroanatomical Correlates," 129.
21. Li et al., "Religious Service Attendance."
22. Koenig et al., "Religion, Spirituality and Mental Health."
23. Koenig, "Religion, Spirituality, and Health," 99.
24. Koenig, "Religion, Spirituality, and Health," 100.

for brief reports of them to be included in a typical university text for psychology undergraduates. David Myers and Nathan DeWall, at the end of a comprehensive chapter on emotion, stress, and health, turn their attention briefly to the association between religiousness, spirituality, and better health. They write, "A 28-year study that followed 5286 Californians found that, after controlling for age, gender, ethnicity, and education, frequent religious attenders were 36 percent less likely to have died in any year. . . . In another 8-year controlled study of 20,000 people, this effect translated into a life expectancy of 83 years for those frequently attending religious services and 75 years for nonattenders."[25]

In the USA, the Pew survey on religion and public life[26] reported that 92 percent of Americans say that they believe in God and 71 percent say they are absolutely certain that there is a God. Of those surveyed, 58 percent say they pray daily and 39 percent say they attend religious services at least once a week. Social and behavioral scientists, noting the importance of religion in the lives of Americans, have studied associations between aspects of religiousness and what is loosely called spirituality with things like better physical and mental health. For example, a 2017 paper by Alyssa Cheadle and Christine Schetter notes that,

> A growing body of research shows that various aspects of religiousness and spirituality are associated with better physical and mental health. Health outcomes that are robustly linked to religiousness and spirituality include the "ultimate" health outcome, mortality, as well as the leading causes of death in the United States, cancer and cardiovascular disease, and also one of the most prevalent mental illnesses in the United States, that is, depression. These findings make religiousness and spirituality of particular relevance to those who study physical and mental health and the many biopsychosocial mechanisms responsible.[27]

Finally, Myers and DeWall draw attention to psychosocial resources, such as optimism, mastery, self-esteem, and gratitude—many of which are valued in spiritual and religious traditions. These resources have well-established associations with health and clearly mediate associations of health and other psychosocial factors. Although the biological processes associated with some forms of religiousness and spirituality have so far been less

25. Myers and DeWall, *Psychology*, 464.
26. Pew Research Center, "U. S. Religious Landscape Survey"; Pew Research Center, "'Nones' On the Rise."
27. Cheadle and Schetter, "Untangling the Mechanisms," 1–2.

extensively researched, it appears that these mechanisms might also help to confer better health—for example, by lowering the production of cortisol in the body and reducing inflammation. Accordingly, some have suggested that biological markers and the associated underlying physiological processes may be possible mechanisms of the link between religiousness, spirituality, and health.

It is important to note that the various mechanisms listed above do not function in isolation. They influence and interact with each other. Much research remains to be done to tease out the relative importance of these various factors, but the major point remains, namely, *an accumulation of evidence demonstrating the link between religiousness, spirituality, and health.* However, it is important to note that *these beneficial effects are what might be called "long term byproducts" of committed religious lives, not sudden one-off healings in contrived highly charged emotional settings.*

HEALTH AND THE RELIGIOUS ENGAGEMENT PARADOX

Writing in the same volume as Harold Koenig, David Myers, referring to Koenig's pioneering studies, draws attention to what he calls "a curious paradox" in the results of the some of these studies. Myers writes, "I have noted a curious paradox in my own quest to explore religion's contribution to human happiness, health, and helpfulness. Across a range of measures, I have asked: is religious engagement associated with humans living well, or with misery, ill-health, premature death, crime, divorce, teen pregnancy, and the like? . . . The answer, to my surprise, differs dramatically by whether we compare places (such as more versus less religious countries or states) or individuals."[28] Myers offers some illustrative examples:

> In Gallup world poll data, I found a striking negative correlation across 152 countries between natural religiosity and national well-being. *People in very religious countries rate their lives as more miserable.* Then I harvested US General Social Survey data and found—as have many other researchers in many other countries (though especially in more religious countries)—*a positive correlation between religiosity and happiness across individuals.*[29]

---

28. Myers, "Frontiers in Psychological Science," 92.
29. Myers, "Frontiers in Psychological Science," 92 (emphasis added).

Myers continued, "This religious engagement paradox appears in other domains as well, including life expectancy, smoking, arrest rate, and teen pregnancy. . . . Princeton economist (and 2015 Nobel Laureate) Angus Deaton and psychologist Arthur Stone (2013) have independently been struck by the same paradox. They have asked, 'Why might there be this sharp contradiction between religious people being happy and healthy, and religious places being anything but?'"[30] Myers, with disarming honesty, concluded his brief review of this paradox by saying,

> These are the sorts of findings that excite behavioral science sleuths. Surely there must be some confounding variables. With the religious engagement paradox, one such variable is income, which is lower in highly religious countries and states. Control for status factors such as income (as my colleagues and I have done), and the negative correlation between religiosity and well-being disappears and even reverses to slightly positive. Likewise, low-income states differ from high-income states in many ways, including social values and also predict voting behavior.[31]

The lesson to be learned: Be careful not to be over dogmatic on unresolved issues. There are dozens of doctoral dissertations to be done to sort out this paradox.

So far, we have reviewed possible long-term associations between religion, health, and healing. This certainly does not threaten to "shrink our faith" in a loving, caring God. Neither does it threaten to "shrink" the God we worship and serve. But what happens if we focus attention on some of the more dramatic claims of the power of God, and of faith in God, to suddenly heal the sick. Claims typical of "healing crusades" and some televangelist ministries?

Miracles of Healing: Historical perspective

As you look at the miracles reported in Scripture one salient feature is that they are not isolated events, but they are events embedded in larger patterns. It is these larger patterns that help us to understand the significance of special events. So, for example, in the first century A.D. thousands of people under the Roman rule in Palestine died a horrifying death on the cross. In one sense, the death of Christ was just another such horrifying death. But for the Christian it was not that because it is embedded in a larger pattern

---

30. Myers, "Frontiers in Psychological Science," 93.
31. Myers, "Frontiers in Psychological Science," 94.

of all the events of Christ's life: his teaching, his miracles of healing, his embodiment of love that preceded that death, and all the events that followed it. The life that was lived by the person who was crucified on Good Friday testified to a wholly different life from the normal person and the fact that this person was seen alive after the crucifixion further testified that this was no ordinary man. It is the pattern in which that event is embedded that gives it its striking and continuing significance. If one searches through Scripture and looks at the so-called miraculous events, we find this same truth that the events gain their significance from the pattern of God's continuing activity within which, in God's providence, these particular events are embedded.

It is not unusual for some presentations of the Christian gospel to be closely linked with dramatic claims about healing miracles occurring during a large-scale evangelistic crusade. The problem is that it is all too easy to make claims when sudden changes in medical conditions occur and one does not take account of the long-term outcome of events.

When we visit our physician, we quite reasonably expect the advice we are given to be derived from evidence-based medicine. This is a perfectly rational expectation given what we know of advances in medical science in recent years. However, at times, things can change suddenly. For example, thanks to the work of the recent winner of the Nobel Prize for Medicine, James Allison, it is possible, though no means certain, that the outlook for a whole group of cancer sufferers may look quite different in ten years' time from what it does now. Oncologist Patrick Hwu, who works closely with the Nobel prize winner has commented, "Fifty years from now, it would be unusual for someone to die of cancer—it would be like pneumonia. And it's our hope that we can compress that time to more like ten or fifteen years."[32] If and when that happens, a deeply thankful patient may quite understandably declare "It's a miracle." We know exactly what they mean. It is their colorful way of expressing their deep relief and gratitude. It is not a way of defining a miracle. To do that, we have to think much more carefully about how the notion of miracle has been viewed by the Christian church in past centuries. There will be lessons to be learned and errors to be avoided.

Healing Miracles in Scripture

Echoing the views of biblical scholar and theologian Beverly Gaventa summarized above, we see that a close examination of the biblical text convinces us that to label an event miraculous does not imply that there are no known natural causes for that event. Against the backdrop of the normal workings

32. Benson, "Immunotherapy."

of nature we expect regular workings of creation. Therefore, it is not surprising that perceiving such unusual events we attach particular significance to them and possibly regard them as miracles. Miracles are certainly not "invasions" by God into an otherwise natural working of creation, for this would deny that in some sense God is there already. Neither are they "merely natural," if by this we imply that God is not active in the whole stream of events moment by moment. They are, rather, special acts of God, and seen to be such—albeit acts in which the secondary means that are responsible for the event are neither more nor less given by God than any other day-to-day occurrences. Some miracles that have unusual, awe inspiring, and distinctive features are regarded as omens or portents of something to occur (for instance, Elijah on Mount Carmel). Nevertheless, their primary purpose is to fix attention upon the message that accompanies the event. Such events are open for all to see, as distinct from events which are miraculous only through the eyes of faith.

Another recurring feature of some miracles is the way in which they are seen as mighty acts of divine power. Clark Pinnock wrote, "The mighty acts of Jesus were performed by one who is himself called the power of God, and these works are entirely appropriate actions to be performed by One who was both Man and God. As some have put it, they serve for him as credentials in the midst of an unbelieving generation."[33] Finally, an all-pervading characteristic of miracles is their importance as signs, tokens, or pledges of an age yet to come; this is true in both the Old and New Testaments. Indeed, some would regard this as the key aspect of miracles. Thus, the healing miracles are seen as a temporary rolling back of the claims of death, which will one day be abolished. All three of these features of miracles are present in the healing recorded in the third chapter of the Acts of the Apostles. We are told that those who observed the miracle were filled with wonder and amazement; the apostles made it clear that this mighty act of divine power was, as they put it, "not by our own power," but by the power of Christ; and finally we may see this as a sign and pledge of an age yet to come, when all disease and sickness will be done away with.

Emotions and Emotionalism in Healing

Feeling emotions and experiencing emotional responses is part of our human nature. Every first-year student taking a course on psychology and neuroscience will be well aware of the way we are made, of our psychobiological make-up—for example, in the comprehensive review chapter in the

---

33. Quoted in Jeeves, *Scientific Enterprise*, 60.

textbook referred to earlier by Myers and DeWall.[34] They will know that our make-up embodies our capacity to respond emotionally to situations and to people. Such students will know that our somatic nervous system controls our skeletal muscles and is constantly keeping our brain updated on the current state of our skeletal muscles and carrying back instructions to them triggering actions you wish to carry out. They will also know about the autonomic nervous system, which controls our glands and the muscles of our internal organs and influences such things as glandular activity, heartbeat, and digestion. The autonomic nervous system is known to serve two important basic and distinct functions. The sympathetic nervous system arouses and expends energy. If you're alarmed or challenged by something the sympathetic nervous system will accelerate your heartbeat, raise your blood pressure, slow your digestion, raise your blood sugar, fill you with perspiration, and make you alert and ready for action. When the stressful situation subsides, your parasympathetic nervous system produces the opposite effects.

It is clear that the various components of our autonomic nervous system constantly work hard in response to changing circumstances and situations. We are all aware of raised emotional feelings when attending an overcrowded sporting event at which we have strong commitments for the success of our own team or when we are attending crowded religious events preceded by stirring music, often in a minor key, and with the message delivered with great conviction by a gifted and persuasive evangelist. It is not unusual at large-scale crusades when the Christian gospel is preached with a very strong emphasis on its power to heal, that such events, deliberately or incidentally, seek through their music, through testimonies, and through the message to generate raised emotions. Hence, the accusation of "emotionalism." Is there any justification for such a criticism?

On the one hand, it is a perfectly understandable reaction to be deeply moved when one hears for the first time that there is someone who loves you with a love beyond your imagination and who has demonstrated his love for you in action, and who invites you to enter into a personal relationship with him through faith, and to experience a new quality of life now and a new hope for the future. That is a perfectly natural emotional response, in some ways not totally dissimilar to the response when one falls in love with another human being. But it is nevertheless different from the kind of heightened emotion generated at large-scale rallies that have been widely publicized as events where miraculous healings will take place. Most would agree that that is quite different.

34. Myers and DeWall, *Psychology*.

In the middle of the twentieth century a well-known British psychiatrist, William Sargant, wrote a controversial book with the title *Battle for the Mind: A Physiology of Conversion and Brain-Washing*.[35] In it, among other things, he narrated his personal experiences when attending and investigating a service held by one of the small Christian snake-handling sects of the southern states of the USA. He writes of how, on one occasion, he found himself so moved emotionally that he felt he had to leave the meeting lest he behave in a way that on quiet reflection he would feel inappropriate. He also narrates how local teenage boys would frequently wait outside the small churches of the snake-handling sects for the young girls to come out of the worship service, knowing that they would be so emotionally aroused that they would be much more prone to the advances of the young men than they normally would.

Even though an evangelist may not deliberately be seeking to raise the emotional temperature of a meeting it may happen nonetheless as a result of the combined effects of a crowded meeting, the repeated singing of worship songs, and the earnest preaching of the skilled evangelist. The question has naturally been raised of whether responses made in such circumstances are as likely to endure as those made at other times and in more sober circumstances. What limited hearsay evidence there is does suggest that there is at times a significant falling away from commitments made at such events as compared with commitments made, for example, quietly in the privacy of one's own room at home. Where such large-scale events have been effectively advertised together with clear expectations that those attending are likely to experience or witness some remarkable healings it is likely that the general level of emotion will likewise be significantly raised. As we shall see later in this chapter, it is therefore not entirely surprising that, on careful investigation, some of the claimed "healings" at one such widely advertised crusade of a healing evangelist sadly turned out to be entirely false claims.

A CONTEMPORARY ILLUSTRATIVE CASE STUDY

Reports of miraculous healings are one of the topics at the interfaces of medicine, science, and Christian faith where differing views are held strongly, sincerely, and for fully understandable reasons. The differences arise not only from the interpretation of claimed miraculous healings, but also different interpretations about what it is claimed that Scripture teaches about such events. These differences emerged recently in the carefully thought out responses, published in the journal *Science and Christian Belief*, to a paper

35. Sargant, *Battle for the Mind*.

by Peter May, reporting his careful and very detailed investigations of a series of dramatic claims of miraculous healings at a crusade held in London by the evangelist Maurice Cerullo. The conversations between those holding differing views will and must continue and on both sides of the debate it is vital to avoid unjustified and uncritical dogmatic statements. These are issues that impact on the lives of ordinary people who personally, or whose loved ones, are facing deeply challenging medical diagnoses. Without doubt, writing about miracles of healing is an extremely emotive and sensitive topic. It is perfectly natural for people to get upset and discouraged if and when some of their personal and deeply held convictions are put under critical scrutiny. This applies particularly if their route to faith has been, in part at least, based upon what they are convinced is a healing miracle within their family, an event that became a persuasive argument leading them to faith in Christ. For this reason, it is doubly important to separate feelings from facts in the ensuing discussion.

May, a medical general practitioner in the UK with forty years of clinical experience behind him, wrote about miracles in medicine.[36] Since the focus of this present book has been on recognizing and evaluating the variety of "gods" on offer today and since some of these "gods" are promoted and validated by, at times, seemingly extreme claims made by television evangelists, the studies by Peter May are directly relevant to our topic. There is a section of Peter May's paper based on the work of one such TV healer, Maurice Cerullo. In 1992, Maurice Cerullo came to conduct an evangelistic campaign in London. His arrival was preceded by posters all over London that implied that at some of the events the blind would see, the deaf would hear, and the lame would walk. In 1992, Dr. May was invited to take part in an ITV News interview with Maurice Cerullo. During the interview, Peter May was able to ask Maurice Cerullo to produce the best three cases from the week that demonstrated acts of divine healing and to put them forward for closer public scrutiny. Eventually Maurice Cerullo offered seven cases, which were then examined by a popular BBC program, *The Heart of the Matter*, hosted by Joan Bakewell. For this discussion Dr. May acted as medical adviser. In brief, what did they find?

- A woman, supposedly healed of low back pain, returned to her orthopedic surgeon who demonstrated that there was no change in her x-rays but that her depression had lifted and she was more mobile.
- A woman anxious that she had a recurrence of a melanoma, actually had a small inflamed cyst that burst and healed itself.

36. May, "Miracles in Medicine."

- A small child had his spectacles taken from him because his parents were told he had been healed. His sight was retested, and the child had his spectacles returned to him.
- A twenty-six-year-old woman had knee pain; her surgeon reassured her there was nothing significantly wrong and her pain settled with physiotherapy.
- A woman believed she was healed of a fibroid, which she had never actually had.

More distressing was a case from the same campaign—but not on the list offered by Cerullo—of a four-year-old girl with a metastatic neuroblastoma. At the evangelistic rally she had been made to run up and down the stage in tears to demonstrate that she was healed. She died of her disease two months later. Another woman, a twenty-five-year-old, "healed" by Cerullo of her epilepsy, stopped her epilepsy medication. She had a fit in the bath six days later and drowned. The coroner stated *"It is a tragedy she went to this meeting and thought she had been cured of everything. Sadly, it led to her death."*

Peter May also reviewed other public investigations of healings, including the miracles of Lourdes and the Vatican miracles. He reminds his readers that the apostle Paul had advised that we should test everything (1 Thess 5:21) and warned of signs and wonders, which cause people to believe what is false (2 Thess 2:9–12). He later adds,

> In our search for truth, we need to read the Book of Nature as well as the Book of Scripture to learn what God is actually doing in the world and how he chooses to fulfil his purposes. If we reduce Christ's miracles to the sort of unverified, anecdotal, subjective vagaries of Alternative Therapy, we will degrade Christ and mislead his people. . . . We must help Christians to have a positive view of the importance of the scientific method in our quest for truth and to see science as a means God has given us to grow in our understanding of reality and our exercise of dominion over the earth, not least in matters of health.[37]

May's references to "reducing Christ's miracles" and to "degrading Christ" further illustrate the "shrunken gods" identified in this present book.

Differing views arise about how to interpret claims of miraculous healings and what Scripture teaches about such events. In conversations between those holding differing views, it is vital to avoid unjustified dogmatic statements. These are sensitive issues that affect the lives of ordinary people

---

37. May, "Miracles in Medicine," 134.

who are facing deeply challenging medical diagnoses, either for themselves or for their loved ones. Such conversations between those holding differing views will continue, and on both sides of the debate it is vital to avoid unjustified and uncritical dogmatic statements. These are sensitive issues which impact on the lives of ordinary people who either personally, or through loved ones, are facing deeply challenging medical diagnoses.

Noting that there is a lack of an agreed definition of a miracle, Peter May focuses on the distinguishing features of Christ's healing miracles. He notes that "Cardinal Lambertini, who went on to become Pope Benedict the 14th, listed them as instantaneous, complete cures of incurable diseases, which would not remit spontaneously and where no other treatment was given. . . . These cures included congenital blindness, a wasted upper limb, a fixed kyphosis of the spine, death of four days duration and paralysis. The nature of the paralysis is not always clear, but in John 5, we learn of a man who had been paralyzed for thirty-eight years."[38] May continues, "What is central to my argument here is that it is events such as these that shape the meaning of the words 'miraculous healing' today. When people speak of miracles, they invariably mean supernatural, Christ-like miracles. To use the word 'miracle' for purely natural events, however wonderful and surprising they may be, devalues the word and confuses its meaning."[39]

There have been systematic attempts to gain a better understanding of Christian healing. Peter May gives the example of a consultation set up in 1991 by Sir John Houghton to organize meetings annually for four years gathering over thirty doctors, healers, bishops, pastors, and theologians who were invited to present and discuss the best cases they could gather from their wide engagement in Christian ministry. Their report claimed doctors and theologians had reached a unique consensus. *They were unable to put forward any case of miraculous healing.*[40]

The views of Paul Marston, who has qualifications in philosophy of science and theology, and of Meric Srokosz, an oceanographer at the National Oceanography Centre in Southampton in the UK, warrant careful thought and the reader is directed to their contributions.[41] However, in my judgment they do not undermine the main thrust of the important contribution made by Peter May with his open evidence-based approach to this controversial topic. In passing, it is noteworthy that May draws attention to

---

38. May, "Response to Marston and Srokosz," 70.
39. May, "Response to Marston and Srokosz," 71.
40. May, "Response to Marston and Srokosz," 72; see also Lucas, *Christian Healing*.
41. Marston and Srokosz, "Response to 'Miracles in Medicine'"; Srokosz, "Response to Peter May."

a recent book by Susan O'Sullivan entitled *It's All in Your Head*,[42] which won the 2016 Welcome Trust Book Prize. May notes that,

> In it, this neurologist vividly describes the medical profession's failure to come to grips with psychosomatic illnesses. I warmly commend it to doctors, healers, pastors and counsellors. It throws enormous light on this common condition [i.e., epilepsy]. This brings to mind the well documented evidence of so-called "top-down" effects referred to in earlier chapters of this book.[43]

Healing and Petitionary Prayer

Peter May's comment about helping "Christians to have a positive view of the importance of the scientific method in our quest for truth," readily brings to mind a series of reports in the last two decades of attempts, using the scientific method, to evaluate the effects of petitionary prayer for those who are sick. David Myers summarized these studies in his 2008 book *A Friendly Letter to Sceptics and Atheists*. Myers identified seven relevant studies published between 1988 and 2006 that showed a consistent pattern—*there was no evidence for any measurable effect of intercessory prayer*. The largest and most recent of these studies was a 2006 study—supported by a grant of $1.4 million from the Templeton Foundation—that examined the effects of prayer on the recovery of 1,800 consenting coronary bypass patients. The patients had been assigned to one of three groups: one that knew it was being prayed for by volunteer intercessors, one that did not know whether it was being prayed for (but was), and a third group did not know whether it was being prayed for (and wasn't). Myers writes "*the simple result: intercessory prayer per se had no effect on recovery.*"[44]

Myers is a committed and actively practicing Christian who prays daily. It is helpful therefore to reflect further on some of his wise and biblically based comments on the efficacy of prayer. He writes, "As Christians recalled during the 1872 British prayer tests controversy, Jesus declared in response to one of his temptations that we ought not to put 'God to the test.'"[45] Reflecting on a proposal to test prayers for randomly selected preterm babies, Keith Stuart Thomson questioned "whether all such experiments come

---

42. O'Sullivan, *All in Your Head*.
43. May, "Response to Marston and Srokosz," 77.
44. Myers, *Friendly Letter*, 214.
45. Myers, *Friendly Letter*, 215.

close to blasphemy. If the health outcomes of the prayed for subjects turn out to be significantly better than for the others, the experiment will have set up a situation in which God has, as it were, been made to show his (or her) hand."[46] When commenting on efforts to prove the effectiveness of prayer, C. S. Lewis argued, "The impossibility of empirical proof is a spiritual necessity. A man who knew empirically that an event had been caused by his prayer would feel like a magician."[47] Myers asks, "If a prayer experiment were to show that the number of people praying or the total number of prayers matter—that distant strangers' prayers boost recovery chances—might rich people not want, in hopes of gaining God's attention, to pay others who will pray for them?"[48] All of this alerts us to the need always to be vigilant and to refute the claims of those whose "God is so small" that they claim that they can manipulate him in some way or another. That is not the God of Scripture where we are confronted with the God, who, as we have said many times, "upholds all things at all times by the word of his power" (Heb 1:3 KJV).

It is relevant here and worth recording the considered views of a dedicated Christian surgeon renowned worldwide for his work on reconstructive surgery on patients suffering from leprosy based on half a century of work. Paul Brand co-authored an article with Philip Yancey on pain and healing published in the *Christianity Today Leadership Journal*. In this article Brand remarked,

> From my experience as a physician I must truthfully admit that, among the thousands of patients I have treated, I have never observed an unequivocal instance of intervention in the physical realm. Many were prayed for, many found healing, but not in ways that counteracted the laws governing anatomy. No case I have treated personally would meet the rigorous criteria for a supernatural miracle.[49]

Healing Miracles and Shrunken "Gods-of-the-Gaps"

It is not uncommon for preachers, when promoting their particular "gods on offer" in the religious marketplace, to appeal to reports of present-day healing miracles to substantiate the case for the God they are offering. Talk

---

46. Thompson, "Revival of Experiments," 534.
47. Lewis, *Miracles*, 216.
48. Myers, "Social Psychology and Faith," 215.
49. Brand and Yancey, "Putting Pain to Work," 123.

of "God intervening" is frequent, but is there biblical warrant for such language? I would argue that such "gods on offer" are, by their very nature, "diminished gods" and "gods-of-the-gaps," and thus we need to scrutinize them carefully. Any discussion of miracles must be set in the wider context of the question of whether it is reasonable for people living in the twenty-first century to believe both in the lawfulness of the natural order and in miracles. Not infrequently such questions are often formulated by asking whether nature "leaves room" for God to "intervene" in the natural order; whether God "uses" natural laws in order to bring about his creative purposes. The reader will recognize ways in which these questions have, in the past, been solemnly asked and firmly answered one way or the other.

Denis Alexander, formerly Director of the Faraday Centre on Science and Religion at Cambridge University and with years of experience as an active research scientist, has written most helpfully on how we can best understand God's providential upholding of the universe he created. Alexander wrote,

> A picture emerges of God as creator, the source and ground of all that exists. Everything that exists apart from God only exists because God brought it into existence. So God is the ground of all existence, and in this view "existence" refers to anything that exists, be they material or immaterial—the laws of nature, quantum vacuums, Higgs bosons, trees, rabbits, mathematical principles, and the elements of the periodic table. If it exists and is not God, then it must by definition be part of the created order within this theistic matrix.[50]

Given the undoubted widespread influence of social media of many kinds we may continue to expect some of these media outlets to continue to be used to promote presentations of the Christian faith, explicitly or implicitly, intended to imply, if not to promise explicitly, significant benefits in terms of health and healing. A balanced view, it has been suggested, is, on the one hand, to recognize that throughout the history of the Christian church there have been sustained attempts to encourage Christians to be at the forefront of developments in healthcare and medicine, seen as part of Christ's calling, while, on the other hand, being careful to avoid excessive claims of dramatic healings that on close scrutiny turn out to be nothing of the kind. The latter kind not only dishonor Christ but also may build walls of resentment against the presentation of the gospel.

---

50. Alexander, "Creation, Providence, and Evolution," 265.

Faith Healing, Embodied and Embedded: A Timely Reminder of the Genuine Article

Each week, the widely read international journal *The Economist* includes one obituary. Normally, this would be of someone such as a national leader, a Nobel Laureate, or some other widely known and internationally esteemed person. The April 8, 2020 edition of *The Economist* included an obituary that documented the remarkable life of an obstetrician named Catharine Hamlin who had died at the age of ninety-six. Remarkably, she was still operating in Ethiopia when she was ninety-two. Catherine, having grown up in a wealthy Sydney family in Australia, went with her husband Reg from New Zealand to Ethiopia in response to an ad in the medical journal the *Lancet*, which called for a gynecologist to set up a midwifery school for nurses in Ethiopia. After arriving, she was faced daily with very young women who, after protracted labor and delivery, were often left so badly injured that the vagina was ruptured, the bladder shredded, and the rectum torn. Catherine Hamlin and her husband settled into a mud brick house in the hospital grounds where she worked. Late into the night they studied intensively all they could find out about the history of "obstetric fistula," as these injuries were known. By the 1970s Catherine had treated more than 25,000 fistula cases. She came to the notice of the high-profile American Oprah Winfrey, who donated $450,000 to cover one year of operating expenses for the hospital. In the midst of all this, she also built the midwifery school that the original advertisement in the *Lancet* had requested. To quote from *The Economist*,

> She did all this, she told Oprah, because she believed that was what God wanted her to do. She was not a missionary doctor, but a doctor who was a Christian. She loved the spirituality of the Ethiopians and was not rigid about where she herself worshipped, moving from church to church wherever she liked the message or the minister. She thought of herself as an ordinary woman. Ethiopians called her *Emaye*. Amharic for mother. They thought of her as a "saint." Through Catherine Hamlin's medical skill and her faith, thousands were healed. This surely is a model for genuine "faith healing."[51]

This was not the work of the multimillionaire evangelist with his private jet flying in with his vast team to conduct a week of healing services, rather, in contrast, it was decade after decade of a Christian physician quietly working out her faith in the healing of thousands. That surely is where

---

51. Economist, "Healing Hands."

the genuine meaning of faith healing should be focused. Catherine Hamlin illustrates how the fruits of real Christian faith are embodied in a life of dedicated service embedded in a needy community. Through her faith and her professional skills, she brought lasting healing to thousands—without massed crowds and exhibitionism.

A Delicate Balance

A pervasive theme in the present chapter, as in previous ones, has been the need for a full recognition of God's moment-by-moment divine upholding of his creation, including ourselves. That being said, if that is the only emphasis, there remains a serious danger of forgetting the equal and important relevance of another pervasive doctrine in Scripture taught and embodied in the life of Christ himself, namely, of *divine emptying*. Both these fundamental truths must be kept in delicate balance. Above all we need to remember how in his incarnation, in his death, and in his crucifixion, Christ preeminently emptied himself to accomplish our full and complete salvation.

11

The Multifaceted Nature of Faith
The Evidence from Scripture

> Think not the faith by which the just shall live
> Is a dead creed, a map correct of heaven.
> Far less a feeling fond and fugitive,
> A thoughtless gift, withdrawn as soon as given.
> It is an affirmation and an act
> That bids eternal truth be present fact.[1]

A CHRISTIAN'S FAITH IS not something to be carefully insulated from the rough and tumble of life and brought out once a week for use in Christian worship. A Christian's faith shows itself in diverse attitudes, not only to Scripture, but also to every new discovery about the remarkable world in which we live, of which we are a part, and that we are privileged and equipped to study and care for. But what do we mean by faith? The evidence from Hebrew-Christian Scriptures and from church history bears eloquent and clear testimony to the richness and multifaceted nature of real biblical faith. If we pass the powerful searchlight beam of faith through the prism of the centuries and the lives of people of faith in every generation, we see that it displays itself in different ways at different times. At times faith involves primarily belief, at times struggling with doubt, at times thankfulness for

---

1. Coleridge, "The Just Shall Live by Faith," 341.

unsought encouraging experiences, at times a call to action, at times facing trials and a renewed call to discipleship.

This theme of faith's richness and multifaceted nature is diminished and debased *whenever faith, in all its wholeness and richness, is shrunk to one small aspect of it.* Such shrinking can happen if faith is presented primarily or exclusively as only one component, such as experience or belief or action. The lives of men and women of faith recorded in Scripture and documented throughout church history make it abundantly clear that real faith includes *all* of these in varied proportions and at different times.

Given the frequency with which we readily use the word "faith" in our religious discourse, it comes as a great surprise to many to discover that, in the entire Old Testament, the word "faith" occurs only twice in the AV and eighteen times in the RSV. Of these eighteen, twelve refer to "breaking faith" or "acting in good faith," while the other six speak rather about "trust." However, while the word "faith" is rare in the Old Testament, the essential ideas surrounding the word are frequent and usually expressed by verbs such as "believe" or "trust" or "hope." Faith is seen preeminently embodied in the life of Abraham, whose whole life radiates trustfulness and a deep faith. In Genesis we read "Abram believed the LORD, and he credited it to him as righteousness" (Gen 15:6 NIV). This same text is taken up by New Testament writers, where the fundamental truth that it expresses is more fully developed. In contrast to the Old Testament usage, in the New Testament the word "faith" is extremely prominent. The Greek noun *pistis* and the verb *pisteuo* both occur more than 240 times while the adjective *pistos* occurs sixty-seven times. In the Synoptic Gospels, faith is often linked with healing episodes, for example, in Matthew 9:22 where we read "Your faith has made you well." In the Fourth Gospel, faith is prominent and is referred to ninety-eight times as the verb *pisteuo*. Given the richness of meaning in the ways the idea of faith is used in Scripture, it is puzzling that, in the discourse of high-profile television preachers, "faith" has such a monochromatic character. How often today, under the influence of the media, do we hear faith presented solely either as adopting a particular form of "behavior" or getting a distinctive "experience" or taking a prescribed "action." We need to pause and ask the question, *is our God too small, not only because our idea of God has shrunk, but also because our understanding of faith has shrunk as well?* Given the importance of that question, in this chapter, we look at the multi-faceted nature of faith. Could it be that, in part at least, our seemingly over-readiness to worship "shrunken gods" is because we have accepted shrunken and unbiblical ideas of what is meant by faith? Faith is not independent of belief, although never identical with it. *Faith in all its fullness involves experience, belief, and action.* In all faith there is implicit or explicit belief. It seems proper therefore to attempt to understand something of the nature of belief and then to examine its peculiar characteristics when associated with the faith state in the Christian life and ask how belief is expressed in action.

One thing is clear: our understanding of our individual differences is a complex problem. That alone should alert us to be suspicious of any simplistic presentations of the Christian gospel, and the life of faith, suggesting that a "one size fits all" approach is acceptable. *Any presentation that in effect "shrinks faith" in all its richness and complexity to a simple formula that says "I have now discovered the way to become and be a Christian, so follow me and my method" should be subjected to the very closest scrutiny.* Some of the brief cameos given in the next chapter of the lives of notable Christians of the past well illustrate this point of the diversity of paths to faith and of ways of living the life of faith. First, however, we must try to get as clear an idea as possible of the varied meanings given historically to the key words "faith" and "belief."

FAITH AND BELIEF

For the sake of clarity in understanding what follows, it may help to remember the various meanings that the words faith and belief have carried in the past. The word "faith" in relation to religion is commonly used in two distinct, though related, senses that are often designated by the Latin words *fides* and *fiducia*. *Fiducia* denotes the worshipper's attitude of practical trust in God. However, this *fiducia* presupposes the occurrence of faith in a different and cognitive sense, namely, *fides*. In turn, some have suggested that *fides* may itself be divided into the sense of "knowing God" and the sense of "believing that there is a God."[2] Following on the work of philosophers such as John Hick, I want to suggest that faith as a whole involves belief of three kinds: belief in the sense of primitive credulity, which I shall call belief-1; belief in the sense of intellectual assent to propositions about God, which I shall call belief-2; and belief as referring to the psychological processes involved in the act of believing, which I shall call belief-3. When I say that belief-3 is tied to the psychological sense of believing, I do not, of course, mean that it is not possible also to consider belief-1 and belief-2 psychologically. I make this distinction because I believe that belief-3 is much more capable of psychological analysis than it is of epistemological analysis. I also believe that the number of variables entering into a psychological consideration of belief-3 is much greater than in the cases of either belief-1 or

---

2. Hick, *Faith and Knowledge*.

belief-2. My beliefs-1, -2, and -3 have an approximate correspondence with "credulity," "credence," and "conviction"—yet I do not wish to identify them with these three terms because of their association with other ideas and theories.

Historically, we find that religious faith has been viewed in several ways. It has been used to describe the primitive credulity of a child or of a savage. It has been used to describe intellectual assent to a proposition. At times, it has been used to describe the state of "believing" in the sense of, in some way, going beyond the immediate evidence. Any analysis of this kind inevitably gives the impression that there are clear-cut differences between different kinds of belief. In practice this is not so. No genuine belief is altogether devoid of feeling and nearly every belief in adult life is in some degree intellectual. The first two kinds of belief, primitive credulity and intellectual assent, are often regarded as constituting the mental attitude we adopt when acknowledging the reality of a given object or a proposition. Such assent frequently is characterized by an accompanying attitude of passivity, whereas the third kind of belief, in the sense of believing and venturing beyond the evidence, is accompanied by an attitude of activity, of affirmation. The first type of belief is regarded as genetically the primary attitude and all of the nonbelieving attitudes depend for their possibility upon its presence. Thus, when the first faint impulse of consciousness awakens within the infant, whatever presents itself to her mind is "real." As yet there is no possible distinction between the real and the "not real" and hence the object is accepted as a matter of course and bears with it the same sort of reality feeling that in later years is restricted to a portion only of one's mental objects. There is, as yet, no awareness of any of the nonbelieving attitudes, although, since belief is possible, so are they also. This feeling of reality in the infant is not only with respect to objects but also to assertions.

FAITH AND DOUBT

Recall the student quoted in the Preface who wrote, "I am a Christian having trouble believing in . . . ." Of course, "I have trouble believing in" something is another way of saying "I have doubts about" that something. So, we must take seriously, and do our utmost to respond to, the appeals for help of any who, for whatever reason, begin to doubt their faith. For some, only after doubt has come can belief, in the sense of intellectual assent, arise. To entertain reasons for believing in the existence of something presupposes the possibility of its non-existence. The strength of intellectual conviction varies considerably between different individuals and different beliefs. Thus while the abstract concept of the reasoned assertion is by itself comparatively poor in so-called reality feeling, it may be so interconnected and entwined with our total "real" world that a refusal to consent to it would work havoc among all our accepted realities, turn our habits of thought upside down, and leave us seemingly not a foot of solid ground on which to stand. At times a conceptual belief may become so firmly entrenched that it may be harder to dislodge than one that is backed by immediate sensory experience. This sort of thing is, reportedly, familiar to the psychoanalyst. For example, in the course of psychoanalysis, it is often reported that there is usually a period when the patient becomes fixated on the analyst and in the subject's eyes the analyst is clothed with an aura of perfection. In one such case the analyst was injured between two sessions and received a black eye. The next time the patient came into the consulting room, he failed to perceive the injury to the analyst. Thus, his overall attitude towards the analyst was such that it dislodged the evidence from his immediate sensory experience. Of the two kinds of belief thus far discussed, the first does not involve in any sense a "leap" beyond the evidence available, and the second, so long as it is dealing with logical propositions clearly defined or with scientific data, does not involve the type of mental activity that is often regarded most characteristic of that involved in religious belief. This is because although a leap may be required, there remains the possibility of closing the gap. In the case of religious belief, considered psychologically as "believing," evidence may come to help to fill the gap from the pragmatic results of "the life of faith" or from the reinterpretation of the evidence thus far available. It is often argued that it is this type of belief that is most characteristic of religious faith.

If the God of religion were a God whose existence had to be proved, then the ordinary religious person who has never heard of the so-called proofs of the existence of God will be convicted of irrationality. Belief will then become a matter of opinion and one thing that religious faith certainly is not is a kind of opinion. In the face of adverse evidence, a woman sticks to her faith but abandons an opinion. Faith is prior to understanding in that the leap must have taken place before the intervening ground can be surveyed from the viewpoint which faith alone can provide. We are indeed told to look upon faith as an interim attitude and that the time will come when faith will no longer be needed. When this happens, the gap will be seen completely filled. We shall then know even as we are known.

FAITH AND TRUST

Faith, then, is not merely a form of belief. Faith involves belief but it is something more than belief. On the other hand, faith is not simply another form of knowledge in the generally accepted usage and meaning of the word "knowledge." Faith is not simply "accepting the theistic hypothesis." It is that, but it is something much more. The ever-present danger is to say that faith is this or that and *nothing but* this or that. This is a danger that besets any attempt at analysis of the kind offered here. It is therefore important to remember that while faith does involve belief, it is something *more than* belief. While faith does involve hypothesis acceptance, it is something *more than* that. And while faith does contain elements of direct and immediate experience, it is something *more than* that. If belief and hypothesis acceptance alone are present, then there is no religious faith. *Religious faith involves the trust (fiducia) or confidence in the God whose existence is thus assented to intellectually (fides).* To move from intellectual assent to religious faith is not an automatic process. Religious faith is a gift. In the act of giving it draws out of the receiver the trust and confidence that transforms his intellectual assent into religious faith. C. S. Lewis, writing around the time that Phillips published his 1952 book, explained,

> By faith we believe always what we hope hereafter to see always and perfectly and have already seen imperfectly and by flashes. In relation to its philosophical premises a Christian's faith is of course excessive: in relation to what is sometimes shown him, it is perhaps as often defective. My faith even in an earthly friend goes beyond all that can be demonstrably proved; yet in another sense I may often trust him less than he deserves.[3]

While the content of beliefs certainly matter, nevertheless obsessive preoccupation with abstract definitions can be soul- and faith-destroying. In the words of N. T. Wright,

> This is why too for every theologian who puzzles that over abstract definitions of "atonement," there are thousands who will say, with Paul, "The Son of God loved me and gave himself for me"—and you get on with the job of radiating that same love out into the world.[4]

---

3. Lewis, *Mere Christianity*, 50–51.
4. Wright, *Day the Revolution Began*, 367.

Wright continues, "It is after all generous love, Jesus-shaped love, that draws people into the Christian family in the first place, not the complex crossword puzzles of subtle theologians."[5]

FAITH AND ACTION

"The basic function of human action," wrote Sir Frederic Bartlett, "is that it attempts to cope with challenges that are issued from the world outside the performer, these being such that if they are not answered, there will be great discomfort and probably speedy extinction."[6] Faith, as it is manifested in action, seeks not only to cope with outward challenges of circumstance but also within with the challenges of conscience. In the face of uncertainty, a natural human reaction is to seek certainty, in the face of insecurity to seek security, in the midst of chaos to look for and strive after order. Basically, humanity is seeking to complete the incomplete. When the mind is trying to evaluate evidence, collected consciously or unconsciously through our natural sensory and perceptual equipment, it is this sense of incompleteness that links religious experience with action and with the operation of the mind.

Religious faith begins with action but in common with other attitudes which involve and entail beliefs, religious faith seeks justification in results, results that indeed are both correlative with and also subsequent to the initial leap of faith. If this appeal to results in action is rejected, then there remain two alternatives for the justification of the beliefs associated with the attitude that results from religious faith. Either, one must fall back upon a purely intuitive position, saying faith's justification is the same thing as its acceptance or faith must rest on the internal consistency within the belief system of that faith. The writer to the Epistle to the Hebrews lists the way in which challenge after challenge was met "by faith." The degree of religious faith may range from high to low, but in every case, however low the degree of faith may be, it is nevertheless capable of directing an enormous output of energy. In one sense, it was in virtue of the energy generated by their faith that the heroes of the eleventh chapter of the Epistle to the Hebrews fulfilled their tasks. "By faith" Noah moved into action, albeit even so, it was because he was first "moved by fear" (Heb 11:7). "By faith" Moses acted in a manner contrary to his own immediate well-being (Heb 11:24). "By faith" is a phrase that on the grounds described in earlier paragraphs might be replaced by the phrase "by going beyond the evidence available and by trusting God"

---

5. Wright, *Day the Revolution Began*, 374.
6. Bartlett, *Religion as Experience, Belief, Action*, 29.

and such a substitution fits very well with the sense of Hebrews 11, for example, instead of "By faith Abraham, when he was tried, offered up Isaac: and he that had received the promises offered up his only begotten son," we could write, "By going beyond the evidence currently available to him and by trusting God Abraham, when he was tried, offered up Isaac: and he that had received the promises offered up his only begotten son."

In his invited chapter to our 2018 book *Psychological Science and Christian Faith,* social psychologist David Myers spells out the evidence for what he labels as "Deep Truths" regarding the relation of faith and action. He writes,

> The two conclusions—that attitudes influence behavior and that attitudes follow behavior—are both true. But like the Christian assumptions that faith feeds action, and that actions feed faith, they are half-truths. In both realms, the deeper truth—and the authentic convergence of social psychology and faith—lies in the reciprocal influence of the attitudes of the heart and the actions of the person. In *The Cost of Discipleship*, Dietrich Bonhoeffer captured this dialectic: *"Only he who believes is obedient, and only he who is obedient believes."*[7]

Most people acknowledge that their *inner attitudes influence their external behavior.* Thus, Myers notes that we need to underline the "Complementary Truth" that our *external behavior influences our inner attitudes* (actions feed faith). He writes,

> We not only stand up for what we believe, we believe in what we have stood up for. *Our attitudes follow our behavior.* Such self-persuasion enables religious believers, political advocates, and even future terrorists to believe more strongly in that for which they have witnessed or suffered. . . . To get people to agree to something big, start small and build. A trivial act makes the next act easier. Succumb to a temptation and you will find the next temptation harder to resist. In dozens of experiments, researchers have coaxed people into acting against their attitudes or violating their moral standards, with the same result: Doing becomes believing. After giving in to a request to harm an innocent victim—by making nasty comments or delivering presumed electric shocks—people begin to disparage their victim. After speaking or writing on behalf of a position they have qualms about, they begin to believe their own words. . . . But this psychological truth also has its counterpart in the language

---

7. Myers, "Social Psychology and Faith," 220 (emphasis in original).

of faith, for faith *is also a consequence of action*. Throughout the Bible, faith is nurtured by obedient action. The Hebrew word for "know" is typically an action verb. To know love, for example, we must not only know about love, we must act lovingly. "Those who do what is true come to the light," said Jesus (John 3:21 NRSV).[8]

Today, we may turn to any collection of the narratives of the experiences of Christian men and women and find that testimony after testimony bears witness of the things that have been done "by faith." The kinds of events most likely to be said to have been wrought "by faith" are those which in terms of expectancy and/or probability were not the most likely to have occurred. This leads on to the unwarranted assumption that in many cases the normal life of the individual is not lived "by faith" but only at special times and in special circumstances.

Faith then manifests itself in action. Such action may be individual or it may be social. There are many small instances in the life of the individual believer that she believes to have been wrought "by faith." Each individual has her own unique experience of God, this she cannot ever fully communicate to her fellow believers. "I teach," said Thomas à Kempis, "without noise of words or clash of opinions, without ambition for honor or confusion of argument."[9] However, in the process of seeking to in some way share these experiences, the person of faith frequently, though not always, seeks the company, friendship, and fellowship of like-minded individuals. The actions that result from such a community of action are as much the actions associated with, resulting from, and relating to the faith attitude, as are the individual actions of the believer. A very deep insight into the nature of any particular faith may be derived from the stories or parables current in the community who profess that faith. Similarly, the actions of such a community can tell us much about the faith of that particular community. The life of Christians such as Dietrich Bonhoeffer is one of many outstanding examples of faith in action. For Bonhoeffer, faith was first and foremost expressed and embodied in discipleship. As James Bryan Smith reminds us, "The early Christians did not refer to their religion as 'Christianity.' In fact, they didn't refer to themselves as 'Christians.' They thought of themselves as 'disciples.' The word *disciple* appears 269 times in the New Testament; the word *Christian* appears only three times—and each time it is used to describe a disciple."[10]

8. Myers, "Social Psychology and Faith," 219 (emphasis in original).
9. Thomas, *Imitation of Christ*, 3.43.
10. Smith, *Magnificent Story*, 147.

Decades of research by social psychologists have established beyond reasonable doubt that our inner attitudes influence our external behavior. Later research in social psychology demonstrated that the opposite is also true: our actions influence our attitudes. These psychological truths have their counterpart in the language of faith, because faith is also a consequence of action. Throughout the Bible faith is nurtured by obedient action. The Hebrew word for "know" is typically an action verb. To know love, for example, we must not only know about love, we must act lovingly. "Those who do what is true come to the light," said Jesus (John 3:21 NRSV). Down the centuries, leading theologians have underlined how faith grows as people act on what little faith they have. John Calvin wrote "Faith is born of obedience."[11] Søren Kierkegaard wrote, "The proof of Christianity really consists in 'following.'"[12] Karl Barth wrote, "Only the doer of the word is its real hearer."[13] To attain faith, argued Pascal, "follow the way by which (the committed) began: by acting as if they believed, taking the holy water, having masses said et cetera. Even this will naturally make you believe."[14] C. S. Lewis agreed with these claims when he wrote, "No conviction, religious or irreligious, will, of itself, end once and for all [these doubts] in the soul. Only the practice of Faith resulting in the habit of Faith will gradually do that."[15]

Not only are actions a manifestation and a justification of religious faith, they are more than that. Faith, so to speak, turns round and fits all of these actions into a new frame of reference. The person of faith looks beyond the immediate evidence of his physical and sociological environment and seeks to view his actions past, present, and future in the light of what he believes to be the will of the God whom he worships and serves. Theologian H. H. Farmer, writing at the same time as Bartlett, wrote, "The man of faith does not demand that God should reveal himself in all situations but sufficiently for all situations."[16] Writing in similar vein but fifty years earlier, W. R. Inge suggested that faith not only provides a new frame of reference for all experience but also that it rearranges all experience. Thus, he wrote,

> Faith rearranges all experience, which is presented to us at first so chaotically, but it leaves nothing out. Every contradiction must be fairly met and overcome. If we edge round it, if we

11. Calvin, *Institutes*, 1.6.2.
12. Kierkegaard, *For Self-examination*, 88.
13. Barth, *Church Dogmatics*, 1.2.792.
14. Pascal, *Pensées*, 233.
15. Lewis, *Christian Reflections*, 61.
16. Farmer, *World and God*, 90.

ignore it or shirk it in any way, we shall enter into life halt and maimed, if we enter at all. Even the claims of piety must give way to the love of truth. To put the needs of the heart before truth is really an act of treason against faith.[17]

FAITH AND DISCIPLESHIP

Throughout the Gospel passages, the outworking of faith is inextricably interwoven with discipleship. Jesus first words to his disciples were not "Come *experience* me." Instead, they were *"Follow* me" (Matt 4:19), with all that entails in living a particular way of life—a life of discipleship. All four Gospels record how our Lord selected and called individuals to follow him and they are referred to throughout as disciples. Christ interrogated his disciples from time to time about what they believed, about their faith. Their faith he said would be manifest very soon in sacrifice; for some, sacrifice even to death. Throughout the Acts of the Apostles and the Epistles the writers repeatedly underline the way that faith and discipleship are inseparable, that faith and discipleship will involve suffering and even death, and that first and foremost faith and discipleship are focused not on an the attitude of "what is in this for me?" but rather, "how may I fulfil my calling and serve my Lord faithfully?"

For example, the apostle Paul, writing to the Christians at Philippi, urged, "Only let your manner of life be worthy of the gospel of Christ" (Phil 1:27 ESV). The book of Hebrews further contextualized and exemplified faith in a list of Old Testament characters who in their lives exemplified the life of faith. Here again the emphasis is on service and sacrifice not fulfilment of needs and felt wants. So once again we discover that the first followers of Christ, like earlier faithful leaders of Israel, repeatedly had to face up to the temptation to shrink discipleship and true faith. Being a disciple would not be an opportunity to ask for a guarantee of a place of privilege with Christ, as some of the disciples mistakenly thought, rather it was a willingness to commit to Christ and follow him on the path of suffering and sacrifice. It was also evident that it was all too easy to shrink discipleship to party allegiance so that already in the early church there were those, we are told, who were saying "I am of Apollos, I am of Paul . . . ." Such a partisan approach to discipleship is sadly all too evident today and whenever it appears it shrinks true faith.

17. Inge, *Faith and Its Psychology*, 537.

AVOIDING SHRUNKEN FAITH

Philip Yancey, that acute observer and analyst of church life in America, writes, "The United States strikes me as somewhere between the extremes, neither honeymoon nor post-Christian. Nearly half of us [Americans] attend church, and Christians have an active presence on university campuses and in every major profession. Even so, churches and parachurch agencies may operate more like industries than living organisms."[18] Yancey suggests that it may well be the case that the USA will follow the path of Europe and witness the church gradually losing influence and drifting to the margins. He asks about reversing the trend and writes,

> As a child in Sunday school I used to sing this song:
> "One door and only one
> And yet its sides are two.
> I'm on the inside
> On which side are you?"
>
> The song captured our church's identity. . . . A long list of rules and beliefs set us apart from those outside the door. It never occurred to me that my faith had something to contribute to the "outsiders." My main obligation was to get them to join us on the correct side of the door. Now, however, *I see that the kingdom of God largely exists for the sake of outsiders, as a tangible expression of God's love for all.*[19]

He suggests, "Instead of fighting a rearguard action against secular opponents, we can communicate our good-news message by living it out among the uncommitted."[20] He discusses three possible ways of doing this, as pilgrim, activist, and artist. He notes further, "Our faith does, after all, have many benefits to offer the world."[21]

This all too brief survey of various attempts at analyzing and describing the nature and complexity of true faith has hopefully shown that we need to be constantly alert to presentations of faith and belief that shrink the all-encompassing quality of true faith to something that would have been unrecognizable to the great heroes of the faith of past centuries. If and whenever faith is described simply as belief, or having a particular fleeting experience, or being a member of a particular denomination, it becomes all too easily linked, in effect, with a presentation of the gospel characterized by

---

18. Yancey, *Vanishing Grace*, 141–42.
19. Yancey, *Vanishing Grace*, 142 (emphasis added).
20. Yancey, *Vanishing Grace*, 143.
21. Yancey, *Vanishing Grace*, 143.

a not too easily disguised hidden agenda of "what's in this for me?" This, in turn, immediately departs from the descriptions of faith in Scripture, where it is inextricably interwoven with discipleship and commitment to the truth. When the concept and meaning of faith and belief has shrunk it leads to an easy and all too ready acceptance of "shrunken gods." One such is in the false contrast between the "reality" claimed to be dealt with by science and the "fantasy" world of faith. Yancey described this false dichotomy this way: "Like a placebo, religious faith may make you feel better, but it has no real substance. For truth about reality you must look to science."[22] The argument of this book is that it is not an "either/or" but a "both/and." To capture the full complexity and wonder of the reality of who we are and of the world of which we are a part, we need the discoveries of science and the insights from a mature and developed religious faith.

Since, we have argued, it is through the eyes of faith that we are able as Christians to understand our work as scientists as part of our calling, and how in doing this we have repeatedly been aware of the pervasive doctrine throughout Scripture that the God in whom we trust is the one who upholds all things at all times by the word of his power (Heb 1:3 KJV), we need to remember that, if this is our only emphasis, we are in danger of forgetting an equally important and pervasive doctrine in Scripture that we also see through the eyes of faith, that the God whom we worship emptied himself, became as a man, suffered on a cross, and taught us that his divine self-emptying gave us a model of key aspects of Christian discipleship. For these reasons the following chapter seeks to set out and keep in delicate balance both God's divine upholding and God's divine self-emptying.

---

22. Yancey, *Vanishing Grace*, 157.

12

The Multifaceted Nature of Faith
The Evidence from Science

> Faith in God now seemed more rational than disbelief. I was beginning to understand from looking into my own heart that the evidence of God's existence would have to come not from science, but from other directions, and the ultimate decision would have to be based on faith, not proof. For a long time I stood trembling on the edge of this yawning gap. Finally, seeing no escape, I leapt.[1]

Perhaps we live today in a time when we fly from the mind, to urge Christians to seek experience, ecstatic phenomena and have their feelings stirred up. Bunyan saw it all with the Ranters and the early Quakers; Luther with the ecstatic prophets of his day. There are, however, hopeful signs of a return to a more balanced life where heart and head act together in a better balance.[2]

PSYCHOLOGICAL PERSPECTIVES ON FAITH

IN HIS RIDDELL MEMORIAL Lectures entitled, "Religion as Experience, Belief, Action," Sir Frederic Bartlett began by suggesting that, "Long ago William James pointed out that probably everything that can be said in

---

1. Collins, "Learning the Language of God," 70–71.
2. Davies, *Genius, Grief, and Grace*, 382.

description of the conditions giving rise to religious experience has been said already, and that there is neither need or place for originality."[3] Be that as it may, there remains the question of whether all those conditions that can give rise to religious experiences have common psychological constituents, and if they do, what are they? If we can discover common psychological constituents to all of the many and varied religious experiences that have been investigated this may help us to understand something more about the nature of religious faith, which is connected with those experiences. Whether the faith precedes experience in a time sequence or vice versa is now a secondary question. History demonstrates at once that the immediate human conditions in which faith may arise are infinitely varied. They may be healthy or diseased. They may express abounding happiness or abysmal misery. They may spring from success or from failure. They may at the time appear to the onlooker as trivial or of the most profound importance. They may be narrowly individualistic or widely socialized. Despite all these wide differences Bartlett thought that most of these experiences seem to have one characteristic in common. It was that a situation, or a state of affairs, is presented in which the individual concerned cannot see through it or think through it to a satisfactory completion that he can then accept as satisfactory. Bartlett recognized that how we try to complete what is felt to be incomplete can vary endlessly. But it is the act of completing the incomplete that is at the core of genuine religious experience.

As the very recent testimony at the head of this chapter from one of today's leading medical scientists graphically underlines, at times, in order to bring about a sense of completeness, a "leap of faith" may be required. One certainly does not have to look very far for confirmatory evidence in support of the importance of this idea of incompleteness as a characteristic of religious experience. In the biblical records, it was as men and women saw and comprehended the life of Christ that they became aware of their own incompleteness and moral imperfection. For example, the apostle Peter exclaims, "Depart from me; for I am a sinful man, O Lord" (Luke 5:8 ESV). And it was not only the case with those who met Christ in the flesh; we also have many recorded religious experiences, over the centuries, where we read of how an individual reading the Gospel narratives and beginning to make comparison of his own life with that of Christ becomes increasingly aware of his own moral imperfections and his incompleteness. Raising awareness of this is what some of the great revival preachers succeeded in bringing out, either consciously or unconsciously. They showed women and men how far they fell short of their own ethical and moral standards and

---

3. Bartlett, *Religion as Experience, Belief, Action*, 7.

followed this up by showing how much further the same people fell short of the absolute standards of perfection embodied in the person and teaching of Jesus Christ.

The sense of shortcoming and moral imperfection that results in us is accompanied by a complementary sense of incompleteness. Not only is there a sense of incompleteness such as Bartlett has suggested, but there will also be a sense of continued inability to turn this incompleteness into a sense of completeness. Indeed, it is often only after prolonged attempts to turn the sense of incompleteness into a sense of completeness that someone comes to recognize his own inability to bring about this transformation from incompleteness to completeness. Through faith a person may, by an initial step, move from the feeling of incompleteness to completeness, but this will often only be temporary since, as the experience of the great saints has shown, there remains, in the process of sanctification, a continuing sense of incompleteness.

So, Paul the apostle, secure in his acceptance with God through faith, nevertheless at the same time could continue to cry out "O wretched man that I am: who shall deliver me from the body of this death?" (Rom 7:24 KJV). If there is any truth in this analysis then we may say further that in every situation that can give rise to religious experience, the mind is trying to round off and complete information or evidence, collected, directly or indirectly, through our natural sensory and perceptual equipment and in so saying we're linking the conditions of religious experience with all other cases of the operation of the mind. Always and everywhere, suggested Bartlett, when it is active, the mind is trying to complete informational evidence that is regarded as so far incomplete. This, he says, is its primary function. In the mid-twentieth century, when J. B. Phillips and C. S. Lewis were writing, those seeking to understand what religious experience can tell us about religious faith were well aware of competing views in the previous half century. These competing views highlighted the mistake of trying to analyze the relation between belief and experience in order to give primacy to one over the other. Certainly, today, with widespread awareness of notions of dynamic feedback, such "either-or" views would be increasingly difficult to defend. I suspect, that both Phillips and Lewis, would have been likely to have been more influenced by the views of Gordon Allport and Sir Frederic Bartlett than of Freud and Skinner.

FAITH EXPRESSED IN COMMUNITY

Except in very rare instances, such as the lonely hermit, faith is lived out in community. This means that the life of faith is fully embedded in our physical, cultural, and social environments. For each of us, the choices we make are embedded within our unique life context and that includes our developmental history and lifetime friendship networks, as well as the broader cultural environment. Thus, our faith is both *physically embodied* and *socially embedded*. Recognizing this, Warren Brown and Brad Strawn have helpfully asked what new insights the advances in neuropsychology and social psychology can provide about how our life of faith in community should be organized and how worship should be conducted. They argue,

> The embeddedness of faith and spirituality requires that churches take seriously the need to combine faith with action. It is not just that what is thought or experienced that occurs in the brain and is expressed in the body, but the impact goes the other direction as well: *actions influence thought*. . . . What we do with our bodies has a profound influence on what we think.[4]

Thus, continue Brown and Strawn,

> To participate in the Eucharist during worship (an extended form of gesture) is for this bodily activity to have a deep influence on our thoughts, feelings, beliefs, and future behavior quite beyond what is said. So, our argument for the role of participation and action in worship is an argument based on the profound embodiment of all thought. Without concurrent action, thought and belief is likely to degenerate into nothing but intellectualism, and worship into mere feelings. Formation of persons will be minimal.[5]

This line of thought leads Brown and Strawn to propose that the commonly held assumption of body-soul dualism actually undermines the message of Jesus that calls Christians to action in the world for the sake of God's kingdom. They write,

> Our premise has been that viewing persons as bodies, not souls inhabiting bodies, *is truer to Scripture, as well as more resonant with modern neuroscience and psychology*. Most Christians believe that humans are souls that *have* bodies, not that we *are* bodies. They presume that the "real me" is not their body or

---

4. Brown and Strawn, *Physical Nature*, 152 (emphasis added).
5. Brown and Strawn, *Physical Nature*, 152.

even their behavior, but is something inside them, in their head or heart—in their mind or soul. Thus, it is possible to be spiritual inside, without being religious in what we do—without participating in the communal religious life of the church. However, Christian life has a very different feel if the essence of the human person is not a ghostly, immaterial soul or spirit that is temporarily trapped in a fleshly body and hidden from view, but is the indivisible composite of the behavior, habits, thoughts, emotions, and personality of the physical body itself.[6]

COMPLETING THE INCOMPLETE AND THE "LEAP OF FAITH"

Although Kierkegaard never used the words "leap of faith,"[7] the notion of *faith as a step beyond the immediate evidence* may be helpful in getting a fully rounded understanding of all that faith involves. Sir Frederic Bartlett's accounts of some of the processes of the mind underlying religious experience and the progression of a person towards the possession of faith,[8] offered from a strictly psychological viewpoint, sound remarkably like a "leap of faith." It is interesting to explore any parallels between such psychological accounts with ones that are typically given in religious language as used by people of faith. Throughout the centuries, Christian theologians have recognized that the movement involved in the acquisition of faith can be a slow, gradual process in some individuals, while in others it occurs in a sudden, dramatic event. In either case, religious conversion may be seen as involving a "leap of faith" or a "crossing of a gap" or chasm in one's life. The change that has taken place in the individual's total interpretation of all her experiences may lead her to exclaim something akin to, "Once I was blind, but now I see," and may feel like being "born again."

Even so, the newly religious person will not be in a position to produce all the evidence necessary to explain the leap in logical or scientific terms. She has jumped out of one frame of reference into a completely new one. What has happened, to quote Bartlett again, is that, "There is the third way, the way of the jump. Here is the incomplete evidence and lo! Coming, perhaps by slow process of unknown accumulation, perhaps by swift dramatic leap, here is the completion!"[9] To use religious terminology, we might

---

6. Brown and Strawn, *Physical Nature*, 159.
7. McKinnon, "Kierkegaard and 'The Leap of Faith,'" 118.
8. Bartlett, *Religion as Experience, Belief, Action*, 10.
9. Bartlett, *Religion as Experience, Belief, Action*, 10.

equally well say, "Therefore, if anyone is in Christ, he is a new creation. The old has passed away; behold, the new has come" (2 Cor 5:17 ESV). The new convert, the young Christian, often sees the evidence for this new creation so vividly that, in her enthusiasm, she is apt to be impatient with those who (again to quote Bartlett) "ought to be able to see that it is different." To use a familiar illustration from a psychology textbook, the new converts' vision will be like that of the man who has been shown a picture containing a hidden figure. After studying the meaningless image, the hidden face or other object suddenly "jumps out" at him, and thereafter he cannot help but see the hidden figure whenever he looks at the picture—and is impatient with anyone who cannot see the figure. But there's something more to religious conversation that cannot be captured by this analogy. Conversion is a total reinterpretation of a person's past and present life experiences that goes much deeper and is much more immersive and subversive than a superficial shift in the perception of a puzzling picture.

The detailed analysis and description that Bartlett, writing as a psychologist, gives of this intuitive "gap crossing" could equally be given in religious terms. The intuition aspect of faith is but the human side of a process that also has a divine side. So "the irresistible strengths" of Bartlett's description has a ready equivalent for a Christian in the love and grace of God. The would-be convert not only leaps toward God, but is simultaneously drawn towards God. Religion has its own set of symbols describing the transformation that takes place when the person takes a leap of faith. These particular symbols are expressed in terms of personal attributes and interpersonal relationships, thus such words as love, trust, commitment, surrender, and confidence are found to be the typical vocabulary of the person who is attempting to communicate an account of a particular religious experience. This, of course, is not to deny that there are several other "spectator" accounts of the same experience that may be given in different language and using different symbols. The fact that a leap has been taken and that a gap has been crossed often comes as a striking realization after the event has taken place. For example, Mortimer Adler, philosopher and editor of *Great Books of the Western World* first came to embrace theism, a belief in God. Philip Yancey, writing about Adler, tells us that,

> Though attracted to the writings of Thomas Aquinas, for decades he resisted calling himself a Christian, a hesitation no doubt influenced by his Jewish heritage. Then in 1984, after a trip to Mexico, he fell ill from a virus that incapacitated him for months. Bedbound, he sank into depression and sometimes would unaccountably burst into tears. During this period an

Episcopal priest visited him faithfully and prayed with him. . . . Adler himself knew only one prayer, the Lord's Prayer, and he repeated it over and over, clinging to every word: "Our Father who art in heaven, hallowed be your name . . . ." As he lay awake in the hospital one night, *he realized he had crossed a bridge without knowing it, a leap of faith to a personal God who hears our prayers*. He rang for the night nurse and scratched out a note which included these words: "Dear God, yes, I do believe, not just in the God my reason so stoutly affirms, but the God to whom Father Howell is now praying, and on whose grace and love I now joyfully rely." Affliction had shown him the way.[10]

THE WHOLE PERSON IS INVOLVED IN REAL FAITH

All mental processes involve cognition, affect, and conation, and faith is no exception. At times a widely held and mistaken belief that the mind functions in a manner other than normal when concerned with religious matters has, in the past, led to investigations of religious phenomena by Christians and non-Christians alike that, in effect, seek to explain and describe religion, including faith, as far as possible in rational and sometimes scientific terms and then to bring in some kind of belief or set of beliefs in a supernatural power *to fill in any gaps that remain*. All such approaches face us once again with a "god-of-the-gaps" and again demonstrate a misunderstanding of the limitations of logical analysis and scientific method, as well as a misunderstanding of the nature of the God of the Christian.

In the mid-twentieth century, one of the most widely known and influential modern psychological systems, Freudian psychoanalysis, applied itself to religion, and made two claims. The first was that all the forms and the original impulses of human religion can be given a complete and full causal explanation within what is called the natural order of events. The second is that there can be therefore no other explanation. Such views should be put alongside those of two other leading twentieth-century psychologists, Gordon Allport at Harvard and Sir Frederic Bartlett at Cambridge. They both shared with the wider public their views on the nature of faith and doubt. Allport was a personality theorist and social psychologist. Bartlett was an experimental psychologist and expert on human memory. Allport's book was *The Individual and His Religion*. Bartlett's contribution was in his Riddell Memorial Lectures.[11] Both wrote about the nature of belief, faith, and

---

10. Yancey, *Vanishing Grace*, 48 (emphasis added).
11. Bartlett, *Religion as Experience, Belief, Action*.

doubt. Both held a constructive view of the relationship between psychology and religion. Gordon Allport, for example, devotes a whole chapter to the nature of doubt. This is important because doubt is as common a sentiment as belief, and certainly in the Christian life doubts creep in from time to time. As Allport states clearly concerning the psychologist's role in studying doubt,

> It is not the function of the psychologist to pass judgement on the legitimacy or illegitimacy of any doubt. His duty is merely to elucidate the process which he finds to be a universal and necessary part of mental life. He holds that if each person understood the doubting process, he would be in a better position to determine the cogency of his own grounds for belief or disbelief. Although each individual has his own history, pattern, and degree of misgiving, of certain modes of doubt that seem especially common.[12]

Allport noted that doubt was particularly evident during the initial phase of religious development. It is relevant here because some of the shrunken presentations of the Christian faith and the Christian life, as we have noted, focus almost exclusively on the personal advantages for the person who becomes a Christian. It is relevant therefore to note Allport's words,

> The child who finds his personal advantage not immediately and satisfactorily served by his prayers may discard his conceptions and terminate once and for all his religious quest. Sometimes issues come to a head only later in life, in conjunction with acute personal need.... Faith centered in self-advantage is bound to break up. To endure at all *it must envisage the universe that extends beyond personal whim and is anchored in values that transcend the immediate interests of the individual as interpreted by himself.*[13]

Those who have studied both the history of personality theories and developments in contemporary research agree that the most illuminating way to study personality is, as with many other psychological phenomena, to study it at multiple levels. This means that there needs to be:

- An awareness of biological influences, which include genetically determined temperaments, variations in autonomic nervous system reactivity, differences in brain structure and function,

---

12. Allport, *Individual and His Religion*, 115.
13. Allport, *Individual and His Religion*, 114 (emphasis added).

- An awareness of psychological influences, which include learned responses, unconscious thought processes, and expectations and interpretations, and
- Recognition of social-cultural influences, such as the effect of childhood experiences, the influence of the present situation, the effect of cultural expectations and the importance of social support.

The way we express our faith varies as widely as our inherited, national, and cultural backgrounds, and our learned individual differences. Some of us are impulsive, some cautious, some anxious, some laid-back. Jesus first disciples were a varied bunch. Peter perhaps inclined to be impetuous, John a bit more reflective. And it helps to be aware of our "natural" tendencies because we can then work on remembering that we all too easily filter all our experiences through them and interpret reality accordingly. It will be more difficult for some than others as they grapple with inbuilt as well as learned ways of thinking and behaving. For example, there is some evidence that the tendency to be overly dogmatic, expressed in the so-called authoritarian personality, and closely linked to a tendency to fundamentalist attitudes, may have biological roots. Wanting Zhong and his colleagues recently gave a detailed account of this possibility in their article titled "Biological and Cognitive Underpinnings of Religious Fundamentalism."[14] Be suspicious therefore of anyone who claims the authority to tell you that "this, and only this" is what faith must be like in your life. Be suspicious of anyone who claims that unless you express your faith in their particular way and not another, it is not true faith. Together these advances have increased our understanding of the biological substrates of cognition and behavior, and that includes faith. They potentially give us new insights into the nature of faith and belief.[15]

This recognition of the need to be aware of how our brains contain multiple systems subserving all our activities, including aspects of our religious lives, is further exemplified by a study underlining the need to be aware of how our basic day-to-day activities depend on the intact functioning of our brains. This includes a better understanding of some of the biological and cognitive underpinnings of religious faith. Some of the fruits of relatively recent research in social neuroscience have, interestingly, revealed that we are indeed made as creatures who possess distinct neural systems subserving personal knowledge and object knowledge. Jason Mitchell, Todd Heatherton, and C. Neil Macrae carried out studies using event-related

14. Zhong et al., "Biological and Cognitive Underpinnings."
15. See Jeeves and Ludwig, *Psychological Science*.

functional magnetic resonance imaging (fMRI) in which they study neural activity as participants were making semantic judgments about people or about objects. They reported that a unique pattern of brain activity was associated with personal judgements and included brain regions previously implicated in other aspects of social cognitive functioning: medial prefrontal cortex, superior temporal cortex, intraparietal sulcus, and fusiform gyrus. They write, "Together, these findings support the notion that person knowledge may be functionally dissociable from other classes of semantic knowledge within the brain."[16] Such studies are a timely reminder that we are complex creatures and that our thinking, believing, and acting are all dependent on the intact functioning of our brains. And since we frequently underline how real faith has at its center a personal relationship with Christ, these findings remind us that our Creator has equipped us with the tools for distinct personal knowledge.

In an earlier chapter, we noted the extremely rapid changes in our understanding of ourselves and the universe in which we live that have occurred since J. B. Phillips published his book in 1952. For example, in the following year the groundbreaking paper by J. B. Watson and Francis Crick spelled out the structure of DNA and continues to have very widespread impact. In the context of this chapter, focusing on the need to be alert to individual differences and how these may affect our response to the Christian gospel, a recent *Nature Neuroscience* report provided new evidence for the link between genetics and mental health. This issue is relevant as we consider the personal struggles of outstanding Christian men and women of the faith from the past—including J. B. Phillips himself, who struggled with depression. This 2019 University of Edinburgh study analyzed the health and DNA records of two million people and pinpointed 260 genes linked to depression.[17] Results from this study identified sections of DNA common in people with depression and also in those who took up unhealthy "lifestyle behaviors" such as smoking. Their findings suggested that depression could be a driving factor leading some people to smoke. They also found that neuroticism—the tendency to be worried or fearful—could lead people to become depressed. Working with the National Institutes of Health Research Mental Health Bioresource and Kings College London, the researchers hope to go on to collect saliva samples and answers to a questionnaire from a further forty thousand people in the UK. Andrew McIntosh, one of the

---

16. Mitchell et al., "Distinct Neural Systems," 53.
17. Howard et al., "Genome-Wide Meta-Analysis."

researchers in the project, concluded, "These findings are further evidence that depression is partly down to our genetics."[18]

NEUROPSYCHOLOGICAL INSIGHTS INTO IMPAIRED FAITH

Any belief that our spirituality, including our faith, is securely protected within a nonphysical part of us (the soul) is challenged by the experiences of individuals who have developed Alzheimer's disease. Some deeply religious people have suffered agonizing distress as they experienced the fragmentation and loss of precious aspects of their religious life. Such distress is equally painful for their loved ones and caregivers. What happens to faith when the brain goes awry? Some of the most important and relevant insights from neuropsychology come from research on how Alzheimer's disease influences the life of faith.

Glenn Weaver, who developed a large research program studying spirituality in Alzheimer's patients, has described some of the changes in these people's experiences of spirituality, religious faith, and meaning in life.[19] The spiritual consequences of Alzheimer's dementia may vary widely across individuals. For some, the loss of independence and control leads to a greater dependence on God. For others, the gradual deterioration of cognitive abilities reduces spiritual interest. Weaver described in detail the experiences of Robert Davis, a Presbyterian minister, a man of deep Christian faith, who was diagnosed with Alzheimer's dementia when he was fifty-three and at the height of his ministerial career. With the help of his wife, he wrote a remarkable account of his experiences well into the middle stages of the disease. How his progressive brain disease affected his spirituality is graphically illustrated in his own words. He wrote,

> My spiritual life was miserable. I could not read the Bible. I could not pray as I wanted to because my emotions were dead and cut off. There was no feedback from God the Holy Spirit. My mind could not rest and grow calm but raced relentlessly, thinking dreadful thoughts of despair.... I can no longer be spiritually fed by sermons. I can get the first point of the sermon and then am lost. The rest of it sends my mind whirling in a jumble of twisted unconnected ideas. Coughing, headache, and great discomfort have attended my attempts to be fed in all the ways I am accustomed to, meeting God through his Word.

18. Salt, "Treasure Trove of 269 Genes."
19. Weaver, "Embodied Spirituality."

... My mind also raced about, grasping for the comfort of the Savior whom I knew and loved and the emotional peace that He could give me, but finding nothing. I concluded that the only reason for such darkness must be spiritual. Unnamed guilt filled me. Yet the only guilt I could put a name on was failure to read my Bible. But I could not read, and would God condemn me for this? I could only lie there and cry "Oh God, why? Why?"[20]

This account should open our eyes to the important role of brain function for the exercise of faith, spirituality, and religious behavior. It is difficult to see how a dualist perspective can accommodate the experiences of patients like Robert Davis. A "soul" or "mind" that is completely separate from the brain and not dependent upon neural functioning should not change (becoming more spiritual or less spiritual) as neurons die and brain tissue deteriorates.

But take heart. Even as I write, James Ainge and his colleagues at the School of Psychology and Neuroscience at St. Andrews University (which I established fifty years ago), working with colleagues at Edinburgh University, have identified the functions of the area of the brain where Alzheimer's disease can begin, raising hopes of a discovery that could lead to treatments.[21] The research is centered on the lateral entorhinal cortex (LEC), which contains layers of cells that form complex connections with other brain regions and has sub-systems with different memory functions. According to these researchers, "When a particular connection between one of the layers of the LEC and the hippocampus malfunctions, episodic memory is affected while simpler forms of memory remain unaffected.... This research is important as it gives us a very specific target when developing treatments and strategies to prevent neurodegeneration in Alzheimer's disease."[22]

A similar story emerges from detailed studies of the faith of sufferers of Parkinson's disease. At Boston University School of Medicine, Patrick McNamara and his colleagues conducted a series of pioneering studies providing new insights into religiosity in patients suffering from Parkinson's disease. With the increase in longevity in the general population producing a corresponding rise in the incidence of late-onset Parkinson's disease, it is important from a pastoral point of view to be aware of any changes in a person's religiosity and spirituality, including their life of faith, that may accompany the development of Parkinson's disease.

20. Weaver, "Embodied Spirituality," 89.
21. Vandrey et al., "Fan Cells in Layer 2."
22. McKee, "Alzheimer's Disease Discovery."

Parkinson's disease is a condition with a clearly defined pathology of the brain involving changes in the activity of dopaminergic neurons. Patrick McNamara, Ramon Durso, and Arial Brown examined the role that prefrontal dopaminergic networks play in maintaining religious beliefs and behaviors. They found that, compared to age-matched controls, individuals with Parkinson's disease scored lower on measures of religious behaviors and expressed less interest in spiritual or philosophical issues.[23] These findings raise the possibility that normal dopamine levels are important for maintaining religious motivation and goal-directed behavior based on religious beliefs and values. Follow-up studies revealed differences in religiosity between Parkinson's patients whose disease symptoms had appeared first on the left side of the body and those who showed earlier onset on the right side, suggesting that the two hemispheres of the brain play slightly different roles in religious behaviors.[24]

However, in a careful review of this area of research, Clare Redfern and Alasdair Coles have pointed out that interpreting the results of such studies is not a straightforward matter. Parkinson's disease produces a wide range of physical, cognitive, and emotional changes, and these symptoms vary in unpredictable ways as the disease progresses and as new treatments are introduced. This makes it difficult to claim that Parkinson's disease itself has a specific negative impact on spirituality.[25]

Take a very simple example. With the progression of Parkinson's disease, mobility is severely limited. Therefore, it is not surprising if a person with Parkinson's shows reduced attendance at worship services. The effort of getting dressed and getting into the worship space may be overwhelming. Thus, a decline in religious behaviors by a Parkinson's patient would not necessarily imply any loss of spirituality or religious faith.

In addition, some research has found a more positive pattern of changes. At least some Parkinson's patients report a strengthened relationship with God and a more intentional search for religious meaning as a way of coping with their disease.[26] These contradictory findings demonstrate the need for rigorous, well-controlled studies mobilizing all the combined skills of neurologists, psychologists, and theologians.

There is clearly much work to be done, but the existing research has already provided new insights into how spirituality, including faith, may be

23. McNamara et al., "Religiosity in Patients."
24. Butler et al., "Side of Onset."
25. Redfern and Coles, "Parkinson's Disease."
26. Redfern and Coles, "Parkinson's Disease."

affected in patients with Parkinson's disease. With a better understanding of what is happening in and to such persons, pastoral care may be improved.

REAL FAITH EMBODIED IN REAL LIVES: A PSYCHIATRIST'S PERSPECTIVE

Contrary to the claims made by promoters of some of today's "shrunken Gods," living the Christian life is not a bed of roses. Only someone totally ignorant of the history of the Christian church could take such a view. Careful historical research has documented in detail the struggles of some great men and women of the faith, revealing a close connection between their personality characteristics, their psychological experiences, and their faith. Awareness of the kinds of influences listed earlier on all our behavior and aware of our increasing knowledge of the biological substrates of all behavior, including changes in brain biochemistry, a distinguished British psychiatrist, Gaius Davies, undertook detailed historical research of the lives of some well-known people of faith of past generations. Men and women who were known to have faced periods of doubt, struggle, and difficulty in their lifelong Christian walk. Davies wrote,

> The question of how temperament and faith are connected is, of course, brought to the fore in every conversion experience. We cannot understand Methodism without knowing something of how John and Charles Wesley found faith and assurance in 1738. Both found Martin Luther a great catalyst: John through Luther's work on Romans, Charles through Luther's commentary on St Paul's letter to the Galatians.[27]

Gaius Davies studied, amongst others, Martin Luther, John Bunyan, John Wesley, William Cowper, Gerard Manley Hopkins, Lord Shaftesbury, and Christina Rossetti. His research made clear that these outstanding leaders who contributed so much also suffered a great deal from anxiety and depression. As John Stott wrote in a Foreword to Davies book, "What I especially admire about Gaius Davies's book is his honesty and realism. He offers no glib remedies. It tells us the truth, that some of God's heroes and heroines have been eccentric and neurotic, and have suffered repeated breakdowns."[28] What is particularly relevant in the present context is Davies's argument—based on recent discoveries about the biological roots of behavior and the impact of psychotropic drugs—that the stories of some

---

27. Davies, *Genius, Grief, and Grace*, 11.
28. Davies, *Genius, Grief, and Grace*, 6.

of these heroes and heroines of the faith may have been quite different had they lived today. Consider a few examples by way of illustration.

Writing of Martin Luther, Davies said, "I believe there was a marked physical and constitutional element in Luther's tendency to depression. I do not see clear evidence that he was ever manic, elated or ill because of an upward mood swing. However, he might now be diagnosed as a cyclothymic personality, with many mood swings which, though significant, were never such as to cause psychosis."[29] Davies documents the evidence that in 1527 Luther was suffering both physically and with depression. Although only age forty-four, he collapsed physically and was expected to die. Luther himself later saw this episode of illness as partly physical and partly psychological.[30] Of John Bunyan, Davies wrote,

> In *Grace Abounding*, Bunyan describes his severe anxiety, and how it often drove him to despair. However, he was not a monk with hours to spend in the confessional. Unlike Luther, he was much more alone with the Bible, and struggled with difficult texts with little help, even allowing for John Gifford and the few books he could obtain.[31]

Davies went on to say about Bunyan, "There could be no clearer example of the severe obsessive-compulsive disorder at work. There are other examples of the same urge to blaspheme. He would want to hold his hand over his mouth or plunge his head into a dung heap rather than give in to the impulse."[32] Later he continued, "Bunyan was remarkable because he suffered so severely from obsessions; he would nowadays be diagnosed as being in need of treatment."[33] Davies not only described the symptoms Bunyan suffered and the way Bunyan obtained relief, but he also showed that great strength may result from overcoming a serious psychological disorder. One can only speculate how much John Bunyan would have benefited by the judicious use of some of today's effective psychotropic drugs.

Writing of William Cowper, Davies said,

> Cowper wanted to break the conspiracy of silence about depression. . . . Cowper was depressed first at the age of twenty-one, and from time to time thereafter for the next ten years. At thirty-one he had his first catastrophic psychotic breakdown, and at

---

29. Davies, *Genius, Grief, and Grace*, 45.
30. Luther, *Letters of Spiritual Counsel*, 115–17.
31. Davies, *Genius, Grief, and Grace*, 65.
32. Davies, *Genius, Grief, and Grace*, 65–66.
33. Davies, *Genius, Grief, and Grace*, 66.

the time of his recovery from it he became a Christian. He was to have four more depressive illnesses before he died at sixty-eight: in between these times he was often amazingly productive as a letter writer and poet.[34]

Near the end of his chapter on William Cowper, Davies wrote, "Why was he not healed? Why should he have suffered six serious depressive breakdowns, several suicide attempts and endured so much mental pain? It is part of the larger mystery of suffering, and there cannot be a final answer. But good came out of the apparent evil of his distress."[35] Again, in the instance of William Cowper we can but speculate what a difference it might have made had some of today's antidepressant medicines been available.

Very relevant to this present book, and in part prompted by the 1952 book by J. B. Phillips, was how Davies described Phillips as someone who had "a special genius for translating and communicating." Yet, Davies concludes, despite all that Phillips achieved, it is clear from his autobiography, *The Price of Success*, that he suffered from recurrent depression. In his sympathetic description of Phillips's many struggles, Davies wrote,

> I find it sad that he was not helped by medication. Nowadays such non-psychiatric forms of treatment as the use of beta-blockers may alleviate the anxiety by stopping the excessive effects of adrenaline on the body: they do this without sedation and without any risk of dependence. By the same token, there are nowadays many forms of antidepressant which might help someone who suffered as much as Phillips.[36]

In the final pages of his book, Davies drew together the threads underlining how his researches had shown repeatedly how individual differences in personality and temperament, were reflected in how someone expresses their faith. Under the heading "Personality and Temperament," Davies wrote,

> My aim in the previous studies in this book has been not only to avoid speculation, but also to draw some conclusions from the facts reviewed. I have tried to show how Martin Luther and John Bunyan were perfectionists who suffered a good deal in their youth from obsessional symptoms. The careful reader will have noted a number of the others—J. B. Phillips, Christina Rossetti,

---

34. Davies, *Genius, Grief, and Grace*, 93–94.
35. Davies, *Genius, Grief, and Grace*, 118.
36. Davies, *Genius, Grief, and Grace*, 320.

Amy Carmichael and Gerard Manley Hopkins were also people with marked traits of obsessionality.[37]

Davies concluded with some profound advice:

> A kind of miracle happens when our heroes find that the water of life, as Christ's gospel has become for them, is turned into a heady wine of doctrinal delight. As C. S. Lewis put it, the heart sings unbidden not with the devotional book but in reading some Christian treatise which speaks to the mind. This may of course become addictive, and systematic theology may be taken as a substitute for the real thing, life in Christ. Perhaps we live today in a time when we fly from the mind, to urge Christians to seek experience, ecstatic phenomena and have their feelings stirred up. Bunyan saw it all with the Ranters and the early Quakers; Luther with the ecstatic prophets of his day. There are, however, hopeful signs of a return to a more balanced life where heart and head act together in a better balance.[38]

The take-home message from Gaius Davies is that our spirituality, including how we demonstrate our faith in our living, is related to and influenced by the functioning of our brains and bodies—a message repeatedly underlined by neuroscience research. C. S. Lewis offered us a subjective, "actor account" when he wrote,

> If I find in myself a desire which no experience in this world can satisfy, the most probable explanation is that I was made for another world. If none of my earthly pleasures satisfy it, that does not prove that the universe is a fraud. Probably earthly pleasures were never meant to satisfy it, but only to arouse it, to suggest the real thing.[39]

---

37. Davies, *Genius, Grief, and Grace*, 372.
38. Davies, *Genius, Grief, and Grace*, 382.
39. Lewis, *Christian Behavior*, 57.

SECTION III

Theological Reflections

13

Divine Upholding and Divine Emptying
An Essential Balance

> Have this mind among yourselves, which is yours in Christ Jesus, who, though he was in the form of God, did not count equality with God a thing to be grasped, but made himself nothing, taking the form of a servant, being born in the likeness of men. And being found in human form, he humbled himself by becoming obedient to the point of death, even death on a cross. (Phil 2:5–8 ESV)

Any dichotomy between creation and redemption carries with it theological dangers, these risks are enhanced when there is an imposed correlation with different divine attributes. The act of creation, of bringing a world into being and maintaining it in being, is clearly an act of great power to which the puny powers of creatures bear no comparison.[1]

Creation is not essentially some distant event; rather, it is the ongoing complete causing of the existence of all that is. At this very moment, were God not causing all that is to exist, there would be nothing at all.[2]

---

1. Polkinghorne, "Kenotic Creation," 90.
2. Carroll, "Aquinas and Contemporary Cosmology," 18.

> Jesus's followers discovered that he was more than a preacher, a healer and redeemer. He was also the Creator and Sustainer of everything.[3]

IN PREVIOUS CHAPTERS, WE have gained an overview of what scientists and biblical scholars tell us about human origins, human nature, and miracles of nature and of healing. Although at first glance, contradictions appeared between what we thought Scripture taught and what advances in science and medicine tell us, we paused to ask whether we may have misinterpreted Scripture or wrongly evaluated new discoveries in science or both. There may be no immediate obvious answers as each puzzle emerges. We have to work at each in the confidence that since the author *both* of Scripture *and* of nature is ultimately the same Author, they will not eventually conflict. We have returned repeatedly to the pervasive biblical theme of our Creator God's divine upholding. But, to underline such upholding without recognizing the centrality of another pervasive theme of Scripture, God's divine self-emptying, would be to shrink the God we worship. James Bryan Smith underlines this when he writes,

> The gospel message—the big story—must include this mind-blowing detail. The shrunken gospels start with me. But now we see that even before I'm in the picture, *Jesus is the center of all things*. The shrunken stories do not include this central truth: Jesus made it all. We sing "Jesus paid it all." He did. But he also made it all.[4]

DIVINE SELF-EMPTYING AND THE WORK OF LOVE

An essential aspect of God's awesomeness is revealed in his self-emptying, technically in *kenosis*. Derived from the Greek verb *kenoō*, used in Philippians 2:7 ("he emptied himself"), the word *kenosis* has many theological meanings. First and foremost, in the context of this present book it refers to a key aspect of creation. It reminds us that *at all times we must keep in delicate balance both God's divine sovereignty and God's divine self-emptying.*

If we are to be faithful to this pervasive theme of Scripture, divine self-emptying, especially prominent with New Testament writers, we must ensure that it figures as prominently in our thinking as the theme of divine upholding. We cannot be satisfied with emphasizing divine upholding

3. Smith, *Magnificent Story*, 96.
4. Smith, *Magnificent Story*, 97 (emphasis in original).

alone. Classically the key doctrine of self-emptying is referred to in Paul's letter to the Christians at Philippi, where he writes, "Have this mind among yourselves, which is yours in Christ Jesus, who, *though he was in the form of God, did not count equality with God a thing to be grasped, but emptied himself, by taking the form of a servant, being born in the likeness of men*. And being found in human form, he humbled himself by becoming obedient to the point of death, even death on a cross" (Phil 2:5–8 ESV). And kenosis is evident in God's revelation of himself and his purposes from the very beginning. Thus, James Bryan Smith wrote,

> Creation was the first act of kenosis: God binds himself to us by creating us and this magnificent world. Covenant was the next act of kenosis. God binds himself to Israel in steadfast faithfulness, despite their infidelity. The incarnation was the next act of kenosis, in which God binds himself to humanity, by becoming human. . . . But now, the most extreme acts of kenosis are about to happen, in what we call Holy Week.[5]

A Timely Consultation

In October 1998, a group of theologians and scientists met in Queens College, Cambridge at the invitation of the President of the College, the distinguished mathematician and theoretical physicist Sir John Polkinghorne, to discuss insights afforded by a kenotic view of creation. A kenotic view underlines the need to remember that creation is brought about by the action of the God of love. The participants later produced a record of their discussions in a volume titled *The Work of Love: Creation as Kenosis*.[6] John Polkinghorne's own chapter, "Kenotic Creation and Divine Action," captured the importance of the central point made in this chapter, namely that to focus exclusively upon divine upholding in creation, with little mention of redemption, is to present an unbalanced view of God's activity in his world. Polkinghorne wrote,

> Any dichotomy between creation and redemption carries with it theological dangers, these risks are enhanced when there is an imposed correlation with different divine attributes. The act of creation, of bringing a world into being and maintaining it in

---

5. Smith, *Magnificent Story*, 115.
6. Polkinghorne, *Work of Love*.

being, is clearly an act of great power to which the puny powers of creatures bear no comparison.[7]

Polkinghorne argued that, "All theological thinking is a precarious balancing act, seeking recourse to the coincidence of opposites in an attempt to use finite human language to discourse about the infinite reality of God. Every assertion seems to stand in need of the qualification of a counter assertion. . . . *The need to do justice both to divine kenotic love and to divine providential power is clearly part of this theological tension.*"[8] Later, identifying specific issues relevant to this book and focused on God's Divine action in creating and upholding, Polkinghorne gives an important reminder:

> If the concept of continuous creation is really to mean what it says, and to consist of more than just a pious gloss on a wholly natural process, then God's providential guiding power must surely also be part of the unfolding of evolutionary history. The kenotic Creator may not overrule creatures, but the continuous Creator must interact with creation. *Thus, kenotic creation and divine action are opposite sides of the same theological coin.* . . . On the one hand, we have science's account of the regularity of the processes of nature. On the other hand, we have theology's claim to speak of a God who acts in history. Can the two be reconciled with each other? I believe so, but achieving this will call for some flexibility from both science and theology in the assessments they initially bring to their dialogue.[9]

Keith Ward, Regius Professor of Divinity at Oxford and a participant in the meeting, underlined the need to remember that, "For Christians, this is not simply a piece of abstract metaphysics. It is a view based firmly on the disclosure of the nature of God in the person of Jesus. As Canon Vanstone has powerfully shown, that nature is revealed in the cross and resurrection of Jesus as one of unrestricted love, and is one that does not simply eliminate suffering, but shares in and overcomes suffering by the patience of love."[10] Ward amplifies his thinking when later he writes, "Jesus's life of healing the sick, forgiving the guilt-ridden, befriending social outcasts, and undermining hypocrisy, is a very good image of the compassionate and pervasive love of God. Because of this disclosure, God can be worshipped not only as the all-powerful source and sustainer of all beings, but as a Father (or indeed a Mother) who cares for finite persons as his children and wishes them to

---

7. Polkinghorne, "Kenotic Creation," 90.
8. Polkinghorne, "Kenotic Creation," 91 (emphasis added).
9. Polkinghorne, "Kenotic Creation," 97 (emphasis added).
10. Ward, "Cosmos and Kenosis," 160.

become fully conscious of his loving presence. In the moment of kenosis, God relates the divine being to creatures who have a proper autonomy and otherness, which it is the divine will not to infringe."[11] Importantly, Ward continues, "But I can think of nothing more important for Christian faith in our day than to recover the truly cosmic sense of redemption that was characteristic both of the biblical writings and of the Church Fathers. Redemption will not be seen as a saving of a few human beings from the destruction of one small planet. It will be seen as a reconstituting of the whole cosmos in the presence of God, in a more glorious form."[12]

Paul Fiddes, another theological participant in the discussions, frequently referenced "the needs of love." This reference to "needs" brings to mind discussions in an earlier chapter of this book where we noted how both psychosociobiological needs and theological needs can be shown to have shaped, at different times, the ways that people have understood the God in whom they believe. It is therefore interesting that Paul Fiddes writes,

> A theological dialogue with science on the concept of need is not then simply a question of clarifying that the true needs of love are neither biochemical deficiencies nor brute instincts. Rather, it should be an exploration of both continuity and discontinuity between "low-level" and "high-level" functions of need. Instead of driving a wedge between "needs" and "love," we may be able to begin to trace the path taken by the creative Spirit of God in luring created beings along the evolutionary trail, until the needs for survival are not cancelled by something "higher," but *transformed* into a means of making truly personal identity. A need that emerges from something "missing" in the context of physical brain structure (for example, a chemical or electrochemical depletion) becomes an altogether different "lack" in the personal realm (for example, the assurance that we are valued).[13]

The Evolutionary Origins and Emergence of Kenotic Behavior

Listen again to a later email sent to me by a student quoted in the Preface. He wrote, "Also I hear that our morals can be completely attributed to scientific evolutionary processes. Do you think this is true? If it is does that make them less valuable/precious?" This is typical of the questions that arise in

11. Ward, "Cosmos and Kenosis," 164.
12. Ward, "Cosmos and Kenosis," 165.
13. Fiddes, "Creation Out of Love," 177.

the minds of thoughtful Christian students taking a course in evolutionary psychology. How would you answer it? Understanding the emergence of kenotic behavior provides a specific example of the general issues raised by this student. My approach is illustrated in my chapter, "The Nature of Persons and the Emergence of Kenotic Behavior," which summarized some of the evidence for the emergence of "self-giving behavior" in the course of biological evolution. To pay attention to what we know of God's *divine upholding* of creation to the exclusion of what has been revealed—in the person of Jesus Christ—about his *divine participating* in creation, would present an unbalanced view of God's relation to his creation that does not do justice to the available evidence. It would shrink God. One illustrative source of relevant evidence pointing to the emergence of elements of kenotic behavior in God's creation comes from contemporary science, which describes the ways in which aspects of self-giving and self-sacrificing behavior are researched and debated by evolutionary biologists, psychologists, and neuroscientists. For example, the evolutionary biologist Frans de Waal wrote that, "aiding others at a cost or risk to oneself is widespread in the animal world."[14] It is instructive to put alongside this statement the words of the theologian Jürgen Moltmann, one of the participants of the Cambridge meeting, who when discussing self-giving, wrote that "God's trinitarian essence, is therefore the mark of all his works."[15]

Moltmann was writing as a systematic theologian, de Waal as a primatologist. This suggests a convergence of thinking on this topic. This reminds us that we must keep in mind the words of Pascal in 1670, "It is dangerous to show a man too clearly how much he resembles the beast, without at the same time showing him his greatness. It is also dangerous to allow too clear a vision of his greatness without his baseness. It is even more dangerous to leave him in ignorance of both."[16]

What happens if we do listen to evolutionary biologists as they reflect on the evolution of aiding others? Evolutionary theory seeks to explain the evolution of aiding others in two general ways:

1. It argues that genes favoring altruism can spread in future generations as their costs to altruists' personal reproductive success is outweighed by the benefits in reproductive success of altruists' relatives carrying copies of the same gene (kin selection). The ratio of these indirect benefits through relatives, versus cost to oneself, needs to be greater

---

14. de Waal, *Good Natured*.
15. Moltmann, "God's Kenosis," 145.
16. Pascal, *Pensées*, 418.

the less closely the altruist is related to those helped—i.e., the lower the likelihood the altruist will be helping copies of their genes in the other.

2. It proposes that genes favoring altruism could spread if the altruism is sufficiently reciprocated (reciprocal altruism).

As regards the first mechanism, examples are widespread in the animal kingdom. Some of its most extreme forms are found, as one might expect, in those odd species where individuals in a colony are usually highly related to each other—social insects like bees and ants, in which workers' genetic relatedness to each other and to the queen is about 75 percent. One of the most graphic examples is honeypot worker ants, who do nothing but hang from the ceiling of the ant colony, acting as receptacles or storage jars for honey, which some workers fill them with, and which the colony draws on when needed. At an individual level, that is indeed self-sacrifice! Examples of reciprocal altruism appear to be much rarer. Humans apart, there are only a handful of examples. A classic one is vampire bats, who are in real danger of starving if they fail to act subtly enough to get their blood meal of an evening, fed in their colony by unrelated nest mates, to whom they are likely to repay the favor on another night.[17]

The examples cited should immediately flash up the warning that we must not assume that because two behaviors look similar, therefore the mechanisms underlying them are similar or identical. We are today familiar enough with our ability to reproduce aspects of human and animal behavior in robots, but no one suggests that the underlying mechanisms producing those behaviors are necessarily the same. Because we may observe self-giving, self-sacrificing behavior in different evolutionary phyla, that in itself tells us nothing about the underlying mechanisms for those behaviors. How, for example, could it be self-giving if there is no awareness of self? Whether, in the case of any particular group of animals, there is awareness of self is a very difficult question to answer. There are some compelling examples, based on anecdotal evidence, that similarities between humans and nonhuman primates may be sufficient that we need strong grounds before we deny that they have no self-awareness of what they are doing. Jane Goodall described examples of chimpanzee behavior that give us pause for reflection. She described, for example, a female helping her mother, who was unlikely to help in return or reproduce again. The anecdotal nature of the observation may be scientifically problematic, but it is certainly different from the ant and bat cases mentioned above. It looks like an unusual episode in

---

17. Wilkinson, "Reciprocal Food Sharing."

which the female recognized her mother is in need of help and worked out a way to help her.[18]

The debate will continue. De Waal has no doubt that, "Evolution has produced the requisites for morality: a tendency to develop social norms and enforce them, to capacities of empathy and sympathy, mutual aid and the sense of fairness, the mechanisms of conflict resolution, and so on."[19] There is thus a good argument for the case that some aspects of self-giving and self-limiting behavior may be seen as developing over the evolutionary phyla, becoming more and more pronounced among the nonhuman primates. De Waal comments, "Once thought of as purely spiritual matters, honesty, guilt, and the weighing of ethical dilemmas are traceable to specific areas of the brain. It should not surprise us, therefore, to find animal parallels. The human brain is a product of evolution. Despite its larger volume and greater complexity, it is fundamentally similar to the central nervous system of other animals."[20]

Those of us who begin from theistic presuppositions, can thus see embedded within creation the seeds, development, and fruits of self-giving behavior. The course of creation has been such that the qualities of self-giving and self-limiting behavior, built into the neural substrates of behavior, may be traced out coming to full flower in humankind. In short, as our knowledge of the effects of divine upholding over the long story of evolution increases, we are beginning to glimpse ways in which the capacity for kenotic behavior may have emerged.

Within the Christian tradition it is not necessary to deny the emergence of elements of kenotic behavior in nonhuman primates in order to defend the uniqueness of the self-giving and self-emptying of Christ. Rather, what we see of the beginnings of kenotic behavior in nonhuman primates, and individual and group human behavior, is demonstrated par excellence and uniquely in the person of Christ. Uniquely, it is by faith we affirm that the ultimate act of Christ's self-giving, by its nature, sets him and it apart from all others. He gave himself, we believe (as the Anglican *Book of Common Prayer* puts it), "as the one full, complete sacrifice, oblation, and satisfaction for the sins of the whole world."[21] Thus, while recognizing our kinship with Christ we at the same time acknowledge his uniqueness since in that act of supreme self-giving, "In Christ God was reconciling the world to himself" (2 Cor 5:19 ESV). At the same time, while we may

---

18. Goodall, *Chimpanzees of Gombe*.
19. de Waal, *Good Natured*, 82.
20. de Waal, *Good Natured*, 96.
21. Episcopal Church, *Book of Common Prayer*, 658.

thankfully marvel that, in creation, we are given glimpses of the emergence of self-sacrificing behavior, we must feel challenged in knowing that our own attempts at following our role model are often so feeble. In the words of the theologian William Sanday at the beginning of the twentieth century, we shall remember that we still believe that Christ is more than human "by the marks which have been appealed to all down the centuries in proof that in him deity and humanity were combined."[22] To repeat the words of Polkinghorne quoted above, *"Thus, kenotic creation and divine action are opposite sides of the same theological coin."*[23]

Divine Upholding and Divine Emptying: An Essential Balance

Divine upholding and divine emptying are both true. If either of them is emphasized to the extent of diminishing or ignoring the other, then we have departed from the clear teaching of Scripture. And such a departure results in shrinking the God in whom we trust. Hence, one recurring theme throughout this book has been the need to be alert to the danger of shrinking our ideas of God by failing to do full justice to the biblical emphasis on God's moment-by-moment divine upholding of the Universe. However, awareness that a central theme of Scripture is God's *divine upholding* must never allow us to forget or diminish an equally central theme of Scripture, namely, the mystery of God's *divine emptying*, demonstrated uniquely in the incarnation of Christ and in his redemptive work. *Divine upholding and divine emptying are both true. If either of them is emphasized to the extent of diminishing or ignoring the other, then we have departed from the clear teaching of Scripture. And such a departure results in shrinking the God in whom we trust.*

Direct reference in Scripture to God's upholding of the natural order is found, for example, in our Lord's own words when he said that God "causes his sun to rise on the evil and the good" (Matt 5:45 NIV), or when he asserted that it is his Father and our Father who feeds the "birds of the air" (Matt 6:26). Neither of these passages states anything extra or contrary to a physical explanation of the movements of the planets or the way birds are fed. What is implied is that when we have finished analyzing the movement of the sun or the feeding behavior of birds in physical terms, there remains a fresh sense to be made of the same pattern of events, if we are to do full justice to the way the world is.

22. Sanday, *Christology and Personality*, 174.
23. Polkinghorne, "Kenotic Creation," 97 (emphasis added).

When Two Accounts May Be Required by the Evidence: Pointers from Science

At times, giving two accounts of the same events is necessary in order to do full justice to the significance of those events. Donald MacKay told an imaginary story of two people sitting on a clifftop looking out to sea.[24] One, a very enthusiastic physicist, so the story goes, even carried some of his scientific equipment with him in the boot of his car. As they sat there on the cliffs, they spotted a light flashing on and off out at sea. The physicist boasted that, given a little time, he would be able to give a full account of all that was happening, the wavelength, emission rate, frequency, and various other characteristics of the flashing light. His friend, however, became increasingly agitated, since in the distant past he had learned the Morse code and was increasingly aware that the light flashes were also communicating a message. In fact, they were saying that the piece of cliff on which the couple were sitting was beginning to crumble and would shortly slide into the sea. One could reasonably expect a physicist to give a complete and exhaustive description, in physical terms, of all that was occurring at the light source, and yet this alone would leave out another, and in the circumstances, arguably more important aspect of the same phenomenon. The meaning and significance in this case were there for those who were able and willing to read it in a different way. The point is that before one assumes that two assertions about the same phenomenon are contradictory, one should be sure that they are not in fact logically complementary.

The history of science illustrates this principle of complementarity well. In the 1800s, the orthodox way of picturing light was in terms of waves spreading through space. The evidence for this was very convincing. It seemed clear that the earlier view of picturing light as a stream of particles was wrong and should be abandoned. But the situation changed again when it was discovered that, in certain previously unexplored situations, light behaved quite differently, like a hail of tiny particles. Which was the true picture, the wave or the particle one? Only after a lot of hard thinking it became clear that the correct answer was that *both pictures could be valid; the two interpretations were not rivals but complements.* The lesson is that we cannot deduce contradictory conclusions by the proper use of the two experimental approaches to the nature of light because they represent answers to different kinds of questions. This principle of "complementarity," first enunciated by the physicist Niels Bohr,[25] *is here being used as an*

---

24. Jeeves and Berry, *Science, Life, and Christian Belief*, 80.
25. Bohr, *Atomic Theory*.

analogy and not in any sense a proof of the necessity of complementarity of Christian and scientific viewpoints. However satisfied we may be that the two pictures are compatible, only the facts of experience can convince us that both are necessary. We are dealing here with a logical point, not a scientific one, but it is one that is open to easy abuse and misunderstanding. For this reason, we need to see clearly the conditions under which it can legitimately be used. Unless we do this, it could easily become an escape hatch that we use when we get into a tight corner in discussions about the relation of science and faith. The somewhat negative point that arises from all this is that before religious and scientific statements are debated as rivals, it is necessary to establish they are not in fact complements. It is also of course equally necessary to realize and to recognize that proof of complementarity would not establish that either account was true.

Underlining the need to recognize that, at times, more than one account of reality is required to do full justice to the whole of our experience, Freeman Dyson in his address at the ceremony in 2000 when receiving the Templeton Prize, called for more respect and understanding between scientists and theologians, noting:

> Science and religion are two windows that people look through, trying to understand the big universe outside, trying to understand why we are here. The two windows give different views, but they look out at the same universe. Both views are one-sided, neither is complete. Both leave out essential features of the real world. And both are worthy of respect.[26]

GOD'S PROVIDENTIAL CARE

Reflecting on theologian Bill Carroll's underlining of God's unceasing divine upholding, Denis Alexander posed the question, "How are we to understand the term 'providence' in relation to God's creation?"[27] Alexander believes that Bruce Ware has provided a useful definition of the term "providence." Ware wrote, "God exhaustively plans and meticulously carries out his perfect will as he alone knows best, regarding all that is in heaven and on earth, and he does so without failure or defeat, accomplishing his purposes in all of creation from the smallest details to the grand purposes of his plan for the whole of the created order."[28]

---

26. Dyson, "Science and Religion," n.p.
27. Alexander, "Creation, Providence, and Evolution."
28. Ware, "Prayer," 128.

Surprisingly, perhaps, for such a central Christian doctrine, when searching for the word "providence" in the NIV translation of the Bible, Denis Alexander noted that it *only* occurred once—in the book of Job:

> Your hands shaped me and made me.
> Will you now turn and destroy me?
> Remember that you molded me like clay.
> Will you now turn me to dust again?
> Did you not pour me out like milk
> and curdle me like cheese,
> clothe me with skin and flesh
> and knit me together with bones and sinews?
> You gave me life and showed me kindness,
> and in your *providence* watched over my spirit. (Job 10:8–12 NIV)

"This passage," wrote Alexander, "provides another example of the immanence of God in the created order, in this context the creation of the human individual. We are reminded of the psalmist's declaration of faith in God: 'For you created my inmost being; you knit me together in my mother's womb'" (Ps 139:13 NIV).[29] Alexander continued,

> God's providence is seen in the Bible as being worked out through the biographies of believers and nonbelievers alike. The Old Testament envisages God moving "the heart of Cyrus king of Persia to make a proclamation throughout his realm" (Ezra 1:1 NIV) just as much as God then moved the hearts of God's people to return to Jerusalem to "build the house of the LORD" (Ezra 1:5).[30]

Divine Upholding and God's Providence

The classic text most often referred to when thinking about God's providential care is in the book of Hebrews where we read, "The Son is the radiance of the glory of God and the exact imprint of his nature, and he upholds the universe by the word of his power" (Heb 1:3 ESV). If we affirm God's moment-by-moment providential upholding of his whole creation, including ourselves, we are rejecting deism, the idea that God created the laws of nature and then removed himself from his creation and from any further active involvement in it. Deism stands in sharp contrast to the type

---

29. Alexander, "Creation, Providence, and Evolution," 272.
30. Alexander, "Creation, Providence, and Evolution," 272.

of Christian theism that resonates with my life experience—the events of which support God's active moment-by-moment involvement in his creation and in the course of my life. That involvement means that without God nothing would exist. Without God, the whole concept of "laws of nature" would not exist. When we talk about laws of nature, we are simply referring to our way of describing our perception of God's faithfulness in his created order, beginning with God's authorship of creation and continuing each day through God's work in maintaining the integrity of that creation.

Another trap when thinking about the meaning of divine upholding is to believe that talk of God's providence necessarily entails determinism. Examples we gave in earlier chapters of God's providential care for his people throughout the exodus and of God's constant provision today for us through the discoveries of modern medicine did not entail any necessary belief in determinism.

Acknowledging that problems remain as we try to hold in delicate balance divine upholding and human freewill, Denis Alexander asks, "How can God providentially move human hearts and ensure that the created order fulfilled his intentions and purposes without subverting genuine human freedom?" His answer,

> We don't know although a voluminous amount of literature addresses precisely that point. Unfortunately, some of it has a strong emphasis on providence and sovereignty at the expense of human free will, whereas other offerings downgrade Providence in an attempt to defend free will. Such dichotomous extremes are quite unnecessary, and Scripture happily illustrates the realities of both genuine human free will and God's providence on virtually every page, seeing no necessary tension between these two essential aspects of the created order. Clearly, what is a problem to our very limited minds is no problem for God.[31]

Alexander summed up his thoughts on this issue this way "The Bible sees God's works occurring equally in the varied manifestations of his activity, whether in the more 'law-like' workings of the natural world (Ps 33:6–11), in chance events (Prov 16:33), or in his control of the weather (Ps 148:8), which we describe today using chaos theory. There is never a hint in the Bible that certain types of events in the natural world are any more or any less the activity of God than any other events."[32]

---

31. Alexander, "Creation, Providence, and Evolution," 273.
32. Alexander, "Creation, Providence, and Evolution," 284.

Maintaining a Delicate Balance: Models to Help our Thinking about Divine Upholding

The challenge remains, can we construct a "thought model" of the relation of God, outside and within his creation? Past attempts have included the models of the creative artist and of the craftsman. Donald MacKay, adapting our thinking about creative artistry to twentieth-century developments in modern technology, enabled us to construct a picture in which our Creator is active within the drama of our day-to-day existence, not only in his creative sustaining power moment by moment, but also in some mysterious way in his personal self-revelation.[33] If we are to begin to do full justice to our understanding of the relation of God to his creation, we need to use a variety of models, each focusing on a particular aspect of the relationship. In the past, the so-called craftsman and creative artist models have helped but they shared a radical shortcoming in that they failed to do justice to the clear biblical teaching that God continues to sustain the universe and to hold it in being moment by moment. They leave us with a picture of the Creator completing his work of art and then leaving it at that. So, the question becomes, how may we come a little nearer to doing full justice to the continuing activity of God in relation to creation? It is at this point that an elaboration of Dorothy Sayers's "author and creative artist" model by the late Donald MacKay is helpful, even though in some respects it remains controversial. MacKay invited his readers to adapt their thinking about creative artistry to modern technological developments of the mid-twentieth century. He asks us to imagine an artist who, instead of using canvas and oils, uses a television screen to display his creation. Furthermore, he uses the transmitting apparatus of a television station in order to generate the display that is portrayed to us. The important difference between this variant of the creative artist model and that of the more traditional artist is that the picture on the screen *continues to exist and to have its present form only as long as our artist continues to generate the program* which expresses his mind. The moment he stops, our picture ceases to exist. This model solves the problem in earlier creative artist models in that it underscores the continuing activity of the artist in holding his creation in being from moment to moment.

With this way of thinking in mind, MacKay wrote,

> Let us imagine the relationship of the author, as a creator, to the literary work which he creates. We can notice certain relevant features of this at once, such that our author, when he eventually conceives and utters his literary work, does so as a single

33. Jeeves, *Scientific Enterprise*, 23.

coherent picture, including the past, present and future of the characters of his story, and the world in which he sets them. This fact helps us to appreciate the logical distinction between the Creator of the drama, who is in this sense a spectator, and that of the actor within the drama. We shall return to the relation between creator-talk and creature-talk, but for the moment we simply wish to note that it is a real distinction. The next step is to imagine a character in a literary work who finds himself addressed by his fellow characters, some of whom claim to speak to him in the name of his creator and their creator. This refers, of course, to the way in which from time to time the prophets spoke and prefixed their statement with words such as "Thus says the Lord."[34]

MacKay continued, "Most amazing of all, the character in our literary work suddenly finds himself confronted by, and personally addressed by, a fellow character who claims to be identical with the creator of the whole literary work and all its characters. Here we are already involved in the mystery of the Incarnation."[35] In this way, MacKay steadily adapted and improved the picture of the creative literary artist, in order to do justice to the biblical teaching that declares that God in eternity, our Creator, is also identical with the one who spoke by the prophets, who was in Christ reconciling the world to himself, and who still today continues to invite personal dialogue and personal relationships with the creatures he has made.

This model of the creative artist, however, has a major inadequacy. Donald MacKay addressed it seeking to come closer to what he believed to be the biblical picture of God's relation to his creation. MacKay believes that we must first recall how the Bible opens with a narrative about the creative activity that gives rise to the existence of our world and its inhabitants. The Bible reminds us frequently (for example Col 1:17 and Heb 1:3) that not only does God uphold creation, including ourselves, in existence, as the continuing activity of the creative word, but also that the whole spacetime meshwork of events are upheld and cohere by and in the same creative word. More important still, the biblical picture teaches that *our Creator is active within the drama of our existence,* not only in his creative sustaining power moment by moment, *but also in some mysterious way in his personal self-revelation.* As Donald MacKay wrote,

> Our Creator is more than simply the creator of our drama, he is also the Creator-participant. With this in mind we must also

---

34. Jeeves, *Scientific Enterprise*, 24–25.
35. Jeeves, *Scientific Enterprise*, 25.

note that nothing we say, on the one hand, about our creatureliness, must be allowed to distort or diminish the truth which is conveyed to us, on the other hand, in the many complementary pictures, which depict us as children of a loving father, as sheep who have gone astray, as prodigal sons and daughters offered a loving welcome home in the home of our father.[36]

We have seen how throughout Scripture God repeatedly affirms his moment by moment upholding of his creation including us. For example, in the Old Testament, Psalm 77 underlines God's providential care for his people. We also saw in an earlier chapter how a very recent and detailed study of the miracles of the exodus vividly illustrates how *God works through "natural events,"* events well-documented to occur in the region where the exodus took place. *The God revealed in Scripture is not a last resort God to go to when all else fails.* He is there all the time upholding his wonderful creation and our lives lived within that creation. *We face the ever-present danger of shrinking the God of creation and the upholder of all things to a convenient God,* shaped by us, for our transitory immediate purposes. When, and if, we do this, *God becomes shrunken* to one we can appeal to support claims we are making for and/or about our particular beliefs to sustain an argument we are making to prove the existence of God by, for example, reference to dramatic, temporary healing events or sudden changes in personal prosperity linked to faith. The message is clear, the God of all this world, the God of Abraham, Isaac, and Jacob, of the apostles, of God incarnate in Jesus Christ, of Paul and the early persecuted Christians, cannot and must not be so manipulated for our purposes. Rather our response is to recognize his awesome majesty and to bow before him and worship.

Looking Back and Looking Forward

Earlier chapters have documented the ways in which, on a series of issues where advances in science impact some traditional and long held Christian beliefs, there has, all too often, been a knee-jerk reaction that results in the God in whom Christians believe being shrunk significantly from the God of Scripture. The God who created all things and holds all things in being is being shrunk to a God who fills in the gaps left after science has done its work. Many different topics could have been selected to illustrate this habitual gap filling, however, I selected, by way of illustration, areas of science in which I have been directly or closely involved for half a century. These included our understandings of human origins, human nature, miracles of nature,

---

36. Jeeves, *Scientific Enterprise*, 24.

and miracles of healing. In every instance I underlined the need to listen as carefully to the reports from dedicated biblical scholars about their fresh understandings of the origins, nature, and proper understanding of Scripture, as to listen to the stream of reports of exciting developments in science.

So far-reaching are the effects of social media today that, certainly in the Western world, few can for long be left unaware of major advances in contemporary science. The way the results of researches are reported is not always neutral. At times it is hijacked for the purposes of propaganda by those who want to use it to support their particular agenda. What this means is that the heartfelt plea for help from the student, illustrated and documented in the Preface to this book, is not going to be an isolated event. As noted, a succession of reviews by large foundations in America such as the Pew Research Center and the Barna Group continue to underline the fact that many serious Christians find themselves challenged in some of their basic beliefs by media accounts of advances in science. Not only do thoughtful young people need help, so do the pastors who are so busy that they simply do not have time to keep up with the media reported rapid advances in science, and more importantly, with their potential implications for some basic Christian beliefs.

Underlying and pervading all our discussions has been the need to recognize the temptation, all too easily and all too often, to depart from the robust understanding of the nature of faith and belief as taught and illustrated throughout Scripture. So prevalent and persuasive are our daily needs and hopes that we all too easily accept presentations of the Christian faith designed to fulfil our temporary felt needs rather than to develop the life of discipleship to which all Christians are called. The desire to fulfil both immediate and long-term needs was illustrated by the work of leading personality theorists of the twentieth century. The list of *psychological needs* suggested by different personality theorists contain common themes, as well as remarkably divergent perspectives on issues such as whether people are basically good or evil, whether human motivation is primarily conscious or unconscious, and whether tension within the personality helps or hinders personal growth. As yet none of the models in the marketplace has succeeded in gaining widespread acceptance amongst psychologists. The fact remains, *we all too easily succumb to presentations of the Christian gospel that focus on our felt needs* such as, for example, the need for healing from our ailments or the need to prosper in our daily lives. For these reasons we devoted a chapter to putting true Christian faith under the microscope and we recalled the need to remember that, as presented and embodied in the life of Jesus Christ and his disciples, living faith above all calls for an all-pervasive response to the call to Christian discipleship.

In conclusion, we underlined *divine self-emptying* as a pervasive theme of Scripture. It is a theme prominent with New Testament writers. We reminded ourselves of the ever-present temptation to tell just half of the story. That means that we cannot be satisfied with emphasizing divine upholding to the exclusion of holding in equal balance God's self-emptying. *We must keep in delicate balance both God's divine sovereignty and God's divine self-emptying. Only by such a balance can we avoid, yet again, "shrinking God."*

Postscript

IN THE PREFACE, I quoted an email from a student struggling to maintain his Christian faith in the face of what seemed to be a series of challenges to it from apparent conflicts between what he was learning in his science lectures at college and what he was hearing from the pulpit in his local church. Numerous surveys in the USA suggest that this is not an isolated incident. The path we have travelled in this book has examined some of the most frequently quoted and most worrying conflicts raised by today's honest and thoughtful students. The approach taken has been an open and yet critical minded look at how a thoughtful and honest Christian, who takes his faith seriously and has a very high regard for Scripture, can be open and honest minded as one challenge after another seems to emerge. We began by reminding ourselves that the temptation to shrink the God in whom we believe in the face of challenges from, on the one hand, science, and, on the other hand, misinterpretations of Scripture is not new. J. B. Phillips wrote about it eloquently seventy years ago. Since then leading theologians and scientists on both sides of the Atlantic have repeated his message.

Perhaps the first and most important lesson we learned was the need to remember that knowledge in all fields moves steadily on. That applies as much to the interpretation of Scripture as to the understanding of the wider implications of advances in science. Advances in both have implications for some of our widely held views of ourselves and of the world in which we live. We took as illustrative examples advances in our understanding of human origins and human nature. Both continue to benefit from new scholarship in science and in biblical studies. We used them as examples of how, on close and detailed scrutiny, they may be mutually enlightening. By bringing them together in a constructive way we were introduced to an even greater and more wonderful Creator and Sustainer God.

On reflection, we discovered how easily and how often faith, as described and exemplified in Scripture, becomes shrunk into just one aspect of it so that it is no longer a fully committed life of trust and discipleship. Faith, we saw, all too easily becomes focused on the claimed uniqueness of a passing emotional experience, on affirming a particular doctrine, of participating in certain actions or fulfilling certain temporary felt needs. A brief look into the lives of some of the great people of faith from the past, both those within Scripture and those whose lives are documented in the history of the Christian church, immediately refutes some of the simplistic caricatures of faith on sale in the religious marketplace today. Sadly, some of these shrunken views of true Christian faith are all too often associated with claims of miraculous healings that on close inspection prove to be totally unfounded. That miracles occur is well documented throughout Scripture and they are seen as manifestations of the ongoing activity of the God who created all things and who moment by moment upholds all things by his power. Miracles are not religious magic. They bear testimony to the ever-present caring activity of a loving God.

Finally, we noted that if we are to begin to do justice to the whole teaching of Scripture, we need always to place as much emphasis on the self-emptying activity of God as on his divine upholding. It is Christ who was before all things, upholds all things, and in his self-emptying and self-giving not only set us an example to follow but achieved on Calvary and in his resurrection our full and complete salvation. In the words of a verse from a Christmas carol, the child born at Bethlehem was indeed,

The Lord of Creation and Savior of all.[1]

---

1. From the hymn "A Maiden Most Gentle," by the Venerable Bede (paraphrased by Andrew Carter).

Appendix

Going Deeper
Guidance for Study and Discussion

ONE PERVASIVE THEME OF this book has been the rich rewards for living the Christian life that accrue from coming, both to science and to Scripture, with an open, seeking, critical mind, always ready to learn more and to move deeper into Christian discipleship and an understanding of Christian faith in all its fullness.

One of the many benefits of group discussion is that each member of the group brings a lifetime of varied experiences in living the Christian life within different historical church traditions, in different contexts, and perhaps in different countries. Each person also possesses unique expertise in different areas of knowledge. Some have historical knowledge, some have specialized scientific knowledge, and perhaps some have familiarity with the languages of the original biblical texts. All of these, taken together, mean that any topic under discussion will benefit from the variety of perspectives taken by those contributing.

This appendix provides some suggestions to facilitate individual study and meaningful group discussion of each chapter, including:

1. Pointers to relevant passages of Scripture;
2. Extracts from the chapter that focus attention on the key issues;
3. Questions for group discussion or for individual meditation;
4. Suggestions for further reading about the issues raised in each chapter.

At a practical level it is suggested that, prior to each discussion meeting, different members of the group undertake to do a bit more reading and research on the main issues raised in the next chapter under consideration.

PREFACE AND CHAPTER 1—IS YOUR GOD STILL TOO SMALL? ECHOES FROM THE PAST

Scripture passages

a. John 1:14—*The Word became flesh*

b. Mark 12:30—*Love the Lord your God with all your heart, your soul, your mind, and your strength*

c. Job 42:3–5—*Things too wonderful for me to understand*

Review and Reflect

How can college students maintain their commitment to truth when authoritative figures in local and national churches seem to be unaware of exciting developments in science that have theological implications at odds with what is preached from pulpits, or who deny the truth or relevance of such new knowledge? (Preface, xi)

The way we come to conclusions about what the Bible teaches is an indispensable part of how we use the Bible. No one comes to the Bible with a blank slate. We come instead with a host of presuppositions and habits of mind, some conscious and deliberate, others products of culture, family, denomination, and our personal fallenness and finitude. The same was true of the classic commentators of the Christian past. (Preface, xiv)

Why do young people who have grown up in church leave it in large numbers in their teens? Why have 50 percent of those who have grown up in the Southern Baptist Church of the USA left the church by the time they are thirty? According to numerous surveys, one of the reasons is that they are asked by their pastors to believe explanations about the world they live in which totally contradict and deny what God has enabled dedicated scientists to discover about the same world and about themselves. Commitment to truth through the diligent use of our minds is a Christian responsibility. (Chapter 1, 3)

Questions for Discussion

1. Do you agree with the assessment that in many Christian circles, attitudes towards science and the relation of science to faith has, in the past, reduced our understanding of God to a "god-of-the-gaps" or a "divine magician" we worship?
2. Can you think of examples of how some presentations of Christianity today continue to shrink God? Does this happen within your local church?
3. Do you agree with N. T. Wright that today there are "plenty of gods on offer"?
4. What characterizes the dominant "gods on offer" in your local cultural and church situation?
5. Which features of modern technology do you think are most influential in shaping the presentation and understanding of the Christian message?
6. Can you identify specific examples of how, within your own Christian community, you can see a tendency to "make God in our own image"? How can you counteract such trends?
7. Is it possible, at the level of the local church, to encourage reading the Bible in its historical and literary contexts? How would you go about that?

Suggestions for Further Reading

Barna Group. "Atheism Doubles among Generation Z." January 24, 2018. https://www.barna.com/research/atheism-doubles-among-generation-z/.

Cootsona, Greg. "Apologetics Needs a 'Systems Upgrade' for Emerging Adults." *BioLogos,* December 18, 2019. https://biologos.org/articles/apologetics-need-a-system-upgrade-for-emerging-adults.

Pew Research Center. "Perception of Conflict between Science and Religion." October 22, 2015. https://www.pewresearch.org/science/2015/10/22/perception-of-conflict-between-science-and-religion/.

Pew Research Center. "Religion and Science." October 22, 2015. https://www.pewresearch.org/science/2015/10/22/science-and-religion/.

Phillips, J. B. *Your God Is Too Small: A Guide for Believers and Skeptics Alike.* London: Simon & Schuster, 1952.

CHAPTER 2—ANYTHING NEW UNDER THE SUN? THE PROLIFERATION OF GODS

Scripture Passages

a. Psalm 8—*How majestic is God's name*
b. Isaiah 2:8—*People worship the idols they have made*
c. Isaiah 44:6–21—*There is no other God*

Review and Reflect

The temptation to thinkingly or unthinkingly mold our idea of God to fit our presuppositions and momentary felt needs is very much in evidence today. It is underlined by the results of numerous surveys in the USA studying the beliefs of contemporary American Christians. (Chapter 2, 30)

Most people, they reported, believe that God agrees with whatever they believe. (Chapter 2, 30)

Questions for Discussion

1. How widespread are the influences as described by James Bryan Smith in shaping how the Christian message is presented in your local church? Is, for example, the "shaming and scary gospel" ever employed in presentations of the gospel?
2. What are some of the dominant "felt needs" in the contemporary world? How might these shape our understanding and sharing of the gospel?

Suggestions for Further Reading

Epley, Nicholas, et al. "Believers' Estimates of God's Beliefs Are More Egocentric Than Estimates of Other People's Beliefs." *PNAS* 106 (2009) 21533–38. https://www.pnas.org/content/106/51/21533.

Margolis, Michele. "When Politicians Determine Your Religious Beliefs." *New York Times*, July 1, 2018. https://www.nytimes.com/2018/07/11/opinion/religion-republican-democrat.html.

Pew Research Center. "When Americans Say They Believe in God, What Do They Mean?" April 25, 2018. https://www.pewforum.org/2018/04/25/when-americans-say-they-believe-in-god-what-do-they-mean/.

Smith, James Bryan. *The Magnificent Story: Uncovering a Gospel of Beauty, Goodness and Truth*. Downers Grove, IL: IVP, 2017.

CHAPTER 3—"GODS" ON OFFER: SAMPLING THE TWENTY-FIRST-CENTURY MARKET PLACE

Scripture passages

a. Micah 6:8—*What does the Lord require?*

b. Luke 4:18–19—*Jesus brings good news of freedom and light*

Review and Reflect

The challenge today, as in the past, is how can we maintain a close relationship with the biblical revelation of God and his nature and not succumb to the temptation of "making gods" only to fulfil our own immediate wants and needs. The God of the Hebrew-Christian tradition is not a shrinking God but an ever-expanding God who expects our spirituality to expand in step with every fresh revelation of the might and majesty of his creation. (Chapter 3, 55)

Questions for Discussion

1. Can you think of specific examples in your community of how the technology available and in use is already shaping how the gospel message is being presented?

2. In what ways has the sharing of the gospel benefitted from the increasing use of modern technology?

3. When using specific technologies, what hazards are there that can distort the content of the message? For example, was Shane Hipps correct that, "This way of doing church . . . reinforces the modern gospel that affirms individualism and the privatization of the faith"?

4. Can you think of any recent advances in science that have the potential to expand our understanding of creation and its relationship to God?

5. What is your view of whether the evidence for an expanding universe has any implications for how we should think about the creation and its relationship to God?

Suggestions for Further Reading

Economist. "Our Father, Who Art in Cyberspace: Churches Turn to the Internet to Reach Their Flocks." *Economist*, April 11, 2020. https://www.economist.com/international/2020/04/11/churches-turn-to-the-internet-to-reach-their-flocks.

Hipps, Shane. *The Hidden Power of Electronic Culture: How Media Shapes Faith, the Gospel, and the Church*. Grand Rapids: Zondervan, 2005. https://vialogue.wordpress.com/2011/12/21/the-hidden-power-of-electronic-culture-notes-review/.

Horne, Marc. "Your DNA Points to Life Expectancy, Say Scientists." *Times* [London], January 15, 2019. https://www.thetimes.co.uk/article/your-dna-points-to-life-expectancy-say-scientists-npp2svjwc.

Wright, N. T. "Hope Deferred? Against the Dogma of Delay." *Early Christianity* 9 (2018) 37–82. https://research-repository.st-andrews.ac.uk/handle/10023/17178.

SECTION II OVERVIEW AND CHAPTER 4—HUMAN ORIGINS: THE EVIDENCE FROM SCIENCE

Scripture passages

a. Genesis 1—*God created the heavens and the earth*
b. Genesis 2—*God breathed the breath of life into humans*

Review and Reflect

We are strange and complicated creatures. We share many traits, including cognitive skills and emotions, with other animals, and increasingly learn that the borders between them and us are murky and permeable. Fresh insights into human nature come from the researches of evolutionary biologists, evolutionary psychologists, social psychologists, cognitive neuroscientists, neurologists, geneticists, archaeologists, and anthropologists. How the human mind achieved its present state and complexity remains a mystery. We are still looking for answers to such questions as: How did consciousness arise? How did language develop? How did the potential for ethical decision making and moral behavior emerge? As we begin to find answers to some of these questions, we must further ask, what is the relationship between these understandings of human nature and understandings of human nature based on the theological concept of humanity being made in the image of God. The understanding of human origins is clearly a multidisciplinary challenge. Diversity of opinion can be a good thing. It may result in a more profound awareness of the complexity of the issues under discussion and of the relevant evidence that needs to be considered. (Chapter 4, 66)

Questions for Discussion

1. Do you think the "knee-jerk" conflict model of science and religion is still present among any of your Christian friends?
2. If it is, why do you think they still hold this view? Do you think it would make a difference to them if they had a better appreciation for the positive relationship that science and religion have had through most of history?
3. Of the various "new insights" into our mysterious human nature listed in chapter 4, which struck you as most important? Why?
4. Does it matter to you that the current evidence points to you being "a bit Neanderthal"? If your answer is, "Yes, it does matter," is it because you think there is biblical basis for this worry? If so, can you elaborate this concern?

Suggestions for Further Reading

de Felipe, Pablo, and Malcolm A. Jeeves. "Science and Christianity Conflicts: Real and Contrived." *Perspectives on Science and Christian Faith* 69 (2017) 131–48. https://www.asa3.org/ASA/PSCF/2017/PSCF9-17deFelipe.pdf17deFelipe.pdf.

Hardin, Jeff. "Biology and Theological Anthropology: Friends or Foes?" *BioLogos Forum*, December 2019. https://wp.biologos.org/wp-content/uploads/2019/12/Biology-and-Theological-Anthropology-Friends-or-Foes.pdf.

Krause, Johannes, et al. "The Complete Mitochondrial DNA Genome of an Unknown Hominin from Southern Siberia." *Nature* 464 (2010) 894–97. https://www.nature.com/articles/nature08976.

Lucas, Ernest C., et al. "The Bible, Science and Human Origins." *Science and Christian Belief* 28 (2016) 74–99.

CHAPTER 5—HUMAN ORIGINS: THE EVIDENCE FROM SCRIPTURE

Scripture passages

a. Genesis 1 and 2—*God as Creator of all that exists*
b. Romans 5:15–21—*Condemnation through Adam, grace through Christ*
c. 1 Corinthians 15:20–58—*Victory over death*

Review and Reflect

Whether we are aware of them or not, we all bring with us a set of assumptions about how we are to understand, to interpret, anything and everything that we read. (Chapter 5, 82)

In an effort to defend the God in whom we believe, we attribute to him direct "interventions" from time to time in his created order. (Chapter 5, 79)

Questions for Discussion

1. Professor Millard asks, "Why do people, especially evangelical Christians, want to find Noah's Ark?" Do you think this is a fair question? If not, why not? Is this a caricature of evangelical Christians? Can you think of any other caricatures of the beliefs of evangelical Christians on science and religion that might be misrepresentative?

2. How have past interpretations of Scripture about human origins had the effect of shrinking our understanding of God's relationship to creation? Can you list some specific examples?

3. Views differ among biblical scholars about whether there was ever an "historical Adam." Does this question matter, and if so, why does it matter?

4. What is your current view about the existence of Adam and Eve? Can you think of any advances in science or in biblical research that would change that view?

5. Do you agree that the most important aspect of what it means to be "made in the image of God" is that God has given us the capacity for a

personal relationship with him? How may we develop this relationship in our day-to-day lives as Christians?

Suggestions for Further Reading

Barna Group. "Six Reasons Young Christians Leave the Church." September 27, 2011. https://www.barna.com/research/six-reasons-young-christians-leave-church/.

Enns, Peter. "Why Young Christians Leave Church." 2016. https://peteenns.com/young-christians-leave-church/.

Kirk, J. R. Daniel. "Does Paul's Christ Require a Historical Adam?" https://fullerstudio.fuller.edu/pauls-christ-require-historical-adam/.

Smith, Samuel. "Wheaton Scholars Pen First 'Origins' College Textbook Bridging the Bible to 'Mainline Science.'" April 1, 2019. https://www.christianpost.com/news/wheaton-scholars-pen-first-origins-college-textbook-bridging-the-bible-to-mainline-science.html.

Than, Ker. "Noah's Ark Found in Turkey?" https://www.nationalgeographic.com/news/2010/4/100428-noahs-ark-found-in-turkey-science-religion-culture/

CHAPTER 6—HUMAN NATURE: THE EVIDENCE FROM SCIENCE

Scripture passages

a. Genesis 1:27—*Humans reflect the image of God*
b. Psalm 8—*What are human beings?*

Review and Reflect

What, for example, is the relation between the mind and the soul? And how do these relate to the brain? If my consciousness and what makes me "me" depend upon the intact working of my brain, what happens to me when I die? Is it legitimate and does it make sense to look to science to give us assurance that there is anything after this present life? (Chapter 6, 95)

Over the past century, biblical scholars also began to move away from a dualistic anthropology in order to recover a more holistic Hebrew view of the human person. The rejection of Platonic dualism provides an opportunity for theologians and psychologists to work together in engaging the neuroscience findings that support a fundamental mind–brain and mind–body unity of the human person. In our view, the most helpful way to move forward is to recognize the mysterious duality of our mental life and physical body, while accepting our essential psychobiological unity as whole, complete persons. (Chapter 6, 103)

Questions for Discussion

1. Before you read this chapter, did you believe that, hidden within you, somewhere in your head or in your heart, you possess "an immortal soul"? If the answer is yes, try to trace how you came to this belief. Was it because your church taught it, or was it because it seemed obvious, or was there some other reason that led you to believe that you have a soul?

2. Has the scientific evidence convinced you of the unity of mind and brain? If you believe that mind and brain are completely separate, how do you respond to medical cases in which brain damage is accompanied by changes in emotions, personality, and moral character?

3. Can you think of any relatives or friends who have suffered a major stroke and whose spiritual life has changed noticeably? Has this chapter helped you to understand better why this might be the case?

Suggestions for Further Reading

Egnor, Michael. "More Than Material Minds." *Christianity Today*, September 14, 2018. https://www.christianitytoday.com/ct/2018/september-web-only/more-than-material-minds-neuroscience-souls.html.

Nature. "Evolution and the Brain." *Nature* 447 (2007) 753. https://www.nature.com/articles/447753a.

Jeeves, Malcolm A., and Thomas E. Ludwig. *Psychological Science and Christian Faith: Insights and Enrichments from Constructive Dialogue*. West Conshohocken, PA: Templeton, 2018.

CHAPTER 7—HUMAN NATURE: THE EVIDENCE FROM SCRIPTURE

Scripture passages

a. Genesis 2:7—*God's breath creates living beings*

b. 1 Corinthians 15—*Resurrection bodies have a new form*

Review and Reflect

To summarize: the term *nephesh* in Genesis 2:7 refers not to a part of Adam's nature, nor to some possession such as a transcendent personal spiritual hypostasis termed a "soul" that lives forever and distinguishes humanity from the animals. Rather, *nephesh hayyah* denotes Adam as a living creature like the animals created in Genesis 1 and 2. It underscores Adam's linkage with the animal creation, not his difference from it. (Chapter 7, 114)

Any attempt to pull together the many and diverse threads of thinking about human nature extending back many millennia will inevitably face the charge of oversimplification. But the attempt must be made if only to see where we have got to at the beginning of the twenty-first century and what are the major challenges that face us today as we continue to think about human nature. (Chapter 7, 119)

Questions for Discussion

1. Have the views of leading biblical scholars summarized in this chapter changed your views in any way? If not, why not? Do you think the biblical scholars have it wrong?

2. Consider N. T. Wright's statement that, "The image of God was not in Genesis 1 intended to refer to some characteristic or special ability or trait of humans but rather a vocation. The vocation in question is that humans were designed by the Creator to have a special role in his governance of the world. Eventually it comes round to using the royal priesthood language which I think is absolutely central." Do you agree or disagree with this statement?

3. What is your own view about the essential nature of a person? If you believe in a bodily resurrection, how do you think a resurrected person would be similar to or different from that person prior to death?

Suggestions for Further Reading

Collins, Francis. "Evolution and the Imago Dei." *BioLogos Forum*, May 11, 2009. https://biologos.org/articles/evolution-and-the-imago-dei.

Enns, Peter. "What Does 'Image of God' Mean?" *BioLogos Forum*, July 27, 2010. https://biologos.org/articles/what-does-image-of-god-mean.

Noll, Mark A. *Jesus Christ and the Life of the Mind*. Grand Rapids: Eerdmans, 2011.

CHAPTER 8—MIRACLES OF NATURE: DIVINE UPHOLDER OR OCCASIONAL GAP FILLER?

Scripture passages

a. Psalm 135:6-12—*God sent signs and wonder to the Egyptians*

b. Romans 1:18-23—*God's power and nature are revealed through the things he has made*

c. Colossians 1:11-19—*Christ is the firstborn of creation, through whom all things were created*

Review and Reflect

The Bible makes clear distinctions between magic and miracles. A lot of the confusion has been caused by failing to observe that Scripture does not sharply distinguish between God's constant sovereign providence and his particular acts. In Scripture, belief in miracles is set in the context of a worldview that regards the whole of creation as continually dependent upon the sustaining activity of God and subject to his sovereign will (see for example Col 1:16-17). In Scripture, we find three aspects of God's divine activity underlined—wonder, power, and significance. They are all found present, not only in special acts, but also in the whole created order (Rom 1:20). (Chapter 8, 130)

We find also that the relation that the miraculous events bear to the wider purposes of God's revelation of his will is emphasized in Scripture. The biblical miracles, therefore, direct our attention to the impression that the event makes upon those who witness it, rather than to theoretical questions, such as whether the cause of a miracle is regular but still unknown to us, or whether it is in some way contrary to our normal expectations. (Chapter 8, 133)

Questions for Discussion

1. How do you react to N. T. Wright's claim that some Christians have a "split-level" view of the world—with God normally outside the created

world, except for occasional miraculous "invasions" into our part of the world? Can you think of examples of how such "split-level" thinking occurs in thinking and talking with fellow Christians about Christian beliefs and practices?

2. Was Philip Yancey exaggerating when he said that Christians often equate magic and faith?

3. Can you think of further examples within Christian thinking of how "explaining" slips into "explaining away"? How can we counteract such a trend?

Suggestions for Further Reading

Kuhn, Gustav. "Experiencing the Impossible." *The Psychologist* 32 (2019) 32–37. https://thepsychologist.bps.org.uk/volume-32/april-2019/experiencing-impossible.

Economist. "Miracles Are on the Rise in Lebanon." *Economist,* December 15, 2018. https://www.economist.com/middle-east-and-africa/2018/12/15/miracles-are-on-the-rise-in-lebanon.

Wright, N. T. *Surprised by Scripture.* New York: HarperCollins, 2014.

Brice-Saddler, Michael. "A Wealthy Televangelist Explains His Fleet of Private Jets." *Washington Post,* June 4, 2019. https://www.washingtonpost.com/religion/2019/06/04/wealthy-televangelist-explains-his-fleet-private-jets-its-biblical-thing/.

CHAPTER 9—MIRACLES OF NATURE: ILLUSTRATIVE EXAMPLES

Scripture passages

a. Joshua 10:12–15—*The sun stood still*

b. Psalm 104:14–24—*God's ordinary daily providence is miraculous*

c. Exodus 14:21–31—*Witnesses to the miraculous escape from Egypt*

d. Mark 3:1–11—*Witnesses to the miracles of Jesus*

Review and Reflect

Given the several millennia covered by biblical history, the total occurrence of miracles in the biblical narratives is surprisingly rare. There are, however, some periods in which the reporting of miracles is frequent. The first is during the exodus and the second such period is during the life of Christ upon earth.... Our purpose in looking at these two periods now is to see what we can discover about any enduring expectations we should have about the nature and frequency of the occurrence of miracles today. (Chapter 9, 147)

Questions for Discussion

1. What has been your reaction and the reactions of your Christian friends to the evidence from science for there being a "natural explanation" for some dramatic events in Scripture, such as the star of Bethlehem, or the sun standing still? Has such evidence weakened or strengthened your faith? If so, why and how?

2. Does it matter to you that there are "natural explanations" for the miracles of the exodus? If so, why does it matter to you? If not, should it matter to you?

Suggestions for Further Reading

Chavalas, Mark W. "Does the Bible Claim that the Sun and Moon Stopped in Their Tracks?" *The Ancient Near East Today* 4 (May 2016). http://www.asor.org/anetoday/2016/05/bible-claim-sun-moon/.

Walton, John H. "Biblical Credibility and Joshua 10: What Does the Text Really Claim?" *BioLogos Forum*, October 15, 2013. https://biologos.org/articles/biblical-credibility-and-joshua-10-what-does-the-text-really-claim.

CHAPTER 10—MIRACLES OF HEALTH AND HEALING: SCRIPTURAL AND SCIENTIFIC INSIGHTS

Scripture passages

a. Mark 1:40-44—*Jesus heals a man with leprosy*

b. Luke 13:10-17—*Jesus heals a woman on the sabbath*

c. John 11:1-44—*Jesus raises Lazarus to life*

d. 1 Thessalonians 5:19-21—*Listen to the prophetic word, but test everything, and hold fast to what is good*

e. *2 Thessalonians 2:9–12—Satan can also use signs and wonders to lead people astray*

Review and Reflect

Today, "shrunken gods" are preached and promoted with, at times, an almost exclusive emphasis on the health benefits of faith and, in some cases, of promises of miraculous healings. (Chapter 10, 154)

Yet we have seen that healing in the Bible, properly understood, is anything but an isolated and extrinsic phenomenon. It is, rather, integral or related to the larger biblical story of God's creation and restoration of humankind. As such, it takes place in the context of human communities of nurture and faith. And it requires discernment and interpretation within and beyond those communities. (Chapter 10, 157)

In the world of the New Testament, healing is an integral part of the mission to the needy. Nearly one third of the Gospel passages are taken up reporting incidents and debates surrounding Jesus Christ's healings. In the history of the Christian church, healing has always been a vital strand within the church's pastoral care. (Chapter 10, 158)

It is not uncommon for preachers, when promoting their particular "gods on offer" in the religious marketplace, to appeal to reports of present-day healing miracles to substantiate the case for the God they are offering. Talk of "God intervening" or of "leaving room for God to act" is frequent. But is there biblical warrant for such language? I would argue that such "gods on offer" are, by their very nature, "diminished gods" and "gods-of-the-gaps," and thus we need to scrutinize them carefully. (Chapter 10, 172)

Questions for Discussion

1. Would Philip Yancey's statement that "more than half the spontaneous prayers I hear in church pertain to the sick" be true of your church?
2. Has reading this chapter changed your views in any way on prayer for healing and if so how?

3. Are there some shared expectations in the church to which you belong about petitionary prayer and healing? Can you summarize these?

4. In the light of this chapter, do you think these beliefs need revising? If so, in what way(s)? How can we maintain a delicate balance between deep trust in God and recognizing our proneness to disease and sickness?

Suggestions for Further Reading

Economist. "Healing Hands: Catherine Hamlin Died on March 18." Obituary in *Economist,* April 8, 2020. https://www.economist.com/obituary/2020/04/08/catherine-hamlin-died-on-march-18th.

May, Peter. "Miracles in Medicine." *Science and Christian Belief* 29 (2017) 127–34.

Miller, Lisa, et al. 2014. "Neuroanatomical Correlates of Religiosity and Spirituality: A Study in Adults at High and Low Familial Risk for Depression." *JAMA Psychiatry* 71 (2014) 128–35. https://pubmed.ncbi.nlm.nih.gov/24369341/.

Myers, David G. *A Friendly Letter to Skeptics and Atheists: Musings on Why God Is Good and Faith Isn't Evil.* New York: Jossey-Bass, 2008.

Pew Research Center. "U.S. Religious Landscape Survey: Religious Beliefs and Practices." June 1, 2008. https://www.pewforum.org/2008/06/01/u-s-religious-landscape-survey-religious-beliefs-and-practices/.

CHAPTER 11—THE MULTIFACETED NATURE OF FAITH: THE EVIDENCE FROM SCRIPTURE

Scripture passages

a. Genesis 15:1–6—*Abram believed God's promises*

b. Matthew 9:18–26—*A woman's faith is instrumental in restoring her to health*

c. Hebrews 11—*Examples of faith in action*

Review and Reflect

This theme of faith's richness and multifaceted nature is diminished and debased whenever faith, in all its wholeness and richness, is shrunk to one small aspect of it. Such shrinking can happen if faith is presented primarily and exclusively as only one component such as either experience, or belief, or action.

The lives of men and women of faith recorded in Scripture and documented throughout church history make it abundantly clear that real faith includes all of these in varied proportions and at different times. (Chapter 11, 177)

Throughout the Gospel passages, the outworking of faith is inextricably interwoven with discipleship. Jesus first words to his disciples were not "Come experience me." Instead, they were "Follow me" (Matt 4:19), with all that that entails in living a particular way of life—a life of discipleship. (Chapter 11, 186)

Questions for Discussion

1. What role does faith play your own Christian journey? How would you describe the essential nature of your faith? Is it, for example, faith as expressed in deep trust, or faith as shown in action, or faith as embodied in discipleship?

2. How can we avoid faith becoming a placebo in attempting to cope with the everyday challenges of life?

Suggestions for Further Reading

Yancey, Philip. *Vanishing Grace: What Ever Happened to the Good News?* London: Hodder and Stoughton, 2014.

CHAPTER 12—THE MULTIFACETED NATURE OF FAITH: THE EVIDENCE FROM SCIENCE

Scripture passages

a. Hebrews 11—*Examples of faith in action*
b. 2 Corinthians 5:11–21—*Being reconciled to God changes everything*

Review and Reflect

Except in very rare instances, such as the lonely hermit, faith is lived out in community. This means that the life of faith is fully embedded in our physical, cultural, and social environments.

For each of us, the choices we make are embedded within our unique life context and that includes our developmental history and lifetime friendship networks, as well as the broader cultural environment. Thus our faith is both physically embodied and socially embedded. (Chapter 12, 192)

Questions for Discussion

1. What lessons have you learned about the nature of "real faith" from some of the accounts given of the lives of great "heroes of the faith" from past generations?
2. In your opinion, to what extent can the exceptional faith of these individuals be explained by their life circumstances?

Suggestions for Further Reading

Howard, David M., et al. "Genome-Wide Meta-Analysis of Depression Identifies 102 Independent Variants and Highlights the Importance of the Prefrontal Brain Regions." *Nature Neuroscience* 22 (2019) 343–52. https://www.nature.com/articles/s41593-018-0326-7.

McKee, Selena. "UK Researchers Make New Alzheimer's Disease Discovery." *PharmaTimes Online,* December 13, 2019. http://www.pharmatimes.com/news/uk_researchers_make_new_alzheimers_disease_discovery_1319837.

Redfern, Clare, and Alasdair Coles. "Parkinson's Disease, Religion, and Spirituality." *Movement Disorders Clinical Practice* 2 (2015) 341–46. https://www.researchgate.net/publication/280915732_Parkinson%27s_Disease_Religion_and_Spirituality.

Salt, Sharon. 2019. "Treasure Trove of 269 Genes Associated with Depression Identified." *NeuroCentral,* February 5, 2019. https://www.neuro-central.com/treasure-trove-269-genes-associated-depression-identified/.

CHAPTER 13 AND POSTSCRIPT—DIVINE UPHOLDING AND DIVINE EMPTYING: AN ESSENTIAL BALANCE

Scripture Passages

a. Job 10:8–12—*We are created and sustained by God's providential care*
b. Psalm 77—*The God who works wonders also cares for us*
c. Psalm 139:1–18—*God knows us and guides us throughout our lives*

d. Philippians 2:5–11—*The Christ who emptied himself has become exalted*

Review and Reflect

An essential aspect of God's awesomeness is revealed in his self-emptying, technically in kenosis. Derived from the Greek verb *kenoō* used in Philippians 2:7 ("he emptied himself"), the word kenosis has many theological meanings. First and foremost, in the context of this present book it refers to a key aspect of creation. It reminds us that at all times we must keep in delicate balance both God's divine sovereignty and God's divine self-emptying. (Chapter 13, 210)

To pay attention to what we know of God's *divine upholding* of creation to the exclusion of what has been revealed—in the person of Jesus Christ—about his *divine participating* in creation, would present an unbalanced view of God's relation to his creation that does not do justice to the available evidence. It would shrink God. (Chapter 13, 214)

Questions for Discussion

1. Focus on the theme of "God's divine upholding of all things at all times." In what ways can this provide a new perspective on your understanding of our human origins and our human nature? How does this theme relate to the idea of God healing through the knowledge and skills he has given to humans within medicine and science?

2. How can the pervasive theme of God's divine upholding be held in delicate balance with the equally pervasive scriptural theme of how God "empties himself," as seen in the incarnation and in how Christ "humbled himself by becoming obedient to the point of death even death on a cross"? (Phil 2:5–8)

3. Explain why you agree or disagree with Polkinghorne's statement, "Thus, kenotic creation and divine action are opposite sides of the same theological coin."

4. What implications for daily discipleship flow from the embodied example of Christ's self-emptying?

5. Are you aware of any additional advances in science, medicine, and biblical scholarship that have been published since this book was written? How might those advances expand upon the stories of mutual enrichment recounted in earlier chapters?

Suggestions for Further Reading

Pew Research Center. "Religion and Science." October 22, 2015. https://www.pewresearch.org/science/2015/10/22/science-and-religion/.

Oord, Thomas J. "Divine Action as Uncontrolling Love." *BioLogos Forum*, June 7, 2016. https://biologos.org/articles/series/divine-action-a-biologos-conversation/divine-action-as-uncontrolling-love.

May we always be able to affirm that we worship a God who is indeed,

The Lord of Creation and Savior of all.

Bibliography

Adorno, Theodor W., et al. *The Authoritarian Personality*. New York: Harper & Brothers, 1950.
Alexander, Denis R. "Creation, Providence and Evolution." In *Knowing Creation: Perspectives from Theology, Philosophy and Science*, edited by Andrew B. Torrance and Thomas H. McCall, 261–85. Grand Rapids: Zondervan, 2018.
———. "Miracles and Science." In *Has Science Killed God? The Faraday Papers on Science and Religion*, edited by Denis R. Alexander, 116–28. London: SPCK, 2020.
Allen, Diogenes. "Persons in Philosophical and Biblical Perspective." In *From Cells to Souls, and Beyond: Changing Portraits of Human Nature*, edited by Malcolm Jeeves, 165–78. Grand Rapids: Eerdmans, 2004.
Allport, Gordon W. *The Individual and His Religion: A Psychological Interpretation*. New York: Macmillan, 1950.
American National Election Studies. "The 2016 Time Series Study." *ANES*, 2016. https://electionstudies.org/data-center/2016-time-series-study/.
Anderson, Emma. "Healing and Ecclesial Response in Nineteenth-Century Catholic France." In *Spiritual Healing: Science, Meaning, and Discernment*, edited by Sarah Coakley, 40–58. Grand Rapids: Eerdmans, 2020.
Aristotle. *De Anima (On the Soul)*. Translated by Hugh Lawson-Tancred. London: Penguin, 1986.
Arnold, Bill T. "Soul-Searching Questions about 1 Samuel 28: Samuel's Appearance at Endor and Christian Anthropology." In *What about the Soul: Neuroscience and Christian Anthropology*, edited by Joel B. Green, 75–83. Nashville: Abingdon, 2004.
Augustine. *Saint Augustine: The City of God*. Translated by Gerald G. Walsh and Daniel J. Honan. Washington, DC: Catholic University of America Press, 1954.
Barna Group. "Atheism Doubles among Generation Z." January 24, 2018. https://www.barna.com/research/atheism-doubles-among-generation-z/.
———. "Six Reasons Young Christians Leave the Church." September 27, 2011. https://www.barna.com/research/six-reasons-young-christians-leave-church/.
Barrett, Justin L., and Matthew J. Jarvinen. "Cognitive Evolution, Human Uniqueness, and the Imago Dei." In *The Emergence of Personhood: A Quantum Leap?* edited by Malcolm Jeeves, 163–83. Grand Rapids: Eerdmans, 2015.
Barth, Karl. *Church Dogmatics*. Edinburgh: T. & T. Clark, 1956.
Bartlett, Frederic C. *Religion as Experience, Belief, Action*. London: Oxford University Press, 1950.

Bauckham, Richard. "For Whom Were the Gospels Written?" In *The Gospels for All Christians: Rethinking the Gospel Audiences*, edited by Richard Bauckham, 9–48. Grand Rapids: Eerdmans, 1998.

Benson, Eric. "Immunotherapy Could Revolutionise Care for Cancer Patients." *Times* [London], November 24, 2018. https://www.thetimes.co.uk/article/immunotherapy-could-revolutionise-care-for-cancer-patients-so-is-this-the-end-of-chemotherapy-as-we-know-it-2cpcmd28d.

BioLogos. "Five Wheaton College Professors Release New Book on Theories of Origins." *BioLogos Forum,* December 4, 2018. https://biologos.org/articles/5-wheaton-college-professors-release-new-book-on-theories-of-origins.

Bloom, Paul. *Descartes' Baby: How the Science of Child Development Explains What Makes Us Human.* New York: Basic, 2004.

Bohr, Niels. *Atomic Theory and the Description of Nature.* Cambridge: Cambridge University Press, 1934.

Boston Cultivator. "Science and Religion." *Boston Cultivator* 7 (1845) 344.

Brand, Paul, and Philip Yancey. "Putting Pain to Work." *Leadership Journal* (Fall 1984) 121–24.

Brice-Saddler, Michael. "A Wealthy Televangelist Explains His Fleet of Private Jets: It's a Biblical Thing." *Washington Post,* June 3, 2019. https://www.washingtonpost.com/religion/2019/06/04/wealthy-televangelist-explains-his-fleet-private-jets-its-biblical-thing/.

Bridge, Mark. "Say a Little Prayer for Me: Alexa App Helps Users to Connect with God." *Times* [London], May 28, 2019. https://www.thetimes.co.uk/article/alexa-say-some-prayers-and-help-me-to-find-god-fokp9v3zv.

Briggs, Andrew, et al. *It Keeps Me Seeking: The Invitation from Science, Philosophy, and Religion.* Oxford: Oxford University Press, 2018.

Brooke, John H. "Historians." In *The Warfare Between Science and Religion: The Idea That Wouldn't Die,* edited by Jeff Hardin et al., 258–78. Baltimore: Johns Hopkins University Press, 2018.

———. *Science and Religion: Some Historical Perspectives.* Cambridge: Cambridge University Press, 1991.

———. "Science and Religion." In *The Cambridge History of Science,* Vol. 4, edited by Roy Porter, 741–61. Cambridge: Cambridge University Press, 2003.

Brown, Warren S., and Malcolm A. Jeeves. "Portraits of Human Nature: Reconciling Neuroscience and Christian Anthropology." *Science and Christian Belief* 11 (1999) 139–50.

Brown, Warren S., and Lynn K. Paul. "Brain Connectivity and the Emergence of Capacities of Personhood: Reflections from Callosal Agenesis and Autism." In *The Emergence of Personhood: A Quantum Leap?* edited by Malcolm Jeeves, 104–19. Grand Rapids: Eerdmans, 2015.

Brown, Warren S., and Brad D. Strawn. "Beyond the Isolated Self: Extended Mind and Spirituality." *Theology and Science* 15 (2017) 411–23.

———. *The Physical Nature of Christian Life: Neuroscience, Psychology, and the Church.* Cambridge: Cambridge University Press, 2012.

Burgess, Kaya. "Thou Shalt Not Tweet in Anger, Says Church of England." *Times* [London], July 1, 2019. https://www.thetimes.co.uk/article/thou-shalt-not-tweet-in-anger-says-church-3hn55rmqf.

Burns, Robert. "The Red, Red Rose." In *A Selection of Scots Songs, Book 2*, edited by Pietro Urbani, 16–17. Edinburgh: Urbani and Liston, 1794.
Butler, Paul M., et al. "Side of Onset in Parkinson's Disease and Alterations in Religiosity: Novel Behavioral Phenotypes." *Behavioural Neurology* 24 (2011) 133–41.
Byrne, Richard W. "The Dividing Line: What Sets Humans Apart from Our Closest Relatives?" In *The Emergence of Personhood: A Quantum Leap?* edited by Malcolm Jeeves, 13–36. Grand Rapids: Eerdmans, 2015.
Calvin, John. *Institutes of the Christian Religion*. Philadelphia: Westminster, 1960.
Campbell, Heidi A., and Stephen Garner. *Networked Theology: Negotiating Faith in Digital Culture*. Grand Rapids: Baker Academic, 2016.
Carroll, William E. "Aquinas and Contemporary Cosmology: Creation and Beginnings." *Science and Christian Belief* 24 (2012) 5–18.
Catholic Church. "In the Image of God." In *Catechism of the Catholic Church, 2nd Edition*, Part One, Section Two, Chapter One, Paragraph 6.366. Vatican City: Libreria Editrice Vaticana, 2012.
Chan, Eva K. F., et al. "Human Origins in a Southern African Palaeo-Wetland and First Migrations." *Nature* 575 (2019) 185–89.
Chavalas, Mark W. "Does the Bible Claim That the Sun and Moon Stopped in Their Tracks?" *Ancient Near East Today* 4 (2016). http://www.asor.org/anetoday/2016/05/bible-claim-sun-moon/.
Cheadle, Alyssa C. D., and Christine Dunkel Schetter. "Untangling the Mechanisms Underlying the Links between Religiousness, Spirituality, and Better Health." *Social and Personality Psychology Compass* 11:e12299 (2017) 1–10.
Christianity Today. "Editorial: No Adam, No Eve, No Gospel." *Christianity Today* 55 (2011) 61.
Clement (of Alexandria). "Stromata (Miscellanies)." *The Ante-Nicene Fathers*, Vol. 2, Section 5, edited by Alexander Roberts and James Donaldson. New York: Scribner's Sons, 1905. Also available at http://www.earlychristianwritings.com/clement.html.
Coakley, Sarah, ed. *Spiritual Healing: Science, Meaning, and Discernment*. Grand Rapids: Eerdmans, 2020.
Coleridge, Hartley. "The Just Shall Live by Faith." In *Poems by Hartley Coleridge*, Vol. 2. London: Edward Moxon, 1851.
Coles, Alasdair, and Joanna Collicutt, eds. *Neurology and Religion*. Cambridge: Cambridge University Press, 2020.
Collins, Francis. "Learning the Language of God." *How I Changed My Mind about Evolution: Evangelicals Reflect on Faith and Science*, edited by Kathryn Applegate and J. B. Stump, 69–74. Downers Grove, IL: IVP Academic, 2016.
Cootsona, Greg. "Apologetics Needs a 'Systems Upgrade' for Emerging Adults." *BioLogos*, December 18, 2019. https://biologos.org/articles/apologetics-need-a-system-upgrade-for-emerging-adults.
Coulson, Charles. *Science and Christian Belief*. London: Fontana, 1967.
Cressey, Martin. "Miracles." In *New Bible Dictionary*. 2nd ed. Leicester, UK: InterVarsity, 1982.
Culkin, John M. "A Schoolman's Guide to Marshall McLuhan." *Saturday Review*, March 18, 1967, 51–53, 71–72.

Curtis, Heather D. "Healing, Belief, and Interpretation in Nineteenth-Century Protestant America." In *Spiritual Healing: Science, Meaning, and Discernment*, edited by Sarah Coakley, 59–83. Grand Rapids: Eerdmans, 2020.

Davies, Gaius. *Genius, Grief, and Grace: A Doctor Looks at Suffering and Success*. Fearn, UK: Christian Focus, 2001.

Dawkins, Richard. "Snake Oil and Holy Water." *Forbes*, October 4, 1999, 235.

de Felipe, Pablo, and Malcolm A. Jeeves. "Science and Christianity Conflicts: Real and Contrived." *Perspectives on Science and Christian Faith* 69 (2017) 131–48. https://www.asa3.org/ASA/PSCF/2017/PSCF9-17deFelipe.pdf17deFelipe.pdf.

de Waal, Frans B. M. *Good Natured: The Origins of Right and Wrong in Humans and Other Animals*. Cambridge: Harvard University Press, 1996.

Draper, John W. *History of the Conflict between Religion and Science*. New York: Appleton, 1875.

Duhem, Pierre. *Essays in the History and Philosophy of Science*. Translated by Roger Ariew and Peter Barker. Indianapolis: Hackett Publishing, 1996.

Dyson, Freeman J. "Complementarity." In *Spiritual Information: 100 Perspectives on Science and Religion*, edited by Charles L. Harper, 52–55. West Conshohocken, PA: Templeton, 2005.

———. "Viewpoint: Science and Religion Can Work Together." *APS News* 9, November 2000. https://www.aps.org/publications/apsnews/200011/viewpoint2.cfm

Economist. "Healing Hands: Catherine Hamlin Died on March 18." *Economist*, April 8, 2020. https://www.economist.com/obituary/2020/04/08/catherine-hamlin-died-on-march-18th.

———. "The Maturing of the Smartphone Industry Is Cause for Celebration: It's Bad News for Apple Shareholders, but Good News for Humanity." *Economist*, January 12, 2019. https://www.economist.com/leaders/2019/01/12/the-maturing-of-the-smartphone-industry-is-cause-for-celebration.

———. "Miracles Are on the Rise in Lebanon." *Economist*, December 15, 2018. https://www.economist.com/middle-east-and-africa/2018/12/15/miracles-are-on-the-rise-in-lebanon.

———. "Our Father, Who Art in Cyberspace: Churches Turn to the Internet to Reach Their Flocks." *Economist*. April 11, 2020. https://www.economist.com/international/2020/04/11/churches-turn-to-the-internet-to-reach-their-flocks.

———. "Pessimism v Progress: Contemporary Worries about the Impact of Technology Are Part of a Historical Pattern." *Economist*, December 18, 2019. https://www.economist.com/leaders/2019/12/18/pessimism-v-progress.

Edit. "Out of This World." *Edit—The University of Edinburgh Magazine* (2019) 28–33. https://www.ed.ac.uk/edit-magazine/editions/2019/out-of-this-world.

Edwards, Jonathan. *A Treatise concerning Religious Affections*. Philadelphia: James Crissy, 1821.

Efron, Noah J. "That Christianity Gave Birth to Modern Science." In *Galileo Goes to Jail: And Other Myths about Science and Religion*, edited by Ronald Numbers, 79–89. Cambridge: Harvard University Press, 2009.

Egnor, Michael. "More Than Material Minds." *Christianity Today*, September 14, 2018. https://www.christianitytoday.com/ct/2018/september-web-only/more-than-material-minds-neuroscience-souls.html.

Eliot, T. S. "The Hollow Men." In *Collected Poems: 1909–1962*. Orlando, FL: Harcourt, 1963.

Enns, Peter. *The Evolution of Adam: What the Bible Does and Doesn't Say about Human Origins*. Grand Rapids: Baker, 2012.
———. *Inspiration and Incarnation: Evangelicals and the Problem of the Old Testament*. Grand Rapids: Baker Academic, 2005.
———. "Why Young Christians Leave Church." 2016. https://peteenns.com/young-christians-leave-church/.
Episcopal Church. *The Book of Common Prayer and Administration of the Sacraments and Other Rites and Ceremonies of the Church*. New York: Appleton, 1845.
Epley, Nicholas, et al. "Believers' Estimates of God's Beliefs Are More Egocentric Than Estimates of Other People's Beliefs." *PNAS* 106 (2009) 21533–38. https://www.pnas.org/content/106/51/21533.
Erikson, Erik H. *Childhood and Society*. New York: Norton, 1950.
Farmer, Herbert H. *The World and God: A Study of Prayer, Providence and Miracle in Christian Experience*. London: Nisbet, 1935.
Farrer, Austin. *Faith and Speculation: An Essay in Philosophical Theology*. London: Black, 1967.
Fiddes, Paul S. "Creation Out of Love." In *The Work of Love: Creation as Kenosis*, edited by John Polkinghorne, 167–91. Grand Rapids: Eerdmans, 2001.
Fields, Howard L. "Meaning in the Neural Investigation of Pain." In *Spiritual Healing: Science, Meaning, and Discernment*, edited by Sarah Coakley, 87–97. Grand Rapids: Eerdmans, 2020.
Freud, Sigmund. *An Outline of Psycho-Analysis*. London: Hogarth, 1949.
Fromm, Erich. *The Heart of Man: Its Genius for Good and Evil*. London: Routledge and Kegan Paul, 1964.
Gallagher, Shaun. *How the Body Shapes the Mind*. Oxford: Clarendon, 2005.
Gaventa, Beverly R. "Healing, Meaning, and Discernment in the Biblical Text." In *Spiritual Healing: Science, Meaning, and Discernment*, edited by Sarah Coakley, 29–39. Grand Rapids: Eerdmans, 2020.
Gibbons, David, ed. *The Time Chart History of the World: Over 6000 Years of World History Unfolded*. Chippenham, UK: Third Millennium, 2014.
Gilson, Étienne. *The Christian Philosophy of St. Thomas Aquinas*. London: Gollanz, 1957.
Gingerich, Owen. "An Astronomical Perspective." In *How Large is God? The Voices of Scientists and Theologians*, edited by J. M. Templeton, 20–43. West Conshohocken, PA: Templeton, 1997.
Goodall, Jane. *The Chimpanzees of Gombe: Patterns of Behavior*. Cambridge: Harvard University Press, 1986.
Graham, Billy. *Wisdom for Each Day*. Nashville: Thomas Nelson, 2008.
Green, Joel. "What Does It Mean to be Human? Another Chapter in the Ongoing Interaction of Science and Scripture." In *From Cells to Souls and Beyond: Changing Portraits of Human Nature*, edited by Malcolm Jeeves, 179–98. Grand Rapids: Eerdmans, 2004.
Haarsma, Deborah. "The Empty Pew: A Christmas Story." *BioLogos Newsletter*, December 5, 2019.
———. "Kids Ask Tough Questions." *BioLogos Newsletter*, December 11, 2018.
Haarsma, Deborah, and Lauren Haarsma. "Christ and the Cosmos: Christian Perspectives on Astronomical Discoveries." In *Christ and the Created Order:*

Perspectives from Theology, Philosophy, and Science, Vol. 2, edited by Andrew B. Torrance and Thomas H. McCall, 227–38. Grand Rapids: Zondervan, 2018.

Harrison, Peter. *The Territories of Science and Religion*. Chicago: University of Chicago Press, 2015.

Harvati, Katerina, et al. "Apidima Cave Fossils Provide Earliest Evidence of Homo Sapiens in Eurasia." *Nature* 571 (2019) 500–504. doi: 10.1038/s41586-019-1376-z.

Hengel, Martin. "Tasks of New Testament Scholarship." *Bulletin for Biblical Research* 6 (1996) 67–86.

Hick, John H. *Faith and Knowledge*. Ithaca, NY: Cornell University Press, 1966.

Hill, Harry, ed. *The Time Chart of Biblical History: Over 4000 Years in Charts, Maps, Lists and Chronologies* Chippenham, UK: Third Millennium, 2002.

Hipps, Shane. *The Hidden Power of Electronic Culture: How Media Shapes Faith, the Gospel, and the Church*. Grand Rapids: Zondervan, 2005.

Hooykaas, Reijer. *Philosophia Libera: Christian Faith and the Freedom of Science*. London: Tyndale, 1957.

———. *Religion and the Rise of Modern Science*. Vancouver: Regent College Publishing, 1972.

———. *Science in Manueline Style*. Coimbra, Portugal: Academia Internacional da Cultura Portuguesa, 1980.

———. "The Rise of Modern Science: When and Why?" *The British Journal for the History of Science* 20.4 (1987) 453–73.

Horne, Marc. "Your DNA Points to Life Expectancy, Say Scientists." *Times* [London], January 15, 2019. https://www.thetimes.co.uk/article/your-dna-points-to-life-expectancy-say-scientists-npp2svjwc.

Horsley, Richard A. *Jesus and Magic: Freeing the Gospels from Modern Misconceptions*. Eugene, OR: Cascade, 2014.

Howard, David M., et al. "Genome-Wide Meta-Analysis of Depression Identifies 102 Independent Variants and Highlights the Importance of the Prefrontal Brain Regions." *Nature Neuroscience* 22 (2019) 343–52.

Humphreys, Colin J. *The Miracles of Exodus: A Scientist's Discovery of the Extraordinary Natural Causes of the Biblical Stories*. London: Continuum, 2003.

———. "The Star of Bethlehem—a Comet in 5 BC—and the Date of the Birth of Christ." *Quarterly Journal of the Royal Astronomical Society* 32 (2017) 389–407.

Humphreys, Colin J., and Graeme Waddington. "Solar Eclipse of 1207 BC Helps to Date Pharaohs." *Astronomy & Geophysics* 58 (2017) 5.39–42.

Huxley, Thomas H. "Darwin on the Origin of Species." *Westminster Review*, 2nd series, 17 (1860) 556.

Inge, William Ralph. *Faith and Its Psychology*. New York: Scribner's Sons, 1910.

Jackson, Joshua C., et al. "The Faces of God in America: Revealing Religious Diversity across People and Politics." *PLoS One* 13 (2018) e0198745.

Jaki, Stanley L. *Bible and Science*. Front Royal, VA: Christendom, 1990.

———. *The Savior of Science*. Grand Rapids: Eerdmans, 1988.

James, William. *The Varieties of Religious Experience: A Study in Human Nature*. New York: The Modern Library, 1902.

Janssen, Luke J. *Standing on the Shoulders of Giants: Genesis and Human Origins*. Eugene, OR: Wipf and Stock, 2016.

Jeeves, Malcolm A. "Brain and Cognitive Processes in Healing." In *Spiritual Healing: Science, Meaning, and Discernment*, edited by Sarah Coakley, 98–117. Grand Rapids: Eerdmans, 2020.

———. "Changing Portraits of Human Nature." *Science and Christian Belief* 14 (2002) 3–32.

———, ed. *The Emergence of Personhood: A Quantum Leap?* Grand Rapids: Eerdmans, 2015.

———, ed. *From Cells to Souls—and Beyond: Changing Portraits of Human Nature*. Grand Rapids: Eerdmans, 2004.

———. "The Nature of Persons and the Emergence of Kenotic Behavior." In *The Work of Love: Creation as Kenosis*, edited by John Polkinghorne, 66–89. Grand Rapids: Eerdmans, 2001.

———. "Psychologizing and Neurologizing about Religion: Facts, Fallacies and the Future." In *Science and Religion in the Twenty First Century: The Boyle Lectures*, edited by Russell R. Manning and Michael Byrne, 75–93. London: SCM, 2013.

———, ed. *Rethinking Human Nature: A Multidisciplinary Approach*. Grand Rapids: Eerdmans, 2011.

———. *The Scientific Enterprise and Christian Faith*. London: Tyndale, 1969.

Jeeves, Malcolm A., and Robert J. Berry. *Science, Life, and Christian Belief*. Leicester, UK: InterVarsity, 1998.

Jeeves, Malcolm A., and Warren S. Brown. *Neuroscience, Psychology and Religion: Illusions, Delusions and Realities about Human Nature*. West Conshohocken, PA: Templeton, 2009.

Jeeves, Malcolm A., and Thomas E. Ludwig. *Psychological Science and Christian Faith: Insights and Enrichments from Constructive Dialogue*. West Conshohocken, PA: Templeton, 2018.

Kierkegaard, Søren. *For Self-Examination/Judge for Yourselves*. Translated by W. Lowrie. Princeton: Princeton University Press, 1944.

Kinnaman, David. *You Lost Me: Why Young Christians Are Leaving Church and Rethinking Faith*. Grand Rapids: Baker, 2011.

Koenig, Harold G. "Religion, Spirituality, and Health: What We Know, What We Need to Know." In *Sir John's Vision: What Do We Know? What is There to Learn?* edited by Paul C. W. Davies et al., 97–110. West Conshohocken, PA: Templeton, 2018.

Koenig, Harold G., et al. "Religion, Spirituality and Mental Health in the West and the Middle East." *Asian Journal of Psychiatry* 5 (2012) 180–82.

Krause, Johannes, et al. "The Complete Mitochondrial DNA Genome of an Unknown Hominin from Southern Siberia." *Nature* 464 (2010) 894–97. https://www.nature.com/articles/nature08976.

Kuhn, Gustav. "Experiencing the Impossible." *The Psychologist* 32 (2019) 32–37.

———. *Experiencing the Impossible: The Science of Magic*. Cambridge: MIT Press, 2019.

Laland, Kevin N. *Darwin's Unfinished Symphony: How Culture Made the Human Mind*. Princeton, NJ: Princeton University Press, 2017.

Laland, Kevin N., et al. "Does Evolutionary Theory Need a Rethink?" *Nature* 514 (2014) 161–64.

Lawrence, T. E. *Seven Pillars of Wisdom*. London: Jonathan Cape, 1935.

Lewis, C. S. *Christian Behavior*. London: Bles, 1945.

———. *Christian Reflections*. Glasgow: Collins, 1981.

———. Introduction to *Athanasius: De Incarnatione Verbi Dei*. New York: Macmillan, 1946.

———. "Is Theism Important? A Reply." In *God in the Dock: Essays on Theology and Ethics*, edited by Walter Hooper, 186–91. Grand Rapids: Eerdmans, 1970.

———. *Mere Christianity*. New York: Macmillan, 1952.

———. *Miracles: A Preliminary Study*. London: Bles, 1947.

Li, Shanshan, et al. "Religious Service Attendance and Lower Depression among Women: A Prospective Cohort Study." *Annals of Behavioral Medicine* 50 (2016) 876–84.

Lindberg, David C. "The Fate of Science in Patristic and Medieval Christendom." In *The Cambridge Companion to Science and Religion*, edited by Peter Harrison, 21–38. New York: Cambridge University Press, 2010.

———. "Review of *The Savior of Science* by Stanley L. Jaki." *Isis* 81 (1990) 538–39.

Lindberg, David C., and Ronald L. Numbers, eds. *God and Nature: Historical Essays on the Encounter between Christianity and Science* Berkeley: University of California Press, 1986.

Longman, Tremper, and John H. Walton. *The Lost World of the Flood: Mythology, Theology, and the Deluge Debate*. Downers Grove, IL: InterVarsity, 2018.

Lossky, Vladimir. *The Mystical Theology of the Eastern Church*. Cambridge: James Clarke, 1991.

Lucas, Ernest. *Christian Healing: What Can We Believe?* London: Lynx, 1997.

———. "Relevance of Genesis for Current Science." *Fliedner Lectures, the Centre for Science and Faith at SEUT School of Theology* (April 21, 2016).

Lucas, Ernest C., et al. "The Bible, Science and Human Origins." *Science and Christian Belief* 28 (2016) 74–99.

Luther, Martin. *Letters of Spiritual Counsel*. Translated by Theodore G. Tappert. Philadelphia: Westminster, 1955.

MacKay, Donald M. *The Open Mind*. Leicester, UK: InterVarsity, 1988.

Maguire, Eleanor, et al. "Navigation-Related Structural Change in the Hippocampi of Taxi Drivers." *Proceedings of the National Academy of Sciences* 97 (2000) 4398–403.

Maiese, Michelle. *Embodiment, Emotion, and Cognition: New Directions in Philosophy and Cognitive Science*. London: Palgrave Macmillan, 2011.

Margolis, Michele. "When Politicians Determine Your Religious Beliefs." *New York Times*, July 11, 2018. https://www.nytimes.com/2018/07/11/opinion/religion-republican-democrat.html.

Marston, Paul, and Meric Srokosz. "A Response to 'Miracles in Medicine.'" *Science and Christian Belief* 31 (2019) 62–69.

Marty, Martin E. "Voices of Theologians and Humanists." In *How Large is God? The Voices of Scientists and Theologians*, edited by J. M. Templeton, 169–202. West Conshohocken, PA: Templeton, 1997.

Maslow, Abraham H. *Toward a Psychology of Being*. New York: Van Nostrand Reinhold, 1968.

May, Peter. "Miracles in Medicine." *Science and Christian Belief* 29 (2017) 127–34.

———. "Response to Paul Marston and Meric Srokosz." *Science and Christian Belief* 31 (2019) 70–77.

McKee, Selena. "UK Researchers Make New Alzheimer's Disease Discovery." *PharmaTimes Online*, December 13, 2019.

McKinnon, Alastair. "Kierkegaard and 'the Leap of Faith.'" *Kierkegaardiana* 16 (1993) 107–25.
McLuhan, Marshall. *Understanding Media: The Extensions of Man.* New York: McGraw Hill, 1964.
McNamara, Patrick, et al. "Religiosity in Patients with Parkinson's Disease." *Neuropsychiatric Disease and Treatment* 2 (2006) 341–48.
Millard, Alan. "Is the Bible Fake News? The Verdict of Biblical Archeology." *Faith and Thought* 67 (2019) 3–14.
Miller, Kenneth R. *Only a Theory: Evolution and the Battle for the American Soul.* New York: Viking, 2008.
Miller, Lisa, et al. "Neuroanatomical Correlates of Religiosity and Spirituality: A Study in Adults at High and Low Familial Risk for Depression." *JAMA Psychiatry* 71 (2014) 128–35.
Milne, Edward A. *Modern Cosmology and the Christian Idea of God.* London: Oxford University Press, 1952.
Mitchell, Jason P., et al. "Distinct Neural Systems Subserve Person and Object Knowledge." In *Social Neuroscience: Key Readings*, edited by John T. Cacioppo and Gary G. Berntson, 53–62. New York: Psychology, 2005.
Mitchell, Piers D. "Anatomy and Surgery in Europe and the Middle East during the Middle Ages." In *Anatomy and Surgery from Antiquity to the Renaissance*, edited by Helene Perdicoyianni-Paleologou, 309–24. Amsterdam: Hakkert, 2016.
Moltmann, Jürgen. "God's Kenosis in the Creation and Consummation of the World." In *The Work of Love: Creation as Kenosis*, edited by John Polkinghorne, 137–51. Grand Rapids: Eerdmans, 2001.
Murphy, Nancey, and Warren S. Brown. *Did My Neurons Make Me Do it? Philosophical and Neurobiological Perspectives on Moral Responsibility and Free Will.* Oxford: Oxford University Press, 2009.
Muthukumar, David W. "Embodied and Socially Embedded 'Self': Understanding Jesus's Bodily Resurrection and Believers' Postmortem Identity and Continuity." *Science and Christian Belief* 32 (2019) 112–30.
Myers, David G. "Cardiac Arrest and the Conscious Experience of Death." *Psychology Community Blog* 30 (October 30, 2019). https://community.macmillan.com/community/the-psychology-community/blog/2019/10/30/cardiac-arrest-and-the-conscious-experience-of-death.
———. "For Irreligious Evangelicals, Christianity Is about Politics—Not God." *Quartz*, November 7, 2017. https://qz.com/1122117/what-does-it-mean-to-be-evangelical-how-the-right-wing-hijacked-christian-identity/.
———. *A Friendly Letter to Skeptics and Atheists: Musings on Why God Is Good and Faith Isn't Evil.* New York: Jossey-Bass, 2008.
———. "Frontiers in Psychological Science." In *Sir John's Vision: What Do We Know? What is There to Learn?* edited by Paul C. W. Davies et al., 83–96. West Conshohocken, PA: Templeton, 2018.
———. "Social Psychology and Faith." In *Psychological Science and Christian Faith*, by Malcolm A. Jeeves and Thomas E. Ludwig, 209–27. West Conshohocken, PA: Templeton, 2018.
Myers, David G., and C. Nathan DeWall. *Psychology.* 13th ed. New York: Worth, 2021.
Myers, David G., and Jean Twenge. *Social Psychology.* 12th ed. New York: McGraw-Hill, 2018.

Nature. "Evolution and the Brain." *Nature* 447 (2007) 753. https://www.nature.com/articles/447753a.
Nicoll, Colin R. *The Great Christ Comet: Revealing the True Star of Bethlehem.* Wheaton, IL: Crossway, 2015.
Noll, Mark A. *Jesus Christ and the Life of the Mind.* Grand Rapids: Eerdmans, 2011.
———. *The Scandal of the Evangelical Mind.* Grand Rapids: Eerdmans, 1994.
Numbers, Ronald L., ed. *Galileo Goes to Jail: And Other Myths about Science and Religion.* Cambridge: Harvard University Press, 2009.
Nur, Amos. "Personal Letter to Colin Humphreys." In *The Miracles of Exodus: A Scientist's Discovery of the Extraordinary Natural Causes of the Biblical Stories,* edited by Colin J. Humphreys, 20. London: Continuum, 2003.
O'Sullivan, Susan. *It's All in Your Head.* London: Chatto and Windus, 2015.
Pascal, Blaise. *Pascal's Pensées (Les Pensées).* New York: Dutton, 1958.
Pennycook, Gordon, et al. "Beyond Reasonable Doubt: Cognitive and Neuropsychological Implications of Religious Disbelief." In *Neurology and Religion,* edited by Alasdair Coles and Joanna Collicutt, 115–29. Cambridge: Cambridge University Press, 2020.
Perrett, David I., et al. "Neurons Responsive to Faces in the Temporal Cortex: Studies of Functional Organization, Sensitivity to Identity and Relation to Perception." *Human Neurobiology* 3 (1984) 197–208.
Peters, Ted. "Astrotheology: Science and Theology Meet ET." *Theology and Science* 16 (2018) 377–79.
Peters, Ted, et al., eds. *Astrotheology: Science and Theology Meet Extraterrestrial Life.* Eugene, OR: Cascade, 2018.
Peterson, Eugene H. *As Kingfishers Catch Fire: A Conversation on the Ways of God Formed by the Words of God.* London: Hodder and Stoughton, 2017.
———. *A Long Obedience in the Same Direction.* Downers Grove, IL: InterVarsity, 2000.
———. *The Message: The Bible in Contemporary Language.* Colorado Springs: NavPress, 2002.
———. *The Message: The New Testament in Contemporary Language.* Colorado Springs: NavPress, 1993.
Pew Research Center. "'Nones' on the Rise: One-in-five Adults Have No Religious Affiliation." October 9, 2012. https://www.pewforum.org/2012/10/09/nones-on-the-rise/.
———. "Religion and Science." October 22, 2015. https://www.pewresearch.org/science/2015/10/22/science-and-religion/.
———. "U.S. Religious Landscape Survey: Religious Beliefs and Practices." June 1, 2008. https://www.pewforum.org/2008/06/01/u-s-religious-landscape-survey-religious-beliefs-and-practices/.
———. "When Americans Say They Believe in God, What Do They Mean?" April 25, 2018. https://www.pewforum.org/2018/04/25/when-americans-say-they-believe-in-god-what-do-they-mean/.
Phillips, J. B. *Your God Is Too Small: A Guide for Believers and Skeptics Alike.* London: Simon & Schuster, 1952.
Plimer, Ian. *Telling Lies for God.* Sydney: Random House, 1994.

Polkinghorne, John. "Kenotic Creation and Divine Action." In *The Work of Love: Creation as Kenosis*, edited by John Polkinghorne, 90–106. Grand Rapids: Eerdmans, 2001.

———, ed. *The Work of Love: Creation as Kenosis*. Grand Rapids: Eerdmans, 2001.

PréCiS. "Interview with Gavin Merrifield." *PréCiS (Christians in Science)* 95 (Spring 2020) 1–6.

Rahner, Karl. *Faith in a Wintry Season*. Translated by Paul Imhof et al. New York: Crossroad, 1990.

Ramakrishnan, Venkatraman. "Scientific Insight." *Times* [London], March 5, 2016.

Redfern, Clare, and Alasdair Coles. "Parkinson's Disease, Religion, and Spirituality." *Movement Disorders Clinical Practice* 2 (2015) 341–46.

Renfrew, Colin. "Personhood: Toward a Gradualist Approach." In *The Emergence of Personhood: A Quantum Leap?* edited by Malcolm Jeeves, 51–67. Grand Rapids: Eerdmans, 2015.

Richards, E. Randolph, and Brandon J. O'Brien. *Misreading Scripture with Western Eyes: Removing Cultural Blinders to Better Understanding the Bible*. Downers Grove, IL: InterVarsity, 2012.

Ritschel, Chelsea. "Aliens Will Likely be Discovered within 30 Years, Nobel Prize-Winning Astronomer Says." *Independent*, October 21, 2019. https://www.independent.co.uk/news/science/aliens-discover-nobel-prize-didier-queloz-physics-exoplanet-astronomer-a9151386.html.

Rogers, Carl R. *Client-Centered Therapy*. Boston: Houghton Mifflin, 1951.

Rokeach, Milton. *The Open and Closed Mind: Investigations into the Nature of Belief Systems and Personality Systems*. New York: Basic, 1960.

Russell, Colin A. "The Conflict Metaphor and Its Social Origins." *Science and Christian Belief* 1 (1989) 3–26.

Salt, Sharon. "Treasure Trove of 269 Genes Associated with Depression Identified." *NeuroCentral*, February 5, 2019. https://www.neuro-central.com/treasure-trove-269-genes-associated-depression-identified/.

Sanday, William. *Christology and Personality*. Oxford: Oxford University Press, 1910.

Sargant, William. *Battle for the Mind: A Physiology of Conversion and Brain-Washing*. London: Heinemann, 1957.

Schule, Andreas. "'Soul' and 'Spirit' in the Anthropological Discourse of the Hebrew Bible." In *The Depth of the Human Person: A Multidisciplinary Approach*, edited by Michael Welker, 147–65. Grand Rapids: Eerdmans, 2014.

Smith, James Bryan. *The Magnificent Story: Uncovering a Gospel of Beauty, Goodness and Truth*. Downers Grove, IL: IVP, 2017.

Smyth, Chris. "New Test Will Reveal Risk of Getting Breast Cancer." *Times* [London], January 15, 2019. https://www.thetimes.co.uk/article/new-test-will-reveal-risk-of-getting-breast-cancer-87c6x06kq.

Srokosz, Meric. "Miracles in Medicine: A Brief Response to Peter May." *Science and Christian Belief* 29 (2017) 135–41.

Stevenson, Leslie, et al. *Thirteen Theories of Human Nature*. New York: Oxford University Press, 2018.

Stone, Lawson G. "The Soul: Possession, Part, or Person? The Genesis of Human Nature in Genesis 2:7." In *What about the Soul? Neuroscience and Christian Anthropology*, edited by Joel B. Green, 47–62. Nashville: Abingdon, 2004.

Stott, John R. W. *The Message of Romans: God's Good News for the World.* Leicester, UK: InterVarsity, 1994.

Sullivan, John E. *The Image of God.* Dubuque, IA: Priory, 1963.

Sylvester, Rachel, and Alice Thomson. "Boris Knows He's Out of His Depth. Suddenly Experts Are Useful Again." *Times* [London], April 4, 2020. https://www.thetimes.co.uk/article/boris-knows-hes-out-of-his-depth-suddenly-experts-are-useful-again-lnjdmmchp.

Tattersall, Ian. *Becoming Human: Evolution and Human Uniqueness.* Oxford: Oxford University Press, 1998.

———. "Human Evolution: Personhood and Emergence." In *The Emergence of Personhood: A Quantum Leap?* edited by Malcolm Jeeves, 37–50. Grand Rapids: Eerdmans, 2015.

———. *Paleontology: A Brief History of Life.* West Conshohocken, PA: Templeton, 2010.

Thiselton, Anthony C. "The Image and the Likeness of God." In *The Emergence of Personhood: A Quantum Leap?* edited by Malcolm A. Jeeves, 184–201. Grand Rapids: Eerdmans, 2015.

———. *The Thiselton Companion to Christian Theology.* Grand Rapids: Eerdmans, 2015.

Thomas à Kempis. *The Imitation of Christ.* Milwaukee: Bruce, 1940.

Thomas Aquinas. *The Summa Theologica of St. Thomas Aquinas.* London: Burns, Oates, and Washbourne, 1912.

Thompson, John L. *Reading the Bible with the Dead: What You Can Learn from the History of Exegesis That You Can't Learn from Exegesis Alone.* Grand Rapids: Eerdmans, 2007.

Thompson, Keith S. "The Revival of Experiments on Prayer." *American Scientist* 84 (1996) 532–35.

Torrance, Alan J. "Retrieving the Person: Theism, Empirical Science, and the Question of Scope." In *The Emergence of Personhood: A Quantum Leap?* edited by Malcolm A. Jeeves, 202–19. Grand Rapids: Eerdmans, 2015.

Turner, Leon. "Disunity and Disorder: The Problem of Self-Fragmentation." In *In Search of Self: Interdisciplinary Perspectives on Personhood*, edited by J. Wentzel Van Huyssteen and Eric P. Wiebe, 125–40. Grand Rapids: Eerdmans, 2011.

Twelftree, Graham H., ed., *The Nature Miracles of Jesus: Problems, Perspectives, and Prospects.* Eugene, OR: Cascade, 2017.

Tyndall, John. *Address Delivered before the British Association Assembled at Belfast.* London: Longmans, Green & Co., 1874.

Uller, Tobias, and Kevin N. Laland, eds. *Evolutionary Causation: Biological and Philosophical Reflections.* Cambridge: MIT Press, 2019.

Valentine, Cyril H. *What Do We Mean by God?* London: SPCK, 1929.

Vallance, Patrick. "How 'Herd Immunity' Can Help Fight Coronavirus." *Spectator*, March 13, 2020. https://www.spectator.co.uk/article/the-case-for-the-herd-immunity-strategy.

Van Till, Howard J. *The Fourth Day.* Grand Rapids: Eerdmans, 1986.

———. "No Place for a Small God." In *How Large is God? The Voices of Scientists and Theologians*, edited by J. M. Templeton, 113–35. West Conshohocken, PA: Templeton, 1997.

Vandrey, Brianna, et al. "Fan Cells in Layer 2 of the Lateral Entorhinal Cortex Are Critical for Episodic-Like Memory." *Current Biology* 30 (2020) 169–75.
Walton, John H. "Biblical Credibility and Joshua 10: What Does the Text Really Claim?" *BioLogos Forum*, October 15, 2013. https://biologos.org/articles/biblical-credibility-and-joshua-10-what-does-the-text-really-claim.
———. *The Lost World of Adam and Eve: Genesis 2–3 and the Human Origins Debate.* Downers Grove, IL: InterVarsity, 2015.
———. "Origins in Genesis: Claims of an Ancient Text in a Modern Scientific World." In *Knowing Creation*, edited by Andrew Torrance and Thomas H. McCall, 107–22. Grand Rapids: Zondervan, 2018.
Walton, Steven. "What Is Progress in New Testament Studies?" Inaugural lecture as Professor of New Testament at London School of Theology, March 6, 2012.
Ward, Keith. "Cosmos and Kenosis." In *The Work of Love: Creation as Kenosis*, edited by John Polkinghorne, 152–66. Grand Rapids: Eerdmans, 2001.
———. *More Than Matter? Is There More to Life Than Molecules?* London: Lion Hudson, 2011.
Ware, Bruce A. "Prayer and the Sovereignty of God." In *For the Fame of God's Name*, edited by Sam Storms and Justin Taylor, 126–43. Westchester, IL: Crossway, 2010.
Watts, Fraser, ed. *Spiritual Healing: Scientific and Religious Perspectives.* Cambridge: Cambridge University Press, 2011.
Weaver, Glenn. "Embodied Spirituality: Experiences of Identity and Spiritual Suffering among Persons with Alzheimer's Dementia." In *From Cells to Souls—and Beyond: Changing Portraits of Human Nature*, edited by Malcolm A. Jeeves, 77–101. Grand Rapids: Eerdmans, 2004.
Welker, Michael, ed. *The Depth of the Human Person: A Multidisciplinary Approach.* Grand Rapids: Eerdmans, 2014.
Wesley, John. *Primitive Physick: Or, an Easy and Natural Method of Curing Most Diseases.* Philadelphia: Prichard & Hall, 1747.
Whipple, Tom. "Who Do You Think You Are? Probably a Little Bit Neanderthal." *Times* [London], August 9, 2019. https://www.thetimes.co.uk/article/who-do-you-think-you-are-probably-a-little-bit-neanderthal-rr52krjdf.
———. "Your Attitude to Risky Sex, Drink and Fast Cars Lies in the Genes." *Times* [London], January 15, 2019. https://www.thetimes.co.uk/article/your-attitude-to-risky-sex-drink-and-fast-cars-lies-in-the-genes-svcn30sqs.
White, Andrew D. *A History of the Warfare of Science with Theology in Christendom.* New York: Appleton, 1896.
———. *The Warfare of Science.* New York: Appleton, 1876.
Whitehouse, Walter A. *Christian Faith and the Scientific Attitude.* Edinburgh: Oliver & Boyd, 1952.
Wilkinson, Gerald S. "Reciprocal Food Sharing in the Vampire Bat." *Nature* 308 (1984) 181–84.
Willis, Thomas. *Cerebri Anatome (the Anatomy of the Brain).* London: Martyn and Allestry, 1664.
Woollett, Katherine, et al. "Talent in the Taxi: A Model System for Exploring Expertise." *Philosophical Transactions of the Royal Society (Biological Sciences)* B 2009 364 (2009) 1407–16.
Wright, N. T. *The Challenge of Jesus: Rediscovering Who Jesus Was and Is.* Downers Grove, IL: InterVarsity, 1999.

———. *The Day the Revolution Began: Reconsidering the Meaning of Jesus's Crucifixion.* New York: HarperOne, 2016.

———. "Hope Deferred? Against the Dogma of Delay." *Early Christianity* 9 (2018) 37–82. https://research-repository.st-andrews.ac.uk/handle/10023/17178.

———. "Idolatry." In *Surprised by Scripture*, by N. T. Wright. New York: HarperCollins, 2014.

———. "Personal Communication." (2011).

———. "Reading Paul, Thinking Scripture." In *Scripture's Doctrine and Theology's Bible*, edited by Markus Bockmuehl and Alan J. Torrance, 59–70. Grand Rapids: Baker Academic, 2008.

———. *Surprised by Scripture.* New York: HarperCollins, 2014.

Yancey, Philip. "Prayer and Physical Healing." In *Prayer: Does it Make Any Difference?* 240–58. Grand Rapids: Zondervan, 2006.

———. *Prayer: Does It Make Any Difference?* Grand Rapids: Zondervan, 2006.

———. *The Resurrection of the Son of God.* London: SPCK, 2003.

———. *Surprised by Hope: Rethinking Heaven, the Resurrection, and the Mission of the Church.* San Francisco: HarperOne, 2008.

———. *Vanishing Grace: Whatever Happened to the Good News?* London: Hodder and Stoughton, 2014.

——— *What's So Amazing about Grace?* Grand Rapids: Zondervan, 1997.

Zeman, Adam. "The Origins of Subjectivity." In *The Emergence of Personhood: A Quantum Leap?* edited by Malcolm Jeeves, 120–42. Grand Rapids: Eerdmans, 2015.

Zhong, Wanting, et al. "Biological and Cognitive Underpinnings of Religious Fundamentalism." *Neuropsychologia* 100 (2017) 18–25.

Zmigrod, Leor, et al. "The Partisan Mind: Is Extreme Political Partisanship Related to Cognitive Inflexibility?" *Journal of Experimental Psychology: General* 149 (2020) 407–18.

Zola-Morgan, Stuart. "Localization of Brain Function: The Legacy of Franz Joseph Gall (1758–1828)." *Annual Review of Neuroscience* 18 (1995) 359–83.

About the Author

MALCOLM A. JEEVES IS Emeritus Professor of Psychology in the School of Psychology and Neuroscience at St. Andrews University in Scotland. He is a past president of the Royal Society of Edinburgh, Scotland's National Academy of Science and Letters, and a Fellow of the Academy of Medical Sciences and of the British Psychological Society. After a long career as a leading experimental psychologist and a pioneer in the fields of cognitive psychology, neuropsychology, and evolutionary psychology, he was honored by Queen Elizabeth II as Commander of the Order of the British Empire for his contributions to science and to neuropsychology. He is the author of numerous books on science and faith, including *Psychology and Christianity*, *From Cells to Souls*, *Rethinking Human Nature*, and *Psychological Science and Christian Faith*.

Name Index

Aaron, 8, 137
Abraham, 10, 127, 177, 183, 224
Abram, 177, 244
Adam, 86, 88–90, 93, 114, 150–51, 236–37, 239, 251, 253, 261–62
Adler, Mortimer, 84, 95
Adorno, Theodor, 9–10, 249
Ainge, James, 200
Alexa, 42, 250
Alexander, Denis, 132–33, 173, 219–21, 249
Allen, Diogenes, 117–18, 249
Allison, James, 164
Allport, Gordon, 191, 195–96, 249
Anderson, Emma, 155, 249
Aphrodite, 11
Applegate, Kathryn, 251
Ariew, Roger, 252
Aristotle, 32, 109, 249
Arnold, Bill, 103, 114–15, 249
Asp, Erik, 122
Athanasius, 27, 256
Atrahasis, 84
Augustine, 39, 45, 52–53, 90, 109, 112, 249
Ayala, Francisco, 69, 104

Bakewell, Joan, 168
Barker, Peter, 252
Barna Research Group, x, 4, 44, 60, 79–81, 225, 231, 237, 249
Barrett, Justin, 76, 104, 249
Barth, Karl, 45, 185, 249
Bartlett, Frederic, 182, 185, 189–91, 193–95, 249

Bauckham, Richard, 24, 250
Baumeister, Roy, 104
Benedict XIV (Pope), 170
Benson, Eric, 164, 250
Berntson, Gary, 257
Berry, Robert J., 218, 255
BioLogos, x, 60, 79, 81–82, 231, 235, 239, 242, 248, 250–51, 253, 261
Bloom, Paul, 112, 250
Bohr, Niels, 218, 250
Bonhoeffer, Dietrich, 16, 45, 158, 183–84
Boyle, Robert, 103, 132, 255
Brand, Paul, 172, 250
Brice-Saddler, Michael, 141, 241, 250
Bridge, Mark, 42, 250
Briggs, Andrew, 139, 140, 142, 250
Bright, Bill, 16–17
Brooke, John, 61, 63, 250
Brown, Arial, 201
Brown, Warren, 70–71, 104, 106, 122, 192–93, 250, 255, 257
Brueggemann, Walter, 47
Brunner, Emil, 45
Bunyan, John, 20, 189, 202–5
Burgess, Kaya, 43, 250
Burns, Robert, 82, 251
Burridge, Richard, 24
Butler, Paul, 201, 251
Byrne, Michael, 255
Byrne, Richard, 69, 74, 104–5, 251, 255

Cacioppo, John, 257
Calvin, John, 110, 159, 185, 251

Campbell, C. A., 104
Campbell, Heidi, 14–15, 17, 43–47, 251
Carmichael, Amy, 205
Carroll, William, 209, 219, 251
Cassius, Dio, 143
Catherine Hamlin, 174–75, 244, 252
Cerullo, Maurice, 168–69
Chan, Eva, 93, 251
Chavalas, Mark, 146–47, 242, 251
Cheadle, Alyssa, 161, 251
Christ, xi–xiii, xv, 5, 9, 12, 16, 24, 29–31, 34, 40, 43–44, 46–47, 52–53, 55–56, 65, 80, 90, 95, 105, 108, 110, 131, 136–37, 143, 147, 158, 163–65, 168–70, 173, 175, 184, 186, 190–91, 194, 198, 205, 209, 211, 214, 216–17, 223–25, 228, 236–37, 240, 242–43, 247, 253–54, 258, 260
Clayton, Philip, 106
Clement (of Alexandria), 30, 251
Coakley, Sarah, 155, 157, 249, 251–53, 255
Coleridge, Hartley, 176, 251
Coles, Alasdair, 120–23, 201, 246, 251, 258–59
Collicutt, Joanna, 120–23, 251, 258
Collins, Francis, 79, 189, 239, 251
Cootsona, Greg, x, 231, 251
Copeland, Kenneth, 141
Coulson, Charles, 21, 251
Cowper, William, 20, 202–4
Cressey, Martin, 131, 251
Crick, Francis, xiv, 20, 49, 198
Culkin, John, 17, 251
Curtis, Heather, 155, 252
Cyrus, 220

Darwin, Charles, 66, 254–55
David, xiv, 127, 135
Davies, Gaius, 189, 202–5, 252
Davies, Paul, 255, 257
Davis, Robert, 199–200
Davison, Andrew, 52
Dawkins, Richard, 88, 125, 252
Deaton, Angus, 163
DeMille, Cecil B., 29

Descartes, René, 105, 109, 112, 117–18, 132, 250
DeWall, C. Nathan, 161, 166, 257
Ditto, Peter, 10
Donaldson, James, 251
Dostoevsky, Fyodor, 94
Draper, John, 61, 252
Duhem, Pierre, 62, 252
Durso, Ramon, 201
Dyson, Freeman, 94, 219, 252

Economist, 13–14, 42–43, 47–48, 138, 163, 174, 234, 241, 244, 252
Edwards, Jonathan, 40, 252
Efron, Noah, 62, 252
Egnor, Michael, 101–3, 238, 252
Elijah, 165
Eliot, T. S., 20, 252
Eliphaz, 141
Emaye, 174
Enns, Peter, 81, 87–92, 237, 239, 253
Epley, Nicholas, 19, 30, 232, 253
Erikson, Erik, 36, 253
Eve, 86, 88, 93, 236, 251, 261
Ezekiel, 137
Ezra, 220

Farmer, Herbert, 185, 253
Farrer, Austin, 21, 253
Felipe, Pablo de, 60, 62, 235, 252
Fiddes, Paul, 213, 253
Fields, Howard, 157, 253
Freud, Sigmund, 11, 36–37, 191, 195, 253
Fromm, Erich, 37–38, 253

Galen, 98, 109
Galileo, xii, 89, 252, 258
Gallagher, Shaun, 106, 253
Garner, Stephen, 14–15, 17, 43–47, 141, 251
Gaventa, Beverly, 155–57, 164, 253
Gazzaniga, Michael, 102
Gibbons, David, 83, 253
Gifford, John, 203
Gilson, Étienne, 39, 253
Gingerich, Owen, 53–54, 253

NAME INDEX

God, x–xv, 3–15, 17–25, 27–36, 38–51, 53–57, 62, 64–68, 76–87, 89–97, 104–5, 107, 110, 113–14, 116–18, 120, 122, 124, 126–34, 136–42, 144–48, 151–52, 154–58, 161, 163–65, 168–69, 171–75, 177–78, 180–85, 187–89, 191–92, 194–95, 199–202, 209–14, 216–217, 219–24, 226–28, 230–41, 243–51, 253–54, 256–58, 260–62
Goodall, Jane, 215–16, 253
Graham, Billy, 29, 44–45, 253
Granquist, Megan, 121
Green, Joel, 103, 115–16, 249, 253, 259
Gutenberg, Johannes, 15

Haarsma, Deborah, 65, 79, 95, 253
Haarsma, Lauren, 95, 253
Hamlet, 20
Hamlin, Catharine, 174–75, 244, 252
Hardin, Jeff, 235, 250
Harper, Charles, 252
Harrison, Peter, 61–62, 254, 256
Harvati, Katerina, 74, 254
Hayes, Vanessa, 93
Heatherton, Todd, 197
Hengel, Martin, 25–26, 254
Hercules, 59
Heymans, Catherine, 51
Hick, John, 178, 254
Hill, Harry, 83, 254
Hipps, Shane, 15–18, 43–44, 233–34, 254
Honan, Daniel, 249
Hooykaas, Reijer, 62–63, 82, 254
Hopkins, Gerard, 202, 205
Horne, Marc, 49, 234, 254
Horsley, Richard, 129–30, 254
Houghton, John, 170
Howard, David, 198, 246, 254
Hughes, Julian, 122
Hume, David, 104
Humphreys, Colin, 135–36, 140, 143–45, 147–53, 254, 258
Huxley, Thomas, 59, 254
Hwu, Patrick, 164

Imhof, Paul, 259
Inge, William, 185–86, 254
Irenaeus, 45
Isaac, 83, 224
Isaiah, 33–34, 46, 232

Jackson, Joshua, 19, 254
Jacob, 224
Jaki, Stanley, 62, 254, 256
James, William, 19, 189, 254
Janssen, Luke, 92–93, 108–9, 254
Jarvinen, Matthew, 76, 249
Jeeves, Malcolm, 60, 62, 67, 94, 103, 106, 134, 157, 165, 197, 218, 222–24, 235, 238, 249, 250–53, 255, 257, 259–63
Jeremiah, 135
Jesus Christ, xii–xii, 5, 9, 24, 34, 56, 65, 105, 108, 135, 158, 191, 214, 224–25, 240, 243, 247, 258
Jesus, xii–xii, 5, 9, 11, 24–25, 29, 31, 34, 41, 44, 46, 54, 56, 65, 105, 108, 118, 125, 127, 129–31, 133–37, 156, 158, 165, 171, 182, 184–86, 191–92, 197, 209–12, 214, 224–25, 233, 240–43, 245, 247, 254, 257–58, 260–62
Jethro, 152
Job, xiv, 137–38, 141, 154, 220, 230, 246
John, xii, 34, 41, 133, 156, 170, 184–85, 197, 230, 242
Joseph, 140–41
Josephus, 143
Joshua, 135, 144–47, 150–51, 241–42, 261
Judge, Stuart, 121

Katie, 101, 103
Kierkegaard, Søren, 185, 193, 255, 257
Kinnaman, David, 80, 255
Koenig, Harold, 159–60, 162, 255
Krause, Johannes, 75, 235, 255
Kuhn, Gustav, 128, 241, 255

Laland, Kevin, 66–67, 255, 260

NAME INDEX

Lambertini, Prospero Lorenzo (Cardinal), 170
Lawrence, T. E., 152, 255
Lawson-Tancred, Hugh, 249
Lazarus, 125, 156, 242
Lewis, C. S., 5–6, 27, 172, 181, 185, 191, 205, 255
Li, Shanshan, 160, 256
Libet, Benjamin, 102
Lindberg, David, 62–63, 256
Longman, Tremper, 91, 256
Lossky, Vladimir, 113, 256
Lucas, Ernest, 19, 35, 87, 91–93, 170, 235, 256
Ludwig, Thomas, xvii, 101, 103, 197, 238, 256–57
Luke, 46–47, 84, 110, 156, 190, 233, 242
Luther, Martin, 16, 20, 159, 189, 202–5, 256

MacKay, Donald, 68, 102, 132, 218, 222–23, 256
Macrae, C. Neil, 197
Magi, 142–44
Maguire, Eleanor, 100, 256
Maiese, Michelle, 106, 256
Mammon, 11
Manning, Russell, 255
Margolis, Michele, 19, 232, 256
Mark, xii, 133, 156, 230, 241–42
Mars, 11
Marsh, Michael, 122
Marston, Paul, 170, 171, 256
Marty, Martin, 22–23, 256
Marx, Karl, 11, 37
Maslow, Abraham, 37, 256
Matar, Louis, 138
Matthew, 56, 135, 143–44, 146, 156, 177, 186, 217, 244
May, Peter, 168–71, 244, 256, 259
McCall, Thomas, 249, 254, 261
McKee, Selena, 200, 246, 256
McKinnon, Alastair, 193, 257
McLuhan, Marshall, 14, 17–18, 251, 257
McNamara, Patrick, 200–201, 257
Meadows, Philip, 46

Melanchthon, Philip, 159
Merrifield, Gavin, xi–xii, 259
Micah, 47, 233
Millard, Alan, 83–84, 125, 236, 257
Miller, Kenneth, 83, 257
Miller, Kevin, 14
Miller, Lisa, 159–60, 244, 257
Miller, Patrick, 103
Milne, Edward, 21, 257
Mitchell, Jason, 197–98, 257
Mitchell, Piers, 158, 257
Moltmann, Jürgen, 214, 257
Morimoto, Takeshi, 122
Moses, 127, 129, 137, 140, 148–49, 151–53, 182
Murphy, Nancey, 105, 257
Muthukumar, David, 106, 257
Myers, David, 2, 9–10, 18–19, 31, 111, 161–63, 166, 171–72, 183–84, 244, 257

Nemesius, 109
Nesteruk, Alexel, 52
Newton, Isaac, 132
Nietzsche, Friedrich, 11
Noah, 83–84, 182, 236–37
Noll, Mark, xiii, 65, 108, 240, 258
Numbers, Ronald, xii, 61–62, 252, 256, 258
Nur, Amos, 150–51, 258
Nurse, Paul, xiv

O'Brien, Brendan, 27–28, 259
O'Sullivan, Susan, 171, 258
Oakes, Peter, 25
Oord, Thomas, 248
Origen, 109

Parnia, Sam, 111
Pascal, Blaise, 185, 214, 258
Paul, Lynn, 70–71, 250
Paul, xiv, 6, 16, 25, 33–35, 54–55, 88–90, 98, 109, 112, 118–19, 137–38, 169, 181, 186, 191, 202, 211, 224, 237, 262
Penfield, Wilder, 102
Pennycook, Gordon, 122, 258
Perrett, David, 99, 258

NAME INDEX

Persinger, Michael, 121
Peter, 156, 190, 197
Peters, Ted, 52, 258
Peterson, Eugene, 3, 8, 10–12, 33, 41, 56–57, 258
Pew Research Center, x, 12–13, 60, 79, 161, 225, 231, 233, 244, 248, 258
Pharaoh, 129, 141, 144–45, 148–49, 254
Phillips, J. B., 3, 6–11, 13–14, 20, 22, 48–50, 181, 191, 198, 204, 227, 231, 258
Pinnock, Clark, 134, 165
Plato, 103, 108–10, 112, 237
Plimer, Ian, 83, 88, 258
Poirot, Hercule, 149
Polkinghorne, John, 97, 209, 211–12, 217, 247, 253, 255, 257, 259, 261
Porter, Roy, 250
Pym, Hugh, xiv

Queloz, Didier, 51, 259

Rad, Gerhard von, 45
Rahner, Karl, 40–41, 259
Ramakrishnan, Venkatraman, 96, 259
Ramesses, 144–45
Redfern, Clare, 201, 246, 256
Renfrew, Colin, 72–74, 77, 259
Richards, E. Randolph, 27–28, 259
Ricoeur, Paul, 104
Ritmeyer, Kathleen, 150
Ritmeyer, Leen, 150
Ritschel, Chelsea, 51, 259
Roberts, Alexander, 251
Rogers, Carl, 37, 259
Rokeach, Milton, 9–10, 259
Rossetti, Christina, 202, 204
Rupe, Richard, 49
Russell, Colin, 60–61, 259
Ryle, Gilbert, 117

Salt, Sharon, 199, 246, 259
Samuel, 114, 249
Sanday, William, 217, 259
Santa Claus, 13
Sargant, William, 167, 259
Sayers, Dorothy, 222

Schetter, Christine, 161, 251
Schule, Andreas, 97–98, 112, 114, 259
Shaftesbury, Lord (Anthony Cooper), 202
Shakespeare, William, 20
Skinner, B. F., 191
Smith, James Bryan, 4, 30–31, 51, 53, 114, 184, 210–11, 232–33, 259
Smith, Samuel, 237
Smyth, Chris, 49, 259
Solomon, 84
Sperry, Roger, 102
Srokosz, Meric, 170–71, 256, 259
Stephen, 110
Stevenson, Leslie, 110, 259
Stone, Arthur, 163
Stone, Lawson, 103, 114, 259
Storms, Sam, 261
Stott, John, 35, 40–41, 202, 260
Strawn, Brad, 106, 192–93, 250
Stuart-Thomson, Keith, 171
Stump, J. B., 251
Sullenberger, Chesley, 126
Sullivan, John, 39, 260
Sylvester, Rachel, xiv, 260

Tappert, Theodore, 256
Tattersall, Ian, 72, 76, 260
Taylor, Justin, 261
Templeton, J. M., 253, 256
The Economist, 13–14, 42–43, 47–48, 138, 163, 174, 234, 241, 244, 252
Theissen, Gerd, 98
Thiselton, Anthony, 104–5, 113, 260
Thomas (á Kempis), 184, 260
Thomas (of Aquino), 39, 109, 194, 253, 260
Thomas, Gunther, 98
Thompson, John, xv, 260
Thompson, Keith, 171–72, 260
Thomson, Alice, xiv, 260
Torrance, Alan, xvii, 105, 260, 262
Torrance, Andrew, xvii, 249, 254, 261
Tranel, Daniel, 122
Trump, Donald, 10, 31–32
Turner, Leon, 65, 260
Twelftree, Graham, 125, 260
Twenge, Jean, 10, 257

Tyndall, John, 61, 260

Uller, Tobias, 66–67, 260
Urbani, Pietro, 251

Valentine, Cyril, 29–30, 32, 260
Vallance, Patrick, xiv, 63, 260
Van Huyssteen, J. Wentzel, 260
Van Till, Howard, 11–12, 92, 260
Vandrey, Brianna, 200, 261
Vanstone, William (Canon), 212
Vesalius, 99

Waal, Frans de, 214, 216, 252
Waddington, Graeme, 144–45, 254
Walsh, Gerald, 249
Walton, John, 78, 84–88, 90–92, 115, 145–46, 242, 256, 261
Walton, Steven, 23–25, 261
Ward, Keith, 111–12, 212–13, 261
Ware, Bruce, 219, 261
Warner, Kelsey, 122
Watson, James, 20, 49, 198
Watts, Fraser, 155, 261
Weaver, Glenn, 199–200, 261
Welker, Michael, 97–98, 112, 259
Wesley, Charles, 202
Wesley, John, 20, 159, 202, 261

Whipple, Tom, 49, 75, 261
White, Andrew, 61, 261
Whitehouse, Walter, 21, 261
Whitty, Chris, xiv
Wiebe, Eric, 260
Wilkinson, David, 52
Wilkinson, Gerald, 215, 261
Willis, Thomas, 99, 261
Wilson, Alan, 93
Winfrey, Oprah, 174
Woollet, Katherine, 100, 261
Wright, N. T., 3, 11–12, 35, 54–55, 103, 113, 118–19, 124–27, 136, 181–82, 231, 234, 239–41, 261–62

Xenophanes, 29–30, 32

Yahweh, 116
Yancey, Philip, 4–5, 127–28, 154, 172, 187–88, 194–95, 241, 243, 245, 250, 262
Yoder, Mark, 4

Zeman, Adam, 71, 262
Zhong, Wanting, 197, 262
Zmigrod, Leor, 10, 262
Zola-Morgan, Stuart, 98, 262

Subject Index

agape love, 105
altruism, 214–15
Alzheimer's disease, 199–200, 246, 256, 261
Anabaptists, 18
animals and humans, 38, 66, 69–70, 75, 87, 98–99, 109, 114, 116, 214–16, 234, 239
anthropology, 39, 65, 67, 71, 96, 98, 103, 113–15, 237
antipodeans, 51–53, 60
astrotheology, 52–53
atheism, x, 88, 92, 94, 171
autonomic nervous system, 166

big bang cosmology, 50, 85
biological substrates, 197, 202, 216
black holes, 51, 54
body-mind problem, 95–96, 98–106, 109–12, 117–19, 122, 192–93, 200, 237–38
body-soul dualism, 98, 103, 105–6, 109–12, 114–15, 118–20, 192, 200, 237
brain-mind link, 94–96, 98–99, 103, 109–12, 117–19, 200
brain, x, 4, 49, 67, 70–71, 75, 94–96, 98–103, 106, 109–12, 115, 121–23, 160, 197–202, 205, 213, 216, 237–38

CAT scans, 101
church attendance, xiii, 31–32, 44, 80, 160–61, 187, 201

community of faith, 16, 44–45, 184, 192, 231, 245
comparative anatomy, 70
comparative psychology, 99
complementarity, 94–95, 218–19
conflict (science vs. religion), x, xii, 24, 59–63, 65, 227
consciousness, x, 26, 53, 66, 94–95, 101–2, 111, 120, 179, 182, 234
constructive doubt, 48
context (social-cultural), 6, 25–27, 61, 81–82, 89–90, 130, 132, 136, 142, 147, 192, 229
conversion, 40, 44–45, 167, 193–94, 202
COVID-19 (coronavirus), ix, xiv, 47, 63
creation, xi–xii, xiv–xv, 11–12, 48, 50, 55, 65, 80, 82, 87–89, 96, 105, 113–14, 116, 119–20, 130–32, 134, 136, 139–40, 144, 157, 165, 175, 194, 209–14, 216–17, 219–24
creative artist (model of God), 222–23

deep truths, 183
deism, 86, 124–25, 220
dementia, 122, 199–200, 246, 256, 261
depression, 46, 160–61, 168, 194, 198–99, 202–4
determinism, 221
disbelief, 113, 127, 134, 165, 189, 196
disembodied human soul, 100–103, 109–10, 119–20, 193
divine power, 134, 165

divine self-emptying, 188, 210, 226, 247
divine sovereignty, 1, 33, 40, 130, 141, 210, 221, 226, 240, 247
DNA, 20, 49, 73, 75, 93, 198, 234
dogma of delay, 55
doubt, 23, 48, 80–81, 122, 141, 176, 179, 185, 195–96, 202
dual-aspect monism, 106, 120
dualism, 98, 103, 105–6, 109–12, 114–15, 118–20, 192, 200, 237
dualistic anthropology, 98, 103, 115, 237
duality, 103, 238

earthquake, 135, 137–38, 150–52
ego, 36, 105
Egypt, 33, 119, 128–31, 135, 140–41, 144–45, 148–49, 240–41
embodied, 99, 121, 192
emergence, 66, 68, 70–73, 76, 93, 104, 106, 213–214, 216–217
emotionalism, 166–67
emotions, 4, 17, 66, 109, 115, 117, 161–62, 166–167, 193, 199–201, 228, 234, 238
Enlightenment, xii, 61, 125–26, 129–30
ethics, 18, 31, 66, 69, 104, 190, 216, 234
evangelistic, 4–5, 16, 44–45, 141, 157, 163–64, 166–69, 174
evolution, x, xii, 60, 66–76, 79–80, 83, 85, 87, 89–90, 105, 212–16
evolutionary biology, 66, 214, 234
evolutionary psychology, xiii, 66, 69, 104, 214, 234
evolutionary theory, 66–67
expanding universe, 50, 52, 87, 234
experiments, 67, 98, 111, 171–72, 183
explaining away, 140, 241

face recognition, 19, 99–100
faith healing, 57, 154–59, 161–75
faith, ix–x, xiii, 6, 15–20, 24, 30, 44–48, 54, 80–81, 137, 158, 168, 176–205, 225, 227–28, 244–46
fake news, 5, 82–84, 125, 128

fall (into sin), xv, 39, 230
false assumptions, 82–83, 126, 184, 192
finiteness (of humans), 20, 98, 212
free will, 101–3, 106, 221
fundamentalism, 92, 197

gap-filling, x, xiv, 12–13, 21–22, 67–68, 70–71, 74, 76–77, 79, 83, 95, 98, 105, 107, 116, 120, 124, 142, 180, 195, 224, 240
Genesis, 35, 53, 84–94, 96, 113–14, 116–17, 177, 234, 236–39, 244
god module (in brain), 122
god-of-the-gaps, x, 5, 21–22, 68, 76–77, 79, 95, 144, 195, 231
grace, 4–5, 39–40, 132, 136, 194–95
Greek thought, 98, 108, 119, 125

healing, 4–5, 7, 23, 33, 57, 129–31, 134–35, 138–39, 154–59, 161–75, 177, 210, 212, 224–25, 228, 242–44, 247
Hebrew thought, 103, 111–17, 119, 121, 125, 129, 237
holocaust, 24
Holy Spirit, 16, 40, 47, 199, 213
Homo erectus, 72, 75
Homo sapiens, 72, 74–75, 93, 108
human existence, 105, 116, 119
human nature, xiii, 22–23, 35–39, 48, 64, 66, 68, 94–95, 106–21, 234–235
human needs, 29–30, 32, 35–43, 55–56, 186, 213, 225, 228
human uniqueness, 38, 68–73, 99, 109, 113–14, 116, 215–16, 234, 239

id, 36
identity, 38, 86, 104, 106, 110, 115, 117, 187, 213
idolatry, 3, 18–19, 32–34, 149, 232
image of God (imago Dei), 19, 39, 46, 53, 66, 82, 93–94, 96, 104–5, 110, 113, 235–37, 239
immanence (of God), 220
immaterial soul, 100–103, 109–10, 119–20, 193

immortality, 33, 97, 137
individual differences, 24, 49, 178, 196–98, 204
intercessory prayer, 4, 128, 154, 171–72, 243–44
intervention (divine), 12, 21, 39, 55, 79, 93, 125, 128, 131–32, 139, 172–73, 236, 243

language development, 66, 69, 104–5, 115, 234
language of faith, 91, 113, 129, 139, 173, 183, 185, 189, 193–94, 212
levels of explanation, 22, 37, 68, 87, 95, 140, 144–45, 151–53, 196, 217–19
limits of science, xiv, 195
localization of brain function, 96, 98–100, 115, 122, 198, 200
localization of mind, 4, 95–96, 98–103, 106, 109–10, 115, 200
localization of soul, 94–103, 110–11, 113, 117–18, 192–93, 200

magic, 4–5, 71, 124, 127–30, 139, 144–45, 172, 228, 231, 240–41
memory, 97, 195, 200
Mere Christianity, 5, 181
mind-body problem, 95–96, 98–106, 109–12, 117–19, 122, 192–93, 200, 237–38
mind-brain link, 94–96, 98–99, 103, 109–12, 117–19, 200
mind, x, xii–xiv, 3–5, 7, 9–10, 12, 16, 20–21, 32, 66–68, 76, 94–96, 98, 100–106, 109–12, 117–19, 167, 179, 182, 189, 191, 193, 195, 199–200, 205, 209, 211, 221–22, 229–30, 234, 237–38
miracles, 4–5, 12, 64, 124–73, 205, 210, 224–25, 228, 240–244
misreading Scripture, 27–28, 89
monism, 105–6, 114, 120
monist anthropology, 114
morality, x, 13, 15, 18, 36, 66, 68–69, 79, 104, 183, 190–91, 213, 216, 234, 238
MRI, 99–100, 159, 198

multiple levels of explanation, 22, 37, 68, 87, 95, 140, 144–45, 151–53, 196, 217–19
mystery, 21–22, 48, 66, 68, 71, 95, 98, 103, 120, 149, 159, 204, 217, 222–23, 234–35, 238

natural selection, 66–69, 76, 214–15
natural-born dualists, 112
naturalistic explanations, 140–42, 144–45, 147, 149, 151–53, 221, 224, 242
Neandertals, 74–75, 235
near-death experiences, 110–11, 122
nephesh (soul), 112, 114–15, 117, 239
networked theology, 15, 17, 43–47
neural networks, 67, 201
neurons, 49, 99, 106, 200–201
neuroscience, xiii, 70, 101, 103, 105–6, 111, 115–16, 120, 165, 192, 197–98, 200, 205, 237–38
New Testament, 7–9, 23–27, 34, 88, 106, 118–19, 129–30, 133–37, 158–59, 165, 177, 184, 210, 226, 243
Noah's ark, 83–84, 236–37
nonreductive physicalism, 106, 120

Old Testament, 8, 26–27, 32, 34, 85, 88, 90–91, 97, 106, 114, 125, 129, 133–34, 137–38, 140–41, 144–45, 147, 156, 159, 165, 177, 186, 220, 224
open minded, 9, 51, 68, 107, 111, 227, 229
out-of-body experiences, 110–11, 122

parable, 184
Parkinson's disease, 200–202
Pentecostals, 18
person, 30–31, 40, 73, 96–98, 101–18, 121–22, 192–98, 237–38
personality differences, 24, 49, 178, 196–98, 204
personality, 9, 35–38, 101, 112, 193, 196–97, 202–4, 225, 238
personhood, 65–76, 101–18, 121–22, 192–98, 214, 237–38

petitionary prayer, 4, 128, 154, 171–72, 243–44
placebo effects, 188, 245
post-Christian era, x, 187
prayer experiments, 171–72
prayer, 4–5, 31, 33, 41–42, 127–28, 154, 171–72, 195–96, 243–244
presuppositions, xiv, 25–28, 30, 35, 85, 89, 92, 125, 178–79, 216, 230, 232
primitive credulity, 178–79
prosperity gospel, 5, 7, 33, 141, 157–58, 224–25
providence, 21, 130, 132, 141, 164, 219–21, 240–41
psychobiological unity, 96, 103, 106, 112, 237–38
psychological needs, 29–30, 32, 35–43, 55–56, 186, 213, 225, 228
psychotherapy, 37

reductionism (physicalism), x, 94, 116, 120
religiosity (religiousness), 162–63, 122, 161–62, 200–201
religious engagement paradox, 162–63
religious ideologies, 10
religious markets (of ideas), 6–7, 14, 17, 22, 33, 42, 139, 141, 172, 228, 243
resurrection, 109–10, 113, 125, 135–37, 212, 228, 238–39
Richter scale, 150

shrinking faith, xiii, 14–15, 45–47, 54, 78, 124, 177, 244
shrinking God, xiii–xiv, 12–14, 45–47, 54–56, 68, 78, 84, 105, 118, 124, 217, 224, 226, 233, 236
social media, 43–47, 173, 225
social neuroscience, 197
social-cultural context, 6, 25–27, 61, 81–82, 87, 89–90, 130, 132, 136, 142, 147, 192, 229
socially embedded identity, 106
soul, x, xii, 4, 76, 94, 99–106, 109–20, 137, 185, 192–93, 199–200, 230, 237–38

Southern Baptist Church, 3, 230
spirit, 47, 54, 97, 99, 110–12, 115–16, 119–20, 129, 193
spiritual healing, 57, 154–59, 161–75
spirituality embedded, 105–6, 174–75, 192–93
spirituality embodied, 105–6, 121, 166, 174–75, 177, 184, 192–93, 199–205
spirituality impaired, 199–205
spirituality, 11, 14, 16, 32–34, 40, 44–46, 55, 96, 105, 110, 113–14, 121, 128, 155, 158–62, 174, 192–93, 199–201, 205, 216, 233, 238–39
split brain, 102
superego, 36
Superman theology, 118
supernatural, 40, 56, 85–86, 118, 125, 129–30, 170–72, 195
superstition, 158

technology, 13–15, 17–18, 26, 43, 45–47, 132, 222, 231, 233
theological presuppositions, xiv, 25–28, 30, 35, 89, 125, 216, 230, 232
theory of mind (mind-reading), 76, 104
transcendence, 37, 40, 114
two books metaphor, 54, 65

unbelief, 113, 127, 134, 165, 189, 196
unconscious, 26, 36, 38, 182, 190, 197, 225
uniqueness (human), 38, 70–72, 99, 113

vocation, 104–5, 113, 116, 118, 239

warfare metaphor, 61, 63
whole persons, 103, 112, 116, 195, 238
worldview, 78, 97, 115, 125–26, 130, 240
worship, 8–9, 11, 14, 29, 32–34, 43, 47, 54, 149, 167, 176–78, 192, 201

www.ingramcontent.com/pod-product-compliance
Lightning Source LLC
Chambersburg PA
CBHW021654230426
43668CB00008B/620